JAPANESE TOURISM

ASIA-PACIFIC STUDIES: PAST AND PRESENT

Series Editors: Xin Liu, *University of California, Berkeley*
Hans Steinmüller, *London School of Economics*
Dolores Martinez, *SOAS, University of London*

The forces of globalization in the Asia-Pacific – the most economically dynamic region of the world – are bringing about profound social, political and cultural changes in everyday lives, affecting the world both within and beyond the region. New social and cultural formations, such as the rise of the middle classes, the spread of new mass-media and virtual technologies and the burden of environmental pressures, present challenges to global social theories. Meanwhile, the past casts a lingering shadow, with historical conflicts adding fuel to current tensions over a wide range of issues. This book series provides an outlet for cutting-edge academic research on the politics, histories, societies and cultures of individual countries in the Asia-Pacific together with overviews of major regional trends and developments.

JAPANESE TOURISM

Spaces, Places and Structures

Carolin Funck and Malcolm Cooper

berghahn
NEW YORK • OXFORD
www.berghahnbooks.com

Published in 2013 by
Berghahn Books
www.berghahnbooks.com

Library of Congress Cataloging-in-Publication Data

Japanese Tourism: Spaces, Places and Structures / Carolin Funck and Malcolm Cooper.
    pages cm. -- (Asia-Pacific studies: past and present; vol.5)
  Includes bibliographical references and index.
  ISBN 978-1-78238-075-7 (hardback: alk. paper) -- ISBN 978-1-78533-029-2 (paperback: alk.
  paper) -- ISBN 978-1-78238-076-4 (ebook)
  1. Japanese--Travel--Foreign countries--History. 2. Tourism--Japan--History. 3. Japan--Social life
and customs. I. Funck, Carolin.
  G332.J38 2013
  338.4'79104089956--dc23

                                                                                    2013006045

British Library Cataloguing in Publication Data
A catalogue record for this book is available from the British Library

ISBN 978-1-78238-075-7 (hardback)
ISBN 978-1-78533-029-2 (paperback)
ISBN 978-1-78238-076-4 (ebook)

Contents

Figures and Tables

Figures

TABLES

ACKNOWLEDGEMENTS

While we were still making changes to this book, the great east Japan earthquake of 11 March 2011 occurred, followed by devastating tsunamis and a very serious nuclear accident that is still not totally under control, which has left deep scars in the country's psyche. It goes without saying that tourism destinations suffered heavily too, and some places mentioned in this book were directly affected. Far worse were the long-term effects, as many Japanese continued to hold back on travel, and foreign tourists shied away from Japan. In March and April 2011, the country saw a reduction in inbound tourism of 50 per cent, and domestic and outbound tourism saw a decline in the desire of locals to travel for pleasure while fellow nationals were suffering from the after-effects of the earthquake. While tourism has been previously seen to bounce back quickly after natural disasters, and most parts of the country were not affected at all, the ongoing nuclear scare still affects tourism in Northern Japan. However, inbound tourism in 2012 had almost returned to pre-earthquake levels. We can only express our hope and sincere wishes that Japan will successfully rebuild itself after this disaster.

More recently, inbound and outbound tourism have both also been affected by the ongoing struggle between Japan and China (and Korea, though to a lesser extent) over territorial claims in the seas between the two countries. As a result of this struggle there was a notable drop in Chinese visitors to Japan since August 2012, and by December, visitor numbers from China had dropped by 34.2% compared to 2011, mainly due to cancellations by group tours (JNTO 2013). Unfortunately, this situation shows little sign of change, and once again we can only hope that this situation does not continue.

Work on this book has been supported by many colleagues and researchers in tourism studies and in geography, both in Japan and elsewhere. Special thanks go to our colleagues and students at Ritsumeikan Asia Pacific University and Hiroshima University, and our families, partners and friends. Special thanks also goes to the team at Berghahn led by Mark Stanton and Charlotte Mosedale, and to Jeremy Eades for his editorial assistance and unfailing support.

The research for this book has been supported by the Japan Society for the Promotion of Science (Grant-in-aid for Scientific Research Projects 17320099 for Kanoh, Mitsunori; and 19520677 and 22520794 for Carolin Funck), and Ritsumeikan Asia Pacific University internal research grants (Malcolm Cooper).

ABBREVIATIONS

FITs	free independent travellers
GDP	gross domestic product
JAL	Japan Air Lines
IATA	International Air Transport Association
JATA	Japan Association of Travel Agents
JNTO	Japan National Tourist Organization
JTA	Japan Tourism Agency
JTB	Japan Travel Bureau
MAFF	Ministry of Agriculture, Forestry and Fisheries
MHLW	Ministry of Health, Labour and Welfare
MLIT	Ministry of Land, Infrastructure and Transport (Tourism was added to the name in 2008, but not reflected in the official abbreviation)
MITI	Ministry of International Trade and Industry
MoJ	Ministry of Justice
NKK	Nihon Kankô Kyôkai (Japan Tourism Association)
NPO	Non Profit Organization
SARS	Severe Acute Respiratory Syndrome
UNWTO	World Tourism Organization
VWC	Visit World Campaign

CHRONOLOGY

Paleolithic	45,000 BC to between 14,000 and 12,000 BC
Jômon period	between 15,000 and 14,000 BC to between 1300 and 500 BC
Yayoi period	between 900 and 800 BC to AD 250
Kofun period	250–710 (including Asuka period 592–710)
Nara period	710–794
Heian period	794–1185
Kamakura period	1185–1333
Muromachi period (Ashikaga Shogunate)	1336–1573
Azuchi-Momoyama period	1568–1603
Edo period (Tokugawa Shogunate)	1603–1868
Meiji period	1868–1912
Taishô period	1912–1926
Shôwa period	1926–1989
Heisei period	1989–present

Note that prehistoric periods often overlap and show strong regional differences.

I

Introduction to Japanese Tourism

Introduction

Many often-repeated stereotypes about the Japanese and their behaviour as tourists – such as 'Japan is a group oriented society in which travel traditionally has been undertaken in groups' (March 2000: 188), or 'the Japanese have a low sense of cultural self-confidence and they usually only travel in groups or visit well-known "culturally approved" attractions' (Graburn 1995: 48) – have long characterized the European and American 'gaze' (Urry 1990) on the Japanese as a tourist-generating nation. In part these stereotypes have arisen as a result of the early pattern of controlled departure from Japan to Europe and North America (see Chapters 2 and 5), and the mass movement of pilgrims and other specific groups internally in the early days of domestic tourism, as well as there being few inbound tourists and locally based commentators in recent years who fully appreciate the actual patterns of Japanese tourism across all sectors, destinations and ages. Recently, however, Japan has been trying to position itself more prominently on the map of international tourism as a destination and origin market for all types of tourists and tourist activities, and Japanese outbound tourists have become much more individualistic in their travel patterns.

In order to achieve this change, the fifty-year-old preoccupation with domestic and outbound tourism, the latter supported initially to help in the promotion of Japanese manufactured goods overseas and then to soak up excess domestic liquidity, will need to move towards a more equal pattern of inbound, domestic and outbound tourism. With the passing of the revised Tourism Nation Promotion Basic Law in 2007, and the approval of the Tourism Nation Promotion Basic Plan (see below, and Chapter 3), this change has accelerated, and it has become even more important in the period since the March 2011 earthquake and tsunami in northern Japan. After this event the government realized that the experience that foreign tourists (including educational tourists) might gain in the rest of Japan could be a powerful tool for reassuring the world of the country's inherent strength and ability to cope with natural disasters, while the promotion of domestic and outbound tourism could both offset the patterns of regional decline that we discuss in Chapters 4 and 5, and reassure the world of the country's continued economic importance (McQueen 1986; Imai 2004).

Japan's tourism policies are being watched with interest by neighbouring countries, since tourism increasingly reaches across borders. In this book we explore the changing patterns of Japanese tourism and views of the Japanese tourist since the Meiji Restoration, and note that these are increasingly coming to resemble the patterns and images held of most tourists everywhere, rather than the limited portrayals of the Japanese in previous works (Cooper and Eades 2007). To assist in understanding these changes, this book provides an in-depth historical, geographical, economic and social analysis of Japanese tourism since 1868.

Importantly, as well as providing a case study of the changing face of global tourism between the nineteenth and twenty-first centuries, this account of Japanese tourism can be used to explore both domestic social relations and international geographical, political and economic relations, especially in the northeast Asian context. In turn, recent changes can be used to shed light on the rise of northeast Asia and the Asia Pacific as prominent tourism arenas on the world stage in the twenty-first century, on the processes of globalization and global governance, on the global reach of market capitalism and big business related to tourism, and on such matters as the challenge of sustainable development, the rural–urban interface, and the impact of events like terrorism, natural disasters and health problems on Japanese inbound and outbound tourism.

The main aim of this book is to enhance the reader's knowledge of Japanese tourism as well as reviewing Japan's role as a destination and a major tourism generating country, but it will also provide important information on the evolving world of tourism in which we all live in the twenty-first century. In this context, tourism is best examined in terms of its social ramifications, and especially its political and economic framework, at different levels of society, including the local, the regional and the global. Tourism is not only a leisure pastime, but also a social, cultural, political, economic and geographical phenomenon, both nationally and internationally. Socio-cultural and geographical analysis thus forms the research framework of this book in three ways: first, there is an emphasis on scale as tourism phenomena and their implications are discussed both in a global context and at the national, regional and local levels; second, the discussion is informed by primary data sources as much as possible such as censuses and surveys, although there are severe limitations on the data available on Japanese tourism, as will be explained in Chapter 4; and third, the incorporation of fieldwork and case studies adds concreteness to the overall picture of Japanese tourism.

Another important aspect of this book is the integration of domestic and international research. While for the latter we draw mainly on English and German sources, we have also included extensive Japanese language material and academic literature in the field of tourism, as illustrated in the following short outline of the main features of Japanese tourism and its background literature.

Patterns of Japanese Tourism

The modern Japanese tourism experience is said to have begun in the Meiji period (after 1868), with the gradual removal of internal travel restrictions, and then, as the economy prospered, a move towards international travel (Manzenreiter 1995). We note in Chapter 2, however, that the Japanese are, and have been for centuries, inveterate tourists (see Bornoff 1991 and Leupp 1995 for a discussion on the importance of the sex tourism aspect of this during the Edo and earlier periods, and Graburn 1983 for the wider aspects). While Japanese international tourism has relatively recently become obvious to other countries, 'it is less well known that the Japanese have had a very long history of domestic tourism' (Graburn 1983: 2). In fact, it is now acknowledged that Japan saw the early development of forms of domestic mass tourism comparable to Europe's, consisting of a combination of pilgrimage and sightseeing, during the Edo period (1603 to 1868) when internal travel was otherwise restricted (Ishimori 1989; Cooper et al. 2008). However, Japan's appearance on the international stage of tourism was actually rather late (post the Meiji Restoration). It is also important to note that traditional elements continue to this day to exert a strong influence on modern forms of travel in Japan (Manzenreiter 1995: 9).

In Japan, like everywhere else, travel for pleasure initially arose as a phenomenon among the upper class. However, as with European countries, it expanded to include much broader sections of the population at a relatively early stage (Ishimori 1989). By the 1600s, even though the feudal system that had dominated Japanese life for centuries had initially allowed no freedom of movement, journeys for special reasons such as pilgrimages or cures had become more common and passes were issued for these purposes. Behind this development stood a growing desire to escape from the strict regimentation of everyday life and a wish for the pleasures of *monomi yusan*, or sightseeing. Travel was made easier for all, regardless of class, by the further improvement of infrastructure along the main highways like the Tôkaidô, which by 1601 had fifty-three post-station towns, each with between thirty and sixty inns, and by the increasing use of ships on the Inland Sea.

The second form of domestic travel, which was equally popular among samurai, farmers and townsmen during the Edo period, was visiting hot springs, the *onsen*. By 1725, for example, the resort of Arima (in today's Hyôgo Prefecture) already had 67 inns (out of a total of 623 buildings) and 130 shops specializing in selling souvenirs (Yamamura 1990: 28). Especially in winter and after the planting of rice in June, when there was little work to be done in the fields, peasants were given permission to visit the hot springs to recuperate from their hard work. This pattern also generated interest in the medical benefits of such tourism, a theme which today is once again attracting interest from policy makers (Yamamura 1995: 30), and in the practices and opportunities for sex tourism, a form of tourism that is now catered for by the large numbers of 'soapland establishments' in many Japanese cities (Eades 2007).

On the opening of the country in 1868 to Western contact (it is worth noting that contact with neighbouring countries like China and Korea had always existed, even during the Edo period) as a result of the end of the Shogunal government and the Meiji Restoration, check points and internal passports were abolished and it became possible to travel more freely. Among the many new influences at this time, the development of alternative means of internal transport and the influence of foreigners on tourism and leisure activities were the most important (Yamamura 1990). In 1872 the first railway line connected Yokohama with Shinbashi in Tokyo, and the rail network quickly spread to cover the whole country. The first Western-style hotel for foreign tourists was built in 1863, and the Japan Tourist Bureau, which is still today a leading travel agency, was founded in 1912 to bring more foreigners and foreign currency into the country. On the basis of this expansion of infrastructure and travel opportunities, Japan experienced a tourism boom, until the shadows of the approaching Second World War brought travel to a halt in the early 1940s (Yamamura 1995: 37).

After the end of the Second World War in 1945 and the cessation of the Occupation by foreign troops in 1952, Japanese tourism took on a different guise. While domestic tourism slowly recovered from the ravages of war, international tourism, first restricted by the Occupation authorities and then by the Japanese government, became outbound rather than inbound from 1964, and since then, academic and government attention has been focused on international travel by the increasingly affluent Japanese. Consistent with previous periods (see Chapters 2 and 3), the government was directly involved in promoting tourism to Japanese holidaymakers from 1952, but only for outbound and domestic tourism, and to the virtual exclusion of any promotional policy for inbound tourists. It was not until the late 1990s that government and the tourism industry began to see any need to change this pattern. In 1997, the first tentative steps were made, which culminated in a government policy document in which inbound tourism once again took equal place alongside domestic and outbound tourism (see MLIT 2009a).

There are four basic policies that underpin this 'new' system: the first is the development of attractive and internationally competitive tourist destinations inside Japan; the second is strengthening the Japanese tourism industry to make it competitive internationally and fostering human resources capable of contributing to the promotion of tourism in Japan; the third is that the promotion of international tourism by Japanese tourists should continue; and lastly, there must be the development of an environment for the promotion of tourism of all types within the nation. Concrete strategies to achieve these changes are found in the national tourism plan of 2012, and include the attraction of eighteen million tourists to the country and increasing the level of outbound tourism to twenty million by 2016 (JTA 2013). These are of course only target levels of activity but appear broadly feasible even if continued disruption by exogenous factors like the global financial crisis, territorial disputes and natural disasters is taken into account (see Chapters 5–8).

Academic Writing on Japanese Tourism

Despite its importance both internally and internationally, Japanese tourism has received relatively little coverage in print. Academic analyses have largely been limited to seeking understanding of the motivations and behaviours of Japanese travellers as they have become more important on the international stage during the past fifty years. A first wave of interest in domestic tourism can be identified among cultural anthropologists starting in the 1980s, when Graburn (1983) coined the phrase 'to pray, pay and play' to describe typical Japanese tourist behaviour. Internally, research concentrated on the reconstruction of rural spaces as pleasure peripheries for urban tourists on the one hand (Moon 1989; Knight 1993; Hendry and Raveri 2002) and the historical development of patterns of tourism on the other (Ishimori 1989; Havens 1994; Vaporis 1995). Major themes in much of this writing were nostalgia and the longing for an idealized *furusato* (hometown) that was actively promoted as a rationale for travel from the late 1980s (Graburn 1995; Robertson 1995). While externally writers were making much of Japan's economic power and the threat this might pose to the European and American economies (rather like the comments now made about China in the twenty-first century), publications on domestic tourism offered a more subtle and nuanced view of the country.

Academic commentaries on Japanese international tourism have concentrated on the motives of tourists travelling to various destinations and the behaviour of Japanese tourists on the international stage (Johnson 1989; ABTR 1990; Bolkus 1991; Mak and White 1992; Mouer and Sugimoto 1995; Asamizu 1998). As Japan entered its 'lost decade' during the economic slowdown of the 1990s, academic interest in Japanese tourism also waned; since 2000 interest has revived, however, as a number of publications prove (Sakai et al. 2000; Slattery 2000; Kobayashi 2003; Sakakibara 2003; Kômoto 2004; Mak et al. 2005; Maksay 2007). Leheny (2003) has discussed tourism and leisure policies, Hendry and Raveri (2005) have offered glimpses of past and present forms of leisure and tourism, while Chon et al. (2000) and Guichard-Anguis and Moon (2009) have edited volumes on cultural aspects of tourism. Others have carried out research on the famous Tsukiji fish market (Bestor 2004), on pearl fishing (Martinez 2004), on Hiroshima and the problems of memorials (Yoneyama 1999), and on the construction of heritage (Brumann and Cox 2010).

In German academic literature, Japanese tourism was first studied by Schöller (1980) and comprehensively analysed by Funck (1999a, 2002, 2004). Publications by Manzenreiter (1995, 2000) and Linhart and Frühstück (1998) have touched upon a variety of issues in the field of Japanese leisure and tourism from a sociological perspective. But in the Japanese literature, tourism has not received as much attention as might be expected, given that it has experienced continuous development since at least the seventeenth century. Reasons for this neglect include the concentration of research in the social and economic sciences on sectors of the economy assumed to be more productive, and Confucian traditions that emphasize work rather than play (Takeuchi 1984). In economics and geography, a lack of reliable data on tourism compared with an abundance of censuses and surveys on other subjects has also deterred interest in tourism.

Aoki and Yamamura (1976), Ishii and Shirasaka (1988) and Tsuruta (1994) have compiled basic bibliographies of writings about tourism in Japanese. However, Ishii and Shirasaka (1988: 146) point to a lack of rigorous statistical methodology and a lack of research on the perception of destinations by tourists and on cultural aspects of tourism. Tsuruta (1994: 74) has noted that since tourism development depends on the private sector in a developed economy like Japan's, there is also a general lack of public literature on aspects of planning (though see Chapter 5 for an outline of the extensive involvement of the state in the development of resorts and other facilities for tourism). Research has mainly focused on two aspects: the spatial patterns of tourist destinations, and tourism development within the wider frame of regional development. A strong emphasis on local case studies contrasts with a paucity of research at the national level. Despite this, the general picture of Japanese tourism can be gained through publications in English by Japanese geographers aimed at an international audience (Suzuki 1967; Tokuhisa 1980; Ishii 1982; Yamamura 1982). Monographs on tourism geography include those by Asaka and Yamamura (1974) and Yamamura (1990, 1995), which draw on Japanese as well as international examples.

If we look at the wider picture of tourism research concerning Japan then, we can distinguish a wave of interest in the early 1970s during the first leisure boom, and in the late 1980s, when the development of tourism and leisure facilities became the target of investment interests during the so-called 'bubble economy', and resort development was promoted as a national project (see Chapters 3 and 5). However, when projects were cancelled or went bankrupt during the ensuing economic downturn, research interest also declined. However, with the arrival of the twenty-first century, tourism has received increasing attention at the policy level, and tourism courses and departments are being established at universities throughout the country. Foreign graduate students and researchers at these new institutions have added new impetus to research on tourism in Japan, finally linking the international and domestic discussions that have so far been connected mainly through the personal links of individual researchers.

Outline of the Book

This introductory chapter has outlined the background of Japanese domestic and international tourism, including a brief introduction to the major patterns of tourism and to the literature in Japanese, German and English. A review of the existing literature related to the development of tourism in the Japanese context indicates that there are significant gaps in knowledge, especially in the English-language literature, some of which this book aims to close.

In the second chapter, we trace and interpret the history of Japanese tourism. Although Japan saw very early internal development of the forms of mass tourism consisting of a combination of pilgrimage and sightseeing (Ishimori 1989; Funck 1999a; Cooper et al. 2008), their appearance on the international stage was rather late. Japan has developed a distinct domestic tourism market based on these earlier influences, upon which the European and American styles of tourism and leisure, especially outdoor leisure introduced by foreigners living in Japan since the nineteenth century, have been grafted, but initially these were mainly for domestic use. It is only recently that domestic destinations have developed distinct strategies for inbound tourism to take advantage of the spread of facilities of an international standard.

Chapter 3 takes a close look at how tourism policy in Japan has developed since the beginning of the Meiji period, and outlines the principal methods of state involvement with respect to tourism promotion, regulatory frameworks authorized by legislation (standards and procedures for development control), state-sponsored industry planning and research, incentive schemes and subsidies for development, and government-supported networks of information providers to tourists. Development policies in Japan have for many years assumed that a transfer of capital and technology overseas must be connected to a strategy of economic upgrading at home, and this is precisely the model we see in the Tourism Nation Promotion Basic Plan 2007 mentioned above.

In Chapter 4 the analysis shifts to domestic tourism and its characteristics and markets. It follows the changing travel flows and travel patterns through the economic ups and downs of the postwar era. While Japan has long been characterized as a market with strong cultural signifiers and well established forms of mass tourism, recent years have seen a diversification of the domestic market that is closely connected to social and demographic changes. We also analyse the multifarious social relations which have characterized local tourism, be they within destinations or between hosts and guests.

The fifth chapter explores in more depth the economic dimensions of Japanese tourism. The structures of the tourism industry, how it intertwines with regional economies, and how it is used as a tool for regional development and as an economic strategy in the context of deindustrialization and an aging society are the focus of this chapter. The interface between tourism and leisure industries in urban areas is also examined. Chapter 6 expands on this discussion in the description of the changing patterns of Japanese outbound tourism. It pays close attention to the issue of national identity and nationalism in the modern world, including the different manifestations and levels of these phenomena as expressed in tourism. In Chapter 6 we examine the process whereby Japanese tourism has become inextricably bound up with national and international social, economic and political processes. The thrust is primarily economic, but in keeping with the argument of the book overall, the emphasis is upon the way in which the political and economic spheres of social life are intimately entwined.

As shown by the recent creation of the Japan Tourism Agency, inbound tourism is becoming more important to Japanese policy makers. Chapter 7 examines inbound tourism within the framework of immigration policies and the conflict between the promotion of inbound tourism and a very restrictive immigration system. A description of the stages of inbound tourism policies is followed by an attempt to trace the movements and motives of international tourists once they are inside Japan. A look at the images provided in guidebooks and on the internet, and a case study of a traditional Japanese town turning into an international destination, round off this chapter.

Chapter 8 is an examination of future relationships between tourism and everyday life in Japan. Changes in society as well as international tourism trends experienced by outbound Japanese tourists have initiated forms of tourism that so far have not been visible in the domestic market, or maybe have not been named. By adapting to domestic structures, eco-tourism, green tourism, marine tourism, youth tourism and so on will develop distinctive patterns, often in strong connection with certain destinations. Our analysis at the local level sheds light on how these influences will play out in the localization of global trends and processes within Japan.

As well as providing a final summary, concentrating on the central argument, Chapter 9 looks again at the implications of Japanese tourism for the rest of Asia and the world. Throughout the study, we have drawn on notable sources of data in four languages: Japanese, English, German and Chinese. In the Conclusion we speculate on a range of pertinent questions that have arisen from those sources, such as 'what is the future of Japanese tourism in light of the growth of China and other neighbouring countries?' and 'what are the implications of *nihonjinron* [theories and discussions about the Japanese] for tourism to Japan?' (Cooper et al. 2007: 74–78). We will end up pointing out that the high diversity of Japanese tourism spaces and their complicated political, economic and social surroundings at the beginning of the twenty-first century do not allow for easy speculation about the future.

THE ROOTS OF JAPANESE TRAVEL CULTURE

The Japanese are inveterate tourists, not only throughout much of the world but particularly within Japan itself, but though the fact of international tourism has been obvious to other countries, 'it is less well known that the Japanese have had a very long history of domestic tourism' (Graburn 1983: 2). In this chapter we trace and interpret the history of Japanese tourism. Although it is acknowledged that Japan saw the very early development of forms of mass tourism consisting of a combination of pilgrimage and sightseeing (Ishimori 1989; Cooper et al. 2008), Japan's appearance on the international stage of tourism is relatively recent. It has therefore developed a distinct domestic tourism market whose patterns increasingly influence neighbouring countries through the desires and practices of Japanese outbound tourists. On the other hand, European and American styles of tourism and leisure, especially outdoor leisure, were introduced in the nineteenth century by foreigners living in Japan. Historical studies show that traditional elements continue to exert a strong influence on modern forms of travel in Japan to this day (Manzenreiter 1995: 9).

The historical development of tourism in Japan is dealt with comprehensively in the Western and English-language literature, both by anthropologists (Graburn 1983; Ishimori 1989; Vaporis 1995) and by geographers (Schöller 1980; Funck 1999a). The standard Japanese works on tourism also contain good summaries (e.g., Ashiba 1994). Because historical geography represents an important branch of this subject in Japan, there is a wealth of source material in the form of guidebooks and travel journals, and numerous detailed geographical studies have also been published.

Changes and Emerging Patterns of Travel: An Overview

In Japan, like everywhere else, travel without external compulsion initially arose as a phenomenon of the upper class. However, in comparison with European countries, it expanded to include much broader sections of the population at a relatively early stage. Ishimori writes that he 'would like to present a hypothesis that in Japan the popularisation of tourism [was] achieved by the early Edo period [the early seventeenth century], which must have been the earliest in the modern world' (Ishimori 1989: 192). Although this hypothesis is certainly not incontrovertible, it does indicate that a strong historical tradition of travel exists in Japan, which we can assume will have exerted an influence on both tourism patterns and the regional distribution of tourist sites to this day.

The earliest written sources mentioning tourism are from the seventh century and tell of emperors recuperating at a summer palace in the mountains near Nara and relaxing at the hot springs of Arima. After the capital moved to Kyoto in AD 794, court nobles visited the temples and shrines of the surrounding area. The range of such religiously motivated journeys was expanded considerably in the eleventh and twelfth centuries by four generations of abdicated emperors, who made the pilgrimage of approximately 300 km from Kyoto to the shrines of Kumano ninety-seven times in a space of one hundred years. These journeys, which were made with an average entourage of one thousand persons, took about a month and represented the beginnings of the Kumano-*môde*, the Kumano pilgrimage (Ashiba 1994: 25). When the government moved to Kamakura in 1192, the Tôkaidô, the road connecting the imperial capital Kyoto with the east and later with Edo (now Tokyo) gained in importance. At this stage it was largely the samurai who undertook pilgrimages. Not until the fourteenth century (the Muromachi period) did the economic situation of the peasants – at least in the region surrounding the capital – improve to a point where they too were able to make short journeys to nearby temples and shrines. The focus of the major pilgrimages then shifted from Kumano to Ise, which is the shrine of the goddess of the imperial family and consequently the highest deity in the land. Active intervention by the priests of Ise gradually established the custom whereby every Japanese person should visit Ise once in their lifetime. Nonetheless, large sections of the population were still discouraged from travelling by political instability, the dangers of highway robbery and piracy, and especially by the countless customs posts. Not until the country was unified under Oda Nobunaga, Toyotomi Hideyoshi and Tokugawa Ieyasu in the late sixteenth and early seventeenth centuries were customs posts changed to check points. With his spectacular cherry blossom festivals, Hideyoshi also cultivated the tradition of *hanami*, excursions to see cherry blossom.

Conditions for travel improved greatly during the Edo period, starting from 1603. The peasants, the social group with the highest status after the samurai, gained in independence and their economic situation improved too through the opening up of new agricultural land and advances in farming techniques. Although the feudal system allowed little freedom of movement because the feudal lords (*daimyô*) feared a drain of resources from their *han* or domains, and therefore of negative repercussions on their food supplies and cash flows, journeys for special reasons such as pilgrimages or cures were authorized and passes issued for the purpose. The result was a growth in forms of travel where, for example, a pilgrimage to Ise was combined with a visit to the sights in Kyoto and Nara – and the religious purpose of the visit became nothing more than a pretext.

Behind this development stood a growing desire to escape from the strict regimentation of everyday life and a wish for the pleasures of *monomi yusan*, or sightseeing.

Whereas the samurai were under the strict supervision of the government and their feudal lords, peasants and townspeople soon discovered that pilgrimage offered a chance to evade such controls. In 1826, towards the end of the Edo period, the German doctor Philipp Franz von Siebold observed that in Japan, like in no other country, the lower their social standing, the more people could travel freely (Siebold 1897: 67). No Japanese overview of the history of travel in Japan fails to include this quote, which so succinctly encapsulates the particularity of the Japanese tradition and supports hypotheses such as that of Ishimori (1989) mentioned above.

Progress was made easier for all, regardless of class, by further improvement of the Tôkaidô, which by 1601 had fifty-three post-station towns providing accommodation along its route, each with between thirty and sixty inns, and by the increasing use of ships on the Inland Sea, now free of pirates. Of course the transport arteries were principally improved for official travellers, like the *daimyô* and their entourages, who had to spend every second year in the capital of Edo and so moved regularly from the provinces to the capital and back again, rather than for the hordes of lower-class pilgrims, but they still benefited.

The second form of travel, which was equally popular among samurai, farmers and townsmen during the Edo period, was visiting hot springs, the *onsen*. By 1725 the renowned resort of Arima (today Hyôgo) already had 67 inns (out of a total of 623 buildings) and 130 shops specializing in selling souvenirs (Yamamura 1990: 28). Especially in winter and after the June rice planting, when there was little work to be done in the fields, peasants were given permission to visit the hot springs to recuperate from their hard work. As medical writings about the effects of the *onsen* became more widely known, the duration of stays settled down to twenty-one days, during which time guests in simpler accommodation catered for themselves. A guidebook from 1810 covering the whole country lists 292 *onsen* (Yamamura 1995: 30).

A combination of the two traditions of pilgrimage and *onsen* lent support and credence to another form of tourism: sex tourism (Eades 2007). During the Edo period, for example, the 'entertainment zone' flourished, although it was built on much earlier traditions. One of the most famous was Yoshiwara in Tokyo, located near one of the largest temple complexes in that city (Bornhoff 1991; Seigle 1993), but also incorporating theatre, wrestling, as well as religion, *onsen* and sex tourism.

After the opening of the country in 1868 as a result of the Meiji Restoration and the end of the Shogunate government, check points and internal passports were abolished and it became possible to travel freely. Among the many new influences at this time, the development of transport and the influence of foreigners on tourism and leisure activities were the most important (Yamamura 1990: 33). In 1872 the first railway line was completed, connecting Yokohama with Shinbashi in Tokyo. The rail network quickly spread to cover the whole country, and the most important lines were nationalized in 1893. Private lines also linked the most important temples, shrines and *onsen* – for example, the Kompira shrine on Shikoku and the Narita shrine near Tokyo, bringing tourists more quickly to their destinations. The first Western-style hotel for foreign tourists was built in 1863, and the Japan Tourist Bureau, which is still today one of the leading travel agencies, was founded in 1912 to bring more foreigners and foreign currency into the country. On the basis of this expansion of infrastructure and travel opportunities, Japan experienced a tourism boom during the 1930s until the shadows of the approaching war brought leisure travel to a halt (Yamamura 1995: 37).

From this short overview, we can distinguish two major transitions in the history of Japanese tourism: the beginning of the Edo period, when stable political conditions and the establishment of transport networks greatly increased opportunities for travel; and the beginning of the Meiji period, when external cultural influences and new transport technology reached the country, thus promoting international tourism. Throughout these changes, two major forms of tourism persisted. Religious travel combined with visits to famous sites underpinned by the tradition of *monomi yusan*, travelling around while sightseeing, while visits to hot springs remained popular as a form of tourism (Erfurt-Cooper and Cooper 2009). These two major traditions will be explained in the following sections as we describe the major changes in the Edo and Meiji periods.

Religious Journeys

Religiously motivated journeys, especially pilgrimages, were of great importance as a basic form of mass tourism in Japan as in other countries (Cooper et al. 2008), so their routes and specific forms of organization are of particular interest. Temples and shrines worked very actively to attract visitors. Shrines in the more remote mountain regions naturally wished to attract as many people as possible, so they sent priests (*sendatsu*, meaning leaders or guides) out across the country to gather pilgrims in the villages and lead them to their temples or shrines as organized groups (Yamamura 1995: 27). Given that they organized the whole trip, including accommodation and the visit to the shrine, and acted as guides, these priests could actually be regarded as precursors of today's travel agents (Ishimori 1989: 186). The expansion of accommodation at shrines and temples was also a major precondition for the growth of pilgrimages. The number of inns at the outer shrine at Ise, for example, grew from 145 in 1594 to 391 in 1671 and to 615 in 1724, before falling again to 357 in 1792, as other shrines and temples nation-wide grew in popularity (Ishimori 1989: 185). In fact this process generated tourist towns with inns as their core, and included shops, restaurants, theatres, souvenir vendors and brothels, besides the temples and shrines. These were the *monzen machi* or temple towns, literally 'towns before the gate'.

The most important institution for supporting pilgrimages, however, was the *kô*; essentially local groups associated with a particular sect, shrine or temple. *Kô* affiliated to the Ise and Kumano shrines were particularly widespread. As religious associations, they served to spread the beliefs of the respective shrines, while as economic organizations they financed the pilgrimages of their members (Ishimori 1989: 182). Members were sent in turn on journeys to distant shrines as representatives of the whole group; this is the origin of the custom of *senbetsu* and (*o-*)*miyage*, parting gifts and souvenirs. The *kô* members gave the pilgrims money for the journey, part of which they used to buy gifts for those who remained at home, mostly amulets from the shrines they visited, which also served as evidence of successful completion of the journey (Graburn 1983: 53). The strong tradition of the *kô* can also be seen as one reason for the tendency to travel in organized groups, which is still apparent in some parts of Japanese domestic and international tourism today (Vaporis 1995: 30). Pilgrims without their own funds or a *kô* to help them financed their journey through alms and begging. In his accounts of two journeys in 1691/92, the botanist Engelbert Kaempfer describes the different types of pilgrim and their ways of asking for alms, which was sometimes a considerable nuisance to other travellers (Kaempfer 1964: 182).

The destinations of pilgrims changed over the centuries. Whereas emperors and court nobles had travelled to Kumano in the eleventh and twelfth centuries, Ise became the most popular destination in the seventeenth century, during the early Edo period. In the latter half of this period, however, destinations diversified to include Zenkô-ji in Nagano, Mount Tateyama in Toyama Prefecture, Kompira shrine in Shikoku, and others. This can be interpreted as a diversification of tourist attractions (Formanek 1998: 169). The outstanding role played by pilgrimage to Ise, the *Ise-mairi*, especially in the Edo period, has already been emphasized; however some details are of interest in explaining the size and function of religious tourism in Japan. It is thought that between two- and four-hundred-thousand people visited the shrine every year (Nishigaki 1987: 260). The figures varied according to the economic situation, especially the success of the harvest.

It should be noted though that only heads of households were organized in the *kô*, so other family members, as well as servants and ordinary townspeople, had no legal authorization to travel to Ise. The only option open to these groups was the *nuke-mairi*, the illegal pilgrimage without travel documents or authorization.

Another variant, which can be understood as a safety valve in this situation, the *okage-mairi* or spontaneous mass pilgrimage, occurred every fifty or sixty years during the Edo period (Shinjô 1971: 195–205). Pilgrims set off for the Ise shrine in their thousands, apparently spurred by rumours that amulets of the shrine had fallen from heaven. They received food and shelter from the people who lived along the way, who regarded this as a way of fulfilling their religious duties. The first such mass pilgrimage occurred in 1650, and it was above all young people and women who surged to Ise from all across the country: 3,620,000 in 1705, 2,070,000 in 1771 and 4,270,000 in 1830 (the latter representing about 10 per cent of the population at the time). The widespread participation in these mass pilgrimages reflects the great pressure of everyday life at the time, for which they represented a safety valve, but also the strength of the Ise creed (Shinjô 1971). Anyone who had been (legally) on a pilgrimage to Ise could be sure that the experience would guarantee them an elevated position in the village community on return. So travel gained a social function at an early stage. This element of reintegration with enhanced status after leaving the group temporarily is a classical element of pilgrimage in all cultures. Unlike the other pilgrimage routes described below, the journey to Ise was a pilgrimage with a specific destination. But here, too, different routes were chosen for the outward and return legs if possible, so it was generally a circular trip lasting at least a month. Most people had the chance to travel only once to such a major shrine in their lifetime so they wanted to see as much as possible (Onodera 1987: 276).

In contrast to the Ise-*mairi*, which took on an increasingly touristic aspect, the great pilgrim trails where several temples were visited in a particular order continued to be frequented by strongly religiously motivated travellers. The two best-known routes, which remain very popular to this day, were the thirty-three Kannon temples in the west (*Saikoku-sanjû-sankasho*) and the eighty-eight temples on the island of Shikoku (*Shikoku-hachijû-hakkasho*). The pilgrimage of the Kannon temples was already established by the twelfth century. It began at Nachi in Kumano, and led through the mountains of Wakayama to Nara and Kyoto, across the Inland Sea, back over the mountains to the coast of the Sea of Japan, finally ending at Lake Biwa. The route was about 900 kilometres long and strenuous, initially the exclusive privilege of monks who had undergone the necessary ascetic training in the mountains. Only in the sixteenth century did lay people begin to undertake the long walk and follow the stone way-markers (Tanno and Tanaka 1993: 107).

The pilgrims received alms along the way and were often exempted from tolls at custom posts and ferries. At each temple they left a kind of wooden visiting card stating their name, town or village and the year. Where these have survived, they tell us a great deal about the number of travellers and where they came from. It turns out that many of the pilgrims of the thirty-three temples came from the eastern regions of Japan, especially what is today's Kantô region, along with other concentrations in today's Kinki (where the temples lie) and southern Honshû and northern Kyûshû regions. So in addition to the time required for the pilgrimage itself, there was also a journey to and from the starting point, so that the whole venture often took about two months. Unfortunately, we only have approximations of numbers: the ferry over Lake Biwa (the way one of the temples was reached) was used by 17,740 pilgrims in 1773, and the Nachi shrine registered 30,000 visitors in 1801, but by 1825 this figure had fallen to just over 10,000 (Tanno and Tanaka 1993: 113).

While the Kannon temples were in the developed and accessible Kinki region, the journey to the eighty-eight temples of Shikoku led through harsh mountainous territory. The route, 1,414 kilometres long, followed the steps of the eighth-century monk Kobo Daishi. Most of the pilgrims came from Shikoku itself. A guidebook, published in 1687 by the main temple on Mount Kôya (Wakayama Prefecture), helped pilgrims to find the way but the Shikoku pilgrimage remained a dangerous undertaking where pilgrims were forced to depend on the goodwill and alms of the locals (Tanaka 1987: 276). Those who were not satisfied with the exertions of these long pilgrimages could attempt the challenge of one of the holy mountains – the belief that certain special mountains were gates to the other world, and therefore sacred, dates back to the Nara period, and probably arose as a coalescence of the nature-based local religion, Shinto, and Buddhism. The Shûgendô sect, for example, which believed in climbing such mountains to experience the other world, has both Shinto and Buddhist elements. As well as Mount Fuji, every region possessed its own mountains that were easily recognized from the plains and were regarded as sacred – for example Tateyama and Hakusan by the Sea of Japan, the three mountains of Dewa in Tohoku and Ôminesan in southern Nara. Settlements sprang up at the foot of each mountain as the 'base camp' from which to start the climb, and temples or shrines were built at the summits. This is where the *yamabushi*, the mountain ascetics, lived while undergoing their strict rituals. The infrastructure has survived to this day, and the rituals are still conducted on a few of the mountains.

It should be noted that this religious interpretation of mountains has never ceased completely in Japan. By virtue of their visual prominence and beauty within the landscape, the holy mountains are today the most popular destinations for climbers, so in that way the tradition of mountain worship lives on in modern leisure activities (Iwabana 1987: 268–269). On many peaks the hiking season starts with the ceremony of *yamabiraki* (opening the mountain). Small shrines can be found on many mountain tops, and training sessions for mountain ascetics in the Dewa mountains, as described by Blacker (1986), remain popular with office workers who want to escape the stress of company life (although Ôminesan in Wakayama Prefecture is still forbidden to women).

Many of the original pilgrimage routes, shrines and temples have survived over the centuries. Nowadays, they are being re-evaluated as cultural heritage sites, some of which have achieved the status of World Heritage sites, like the pilgrimage routes of Kumano in Wakayama. In the case of Mount Fuji, where registration as a natural World Heritage Site is impossible due to insufficient environmental conservation and the roads, housing developments and military bases around the mountain, religious tradition has been revived as an alternative way of claiming heritage status for Japan's national symbol. The pilgrimage route of the eighty-eight temples on Shikoku has also led to a campaign promoting the island as a place of recuperation from the hectic pace of modern urban life, sponsored by the Japan Tourism Bureau. In fact, already in the Edo period, pilgrimage had begun to undergo a process of secularization, and religious journeys had developed into a highly organized form of travel that allowed for sightseeing along the way. Japanese pilgrims or tourists could be away from their normal daily life for quite an extended time, during which they had ample opportunities for new discoveries and experiences. It seems that commoners in early modern Japan had more freedom to enjoy their leisure than their modern counterparts (Formanek 1998: 183).

Travel to Hot Springs

Onsen, hot springs or spas, are mentioned in the first chronicles from the eighth century AD (Erfurt-Cooper and Cooper 2009). The three most famous hot springs at that time were the waters of Iyo in Dôgo, now part of Matsuyama City on Shikoku Island, Arima in Hyôgo Prefecture, and Muro, now part of Shirahama in Wakayama Prefecture. Legends surrounding the discovery of healing waters, often connected to a wounded bird or other animal, abound just as they do in Europe. The development of hot springs was closely connected to shifts in the political centre because they were frequented by the political and social elites. Thus, until the Kamakura Shogunate shifted the locus of power to the east in the late twelfth century, hot springs in western Japan flourished as destinations. Spas also had a strong connection with religion, as visitors would rely equally on prayers and on the waters for healing their diseases.

Over the centuries, famous spas experienced ups and downs, as they were vulnerable not only to natural disasters like fires, earthquakes and landslides, but also to the changing tastes of their noble clientele. Also, each spa developed a different character depending on geographical features and management structures. Guichard-Anguis (2002) sketches the history of Arima, which is already mentioned in the *Nihon shoki* chronicles from AD 720 and the poetry collection *Manyôshû* from around 750. According to these chronicles, several emperors stayed in Arima in the seventh century for two or three months each, hoping to cure fertility problems. However, as hot springs are by their very nature located in seismically active areas, often in the mountains, they are prone to earthquakes and inundations by mountain streams. Arima is no exception: about every 500 years, earthquakes cause severe damage, the latest in 1995. In the twelfth century, a monk helped to rebuild the spa and create temple lodgings for sick people and travellers. In the sixteenth century, Hideyoshi had taken a liking to the *onsen* which he visited yearly and he supported reconstruction after an earthquake in 1569. At that time, a common bath, twenty temple lodgings each with several inns, souvenir shops, prostitutes and artistic entertainers were available for visitors. From the records of donations for reconstruction of the main temple in 1695 it can be seen that donors came mainly from the Kansai area, but also from Shikoku, Kantô, western Honshû and Kyûshû, giving proof of the popularity of Arima. In 1725, 67 inns, 47 simple lodgings and 130 souvenir shops catered for the tourists (Yamamura 1998: 29, 44). When a railway line was opened between Kobe and Osaka in 1874, visitor numbers increased and Arima became a recreational area for inhabitants of these cities. A similar pattern can be discerned for Beppu on the island of Kyûshû (Cooper and Erfurt-Cooper 2009).

In the beginning, hot springs were managed by nearby temples, but in the middle ages, feudal domains became involved too. In the Edo period, the feudal domains took over control of the administration, which was then entrusted to villages or feudal officials. Basically, spas can be divided into places where a few lodges had a monopoly on the hot water, like in Beppu (also used by the Shogunate to assist in the healing of wounded warriors) and Atami, and settlements where the hot spring was provided to visitors in a public bath, as in the case of Arima or Dôgo. The right to run an *onsen* included control of the water, all kinds of services for visitors and entrance fees for the spa. Part of the income gained through entrance fees had to be handed over to the domain where the hot spring was located. *Onsen* rights thus were a contested source of income. Takahashi (2004) describes the case of a hot spring in northern Japan, where five legal battles were fought about *onsen* rights during the eighteenth century. In most of these cases, nearby villagers challenged the right of a noble family to monopolize the spa resource. They argued that they had to provide horses for official visitors, especially samurai, as a free service and didn't gain anything in exchange, as goods provided to *onsen* guests were bought in another village. This indicates that spas had already developed into an important factor in local economies and had created their own market positions. Domain administrations, which had to judge the cases, usually decided in favour of noble families, but used each opportunity to raise the amount paid in exchange for *onsen* rights.

In the Edo period, visiting hot springs became common not only among feudal lords and samurai but also common people, and the basic structures of today's spa settlements were completed. Domains struggled to attract visitors for economic reasons while at the same time they set up rules to control order. Commoners looking for a cure at a hot spring first had to receive permission from their domain. After often quite exhausting travel, they would reach their destination and check in at an inn, where they borrowed bedding and cooking utensils. Stays extended over several weeks and people prepared meals in their lodgings, buying ingredients from local stalls. It was also possible to entrust personnel at the lodgings with cooking. Visitors took several baths a day, and it was not uncommon that a too strong wish for a cure led to death from immersion in too hot water (Yamamura 1998: 42).

In the eighteenth century, medical publications and guidebooks helped to increase the popularity of hot springs. Several authors compiled lists of *onsen* to describe their medical value or serve as a guide for travellers. In 1738, a doctor published information on 214 hot springs around the country, judging their quality by their water temperature, although information on the northern provinces is lacking in this list (Yamamoto 2004). In 1794, another doctor contested the theory of hot *onsen* being the best for cures and explained in his own publication that even different springs within a single spa location could have different medical effects, thus suggesting that hot springs should be chosen according to the illness to be cured. Information on hot springs was published not only for people with ailments but also for travellers looking for a relaxing soak. A guidebook from 1810 introduced 292 *onsen* around the country, listed by province along the major travel routes. It includes information on distances from the nearest post stations or castle towns, the effects of the waters, special products, and even the availability of prostitutes. By the late Edo period, *onsen* rankings in the form of pamphlets bought as souvenirs became increasingly popular. The oldest known pamphlet dates from 1817 and lists ninety-six hot springs arranged like a Sumo tournament ranking, with the springs of the 'east' competing against the 'west'. As hot springs became more concentrated in the eastern part of Japan, eastern 'competitors' had to appear in the western section to make numbers even. Arima, Kinosaki (Hyôgo Prefecture) and Dôgo led the 'west'; Kusatsu, Gunma (Gunma Prefecture) and Suwa (Nagano Prefecture) the 'east' (Yamamoto 2004).

In the Meiji period, when travel became easier due to the introduction of railways, *onsen* experienced a boom too. The number of *ryokan* inns in Beppu (Kyûshû) soared from 24 in 1888 to 286 in 1911, most of which piped hot spring water directly to their own bathhouses. In addition there were also twenty-four public bathhouses. Whereas the rural resorts were visited by peasants during the agricultural off-season, city dwellers recuperated at springs near the cities. Some of these developed into major entertainment districts. Numerous new springs were tapped and developed (Yamamura 1995: 33–36). Up to the present day, it is not an exaggeration to say that *onsen* are perhaps the most distinctive feature of Japanese domestic tourism. The rush to dig for hot springs all over the country during the years of the bubble economy illustrates their importance: while the number of natural hot springs actually declined between 1963 and 2001 from 5,757 to 5,186, artificially drilled springs increased three-fold from 4,638 to 13,063 (Yamamoto 2004: 24). For Japanese-style accommodation facilities, *onsen* water is almost a necessity for success, while in recent years Japanese hot springs have developed into a major tourist attraction for visitors from China, Taiwan and Korea.

Official Travel

The two major forms of – at least partly – pleasure travel described above made use of transport networks originally created for the purposes of official travel. It should not be overlooked that the physical landscape of Japan does not lend itself easily to travel. The land surface is mountainous and deeply dissected, and coastlines are rugged and often wracked by storms. In the Seto Inland Sea, one of the major transport routes, strong tides inhibit sailing. On the other hand, for any form of central state trying to control at least the main islands of Honshû, Kyûshû and Shikoku, it was vital to develop some kind of transport network. Facilitating official travel, spreading control and information from the centre, and transporting goods and taxes from the provinces were the major reasons for the establishment of roads, harbours and shipping routes. When Japan was gradually transformed into a more centralized state modelled on that of China from the seventh century onwards, the road and way-station system was also introduced and a transport network covering the whole country established.

The importance of official travel holds especially true for the Edo period, which was characterized by more than 250 years of relative political stability and coherence from 1603 to 1868 under the Tokugawa Shogunate. It is no exaggeration to say that this coherence was possible due to the continuous movement of information and people through an elaborate system of official travel and control. The most important type of official travel was generated through the system of *sankin kôtai*, which formed an essential pillar of the government and furthered integration at multiple social levels (Brown 2009: 76). It was established between 1635 and 1642 and basically forced all *daimyô* throughout the country to spend half of their time in Edo serving the Shogunate and the rest in their home province. Their wives and children had to stay in Edo permanently as hostages of the government, which was also an important element in the growth of Edo into one of the world's largest cities as their entourages added significantly to the population. Through this system of alternate attendance, the Shogunate was able to control the whole country thoroughly. Different types of *daimyô* had to travel to Edo at different intervals, at different times of the year (April, February, August) and for different periods (six or twelve months). Attendance not only controlled but also weakened the *daimyô* because it forced them to spend great sums on their residence in Edo and their processions back and forth.

The number of retainers that travelled with them was regulated according to the income of each domain. In the case of the extremely rich Kanazawa domain, up to 2,500 persons travelled together; it took them three days to pass through one station on their route. On average, most *daimyô* travelled with a company of 150 to 300 persons. Combining traffic records of all major routes, about 250 *daimyô* processions were counted per year (Kodama and Toyoda 1970: 136–37). As the stay in Edo was also usually very costly, *daimyô* tried to save money on their way back home by avoiding the official roads or stations, reducing the number of retainers and even the number of dishes served during the trip (Kodama and Toyoda 1970: 139). On the other hand, causing financial difficulties for *daimyô* was one major purpose of the whole system. Towards the end of the Edo period, discussions occurred as to whether the system was too costly and should be abolished. However, it kept the *daimyô* busy travelling and deprived them of the time, energy and financial means that otherwise might have been used for stronger regional independence or even direct opposition to the central government. This strategic management of official travel was therefore indispensable for the Shogunate. On the positive side, it also furthered the exchange of ideas, policies and administrative reforms among the *daimyôs* while residing in Edo (Brown 2009: 77).

Other official opportunities for travel included visits by the Shogun to the shrine in Nikkô on Tokugawa Ieyasu's memorial day in April or on the ceremonial delivery of the first green tea from Uji near Kyoto to the Shogun. All these types of official travel served to establish and maintain control by the central government throughout the country and to symbolize the position of the Shogunate through ceremonial processions. A well-organized road and way-station network was therefore a political necessity.

The Infrastructure of Travel

The great growth of travel during the Edo period can thus be attributed above all – alongside social shifts and economic changes – to improvements in infrastructure (Yamori 1987: 268). As Ishimori puts it, 'One of the most important elements of the infrastructure, which contributed to the development of tourism in the Edo period, was the improvement and expansion of road networks' (Ishimori 1989: 184). The main arteries were the five great roads leading to Edo: the Tôkaidô to Osaka and Kyoto; the Nakasendô leading through the mountains of Nagano and the Kiso Valley to Lake Biwa and Kyoto; the Nikkôdôchû connecting Edo and Nikkô; the Ôshudôchû travelling north into present Fukushima Prefecture; and the Kôshudôchû, which leads through today's Kanagawa and Yamanashi Prefectures to join the Nakasendô near Suwa in Nagano. All were provided with post stations a day's march apart. The most important of these roads was the Tôkaidô, whose intensive use also came to the attention of the German traveller Engelbert Kaempfer when he travelled to Edo in 1691:

> There are incredibly so many people travelling on the main roads in this country, and in several seasons roads are flooded with the people just as in the big cities of Europe . . . There are at least two reasons why so many people travel in this country. Firstly, because of the big population of this country, and secondly because of the people's fondness for travelling compared with the peoples of other countries. (Kaempfer, cited in Ishimori 1989: 179)

Or as Tanno and Tanaka put it, 'The Tôkaidô is the connecting line between the two regions Edo-Kamakura and Kyoto-Osaka, and its importance as Japan's main artery remains unchanged to this day' (Tanno and Tanaka 1993: 136).

For reasons of security, the government in the Edo period forbade even *daimyô* from using wheeled vehicles. The building of large ships and bridges was also restricted, because they, too, could have been used for military action against the central government. So all strata of society had to rely on horses or their own legs, and the roads and post stations were constructed accordingly. Paradoxically, this underdevelopment of transport turned out to be a factor that allowed even ordinary citizens to travel (Ishimori 1989: 190) at a time when incomes were generally very low. Another interesting pattern in modern Japanese travel derives from the fact that travellers who were on foot during the Edo period wanted to carry as little baggage as possible. Consequently, at a very early stage a service was set up to send luggage in advance – for example, from Ise to an accommodation house in Kyoto or Maibara, and have it collected from there and taken back to Edo before the return journey (Ishimori 1989: 188). To this day most Japanese prefer to travel without luggage, which they send in advance using the modern version of this service, the *takuhaibin* (home delivery service).

A broad spectrum of different lodging types grew up around these transport and travel patterns. As well as residences that were reserved for the *daimyô* and their entourages, there were also various different kinds for ordinary citizens. In the simpler type of accommodation, the *kichin yado*, the guest paid only for the firewood with which to cook meals, but growing numbers of *hatago* (type of accommodation offering meals) also provided meals. As well as making the luggage lighter, variations in the food at different places on the way, where the strict religious rules of the shrines did not apply, became an additional attraction of the journey (Shinjô 1971: 65). Growth in the numbers of serving girls also led to a flourishing trade in prostitution, to which the government in the end responded by restricting the number of girls an inn was allowed to employ (Ishimori 1989: 185). In another type of response to the regular problems with drunkards and prostitution, a number of inns joined together in 1804 to form the Naniwa-kô, which offered its guests safe, quiet accommodation. Prostitution, gambling and excessive consumption of alcohol were forbidden in the inns run by members of this organization, and lamps and fires were checked regularly. Other similar organizations arose later, and their efforts to guarantee guests particular standards represented the precursors of today's hotel and *ryokan* associations (Ashiba 1994: 27). Accommodation was not cheap, of course, but there were few other costs and anyway a journey of this kind was generally made only once in a lifetime (Tanno and Tanaka 1993: 132).

Alongside religion and pleasure, another important motivation for such journeys was to visit places that had become famous through literature: 'Travel and poetry cannot be separated' (Tanno and Tanaka 1993: 134). In Japan, famous poems have always been important bearers of information about beautiful landscapes and historically important places. This tradition begins with the *Manyôshû*, a ninth-century collection of poetry singing the praises of the beauty of the Asuka region, continues in subsequent travel journals, which often contain poems, and finds its culmination in the wanderings of *haiku* poets like Matsuo Bashô. Once a place had been extolled and thus made into a *meishô* or 'famous place', there were soon imitators who visited the same place themselves, sometimes to leave their own poems there, often simply to enjoy the atmosphere. In this way, a chain of sites grew up whose names gained a fame lasting through the centuries, even if their character altered over the years. Today, even where all that remains of places celebrated by poets is in fact their names, they are still visited for their 'name value'.

The travel guides that appeared from the seventeenth century onwards were more practically minded, providing information on accommodation, prices, routes, distances and sights. The first book with drawings, the *Illustrated Book of the Sights of Kyoto*, appeared in 1780 in an edition of 4,000 which sold out within a year. Descriptions of the Tôkaidô and many other famous places followed. Illustrated small-format maps were also invaluable aids for travellers (Ashiba 1994: 29–30). Siebold noted in the nineteenth century that maps and travel guides were used more frequently in Japan than in Europe (Siebold 1897: 61). The increasing numbers of such illustrated guides in the late Edo period show that travel was becoming ever more popular at the time. Of course journeys, especially along the Tôkaidô, also became the subject matter of novels, *kabuki* theatre and woodcuts. Illustrations by the woodblock artist Hokusai of the fifty-three stations of the Tôkaidô from 1804 are famous. Thus art and literature not only encouraged contemporaries to travel but also represent important sources on the history of travel in Japan.

The fact that a *kô* made it possible even for peasants from remote villages to travel to the capital also gave a great boost to the dissemination of knowledge and technology during the Edo period. Traders and tourists used the same road network, which helped the Japanese economy to integrate. And the exchange of information between the remote provinces of Satsuma, Tosa and Chôshû, which ultimately toppled the Edo government, was made possible by the travels of a number of active samurai: 'The mass development of tourism in Japan was related to unification, indeed the creation of Japan as a modern nation' (Ishimori 1989: 192). Leheny (2003: 53) on the other hand points out that a tendency to tolerate pleasure travel under the name of pilgrimage and an increasing commercialization of this over the years do not necessarily mean that pre-Meiji Japan had a functioning tourism industry. According to his view, the necessary travel permits, high costs and long duration of trips prevented the travel market from moving out of a relatively nascent stage of development. However, this view stands in contrast to the observations of the few foreign visitors at the time as mentioned above, and of most researchers who emphasize the high level of systemization and popularization of travel in Edo-period Japan (Ishimori 1989; Vaporis 1995).

It should be noted that travel and the information thus gained was restricted mainly to Japan itself because there were very few contacts with foreigners. However, regular visits by Korean and other delegations during the Edo period have often been overlooked by European and American historians. They too made use of the extensive travel infrastructure available in the Edo period.

Travel by Foreigners: Korean Delegations

It is a well-known fact that during the Edo period, after the edicts banning foreign access to Japan came into place between 1624 and 1641, travel by foreigners was restricted to a few official occasions. At the same time, Japanese were forbidden to travel abroad in 1637. Except for a few authorized Chinese traders and the Dutch who were confined to their small settlement of Dejima in Nagasaki, it is often said that as a result Japan cut itself off from communication with the world at large. However, it is often overlooked that delegations from Korea visited regularly and travelled the length of the country from Kyûshû to Edo, exchanging culture and ideas with the regional elites along their route, even during this period.

During the fourteenth and fifteenth centuries, Korea and Japan had established frequent exchanges as equal nations. These included not only relations between the two governments but also trade and exchange involving regional feudal lords and merchants in south-west Japan. Situated on islands half way between Kyûshû and Korea, the domain of Tsushima profited especially from this situation. The official missions going back and forth were known under different names over the years. However, during a period of especially positive relations in the middle of the fifteenth century, three Korean delegations were given the name *tsûshinshi*, which in Chinese characters means 'delegation to convey trust'. Even though relations deteriorated when Hideyoshi invaded Korea in 1592 and 1597, abducting several tens of thousands of Koreans to work in Japan, among them potters who later established the famous brands of Japanese pottery, once

Tokugawa Ieyasu had established his rule in 1600 he started to revive connections with Korea through the lords of Tsushima. Relying on the opportunity to trade with Korea, Tsushima desperately tried, and finally succeeded, in inviting the first visitors in 1607. Throughout the Edo period, twelve envoys from Korea visited Japan. The first three delegations concentrated on repatriating about 1,900 of the abducted Koreans. The remaining nine visiting between 1636 and 1811 took the name of *tsûshinshi*.

The Korean delegations, which consisted of between 300 and 500 persons on six large ships, formed an important part of relations between the two countries and are well researched, based on numerous picture scrolls and records from participants as well as observers at the time. The ninth delegation in 1719, for example, was to congratulate the new Shogun Yoshimune and was recorded in detail by one of the delegates. The convoy of 457 participants left Seoul on 11 April and Pusan in the middle of June, and then stayed in Tsushima until the middle of July. They continued to Ainoshima Island, facing Fukuoka, and then to Shimonoseki at the western end of Honshû, where they engaged in cultural exchanges before entering the Seto Inland Sea on 24 August. After stopping at the islands of Kaminoseki and Shimokamagari, they reached Tomonoura on 28 August and enjoyed the landscape and their reception by the officials of Fukuyama domain. After a short stop at Ushimado in Okayama and Murôtsu in the province of Harima (now Hyôgo Prefecture), they left their ships in Osaka to continue up the Yodogawa River to Kyoto in smaller boats provided by the Shogunate, and then to Edo on foot. Alongside Lake Biwa they were allowed to use a different road from the ordinary *daimyô*, one which was reserved for the Shogun travelling from Edo to Kyoto.

Different convoys stopped at different ports, but they always enjoyed lavish receptions by several hundred boats and exchanges of poetry, arts and knowledge. Whereas officials of the delegations stayed in accommodation used by *daimyô* or in temples, retainers were spread all over the villages. As Japan received little information from the rest of the outside world during the Edo period, the Korean delegations were welcomed as opportunities for exchange and entertainment by local officials and cultural circles. Receptions, accommodation, food, ships and retainers were all provided by the larger domains along the route. Preparations for this big event had to start almost half a year beforehand and the cost for each domain housing the delegates was immense (Hamada 1999: 73). The last delegation in 1811 only went as far as Tsushima, one reason being the high cost of travel and receptions.

Western Influences and the Spread of Outdoor Recreation after 1868

When Japan opened its doors to foreigners in 1868, they were only allowed to settle in a few restricted places, mainly Kobe and Yokohama. Here, specialists in all kind of fields, including engineers, doctors, military advisors and professors from Western countries, gathered to form cultural enclaves where they enjoyed their own imported lifestyles and leisure activities. This included summer retreats and different types of sport and outdoor recreation. For foreigners living in Yokohama and the Tokyo area, the areas around Hakone, Nikkô and Karuizawa became their refuge from the hot, humid summers. In 1886, for the first time in Japan, a Canadian priest established a second house in Karuizawa, soon to be followed by others. In the Rokko mountain range adjacent to Kobe City, the first golf course was created in 1903, accompanied by second houses. Cricket, tennis, sailing regattas, golf, rugby and so on soon became organized in clubs, often with overlapping memberships (Manzenreiter 2000: 53). Mountaineering became popular when the beauty of Japanese mountains was discovered, and the country's main mountain range was given the somewhat familiar name of the 'Japanese Alps'. Around the same time, beach development started along the coasts close to Tokyo, Yokohama and Kobe, induced by the discovery of the healthy effects of saltwater therapy.

Western ways of spending holidays and leisure, however, soon spread among the elites of Japan, either through their own experiences abroad, their personal relations with foreigners, or through the transfer and imitation of ideas. Differences in the import process and the prices of sporting gear and equipment, in the facilities and conditions that were necessary to enjoy an activity, and in the social strata that first came into contact with these new forms of recreation and whether they were integrated into the educational process in schools, all influenced the speed and extent of a particular activity's spread in Japan. Some activities gained popularity while others did not; but the idea of outdoor recreation transformed Japanese society and tourism, and the Japanese in turn adjusted the activities to their own social needs.

Summer Resorts

Hill stations and summer resorts were a common feature of European colonies in sub-tropical and tropical climates. Although Japan was not a colony, the foreigners who came from a more temperate climate introduced the concept of summer retreats as a way of escaping the hot, humid summers in much of the lowland areas of the country. Naturally, they chose places close to their settlements, such as Hakone and the areas around Mount Fuji west of Tokyo, and Nikkô and Lake Chûzenji to the north. Both regions were within easy reach of Yokohama and Tokyo and were already well established as Japanese domestic tourist spots because of their hot springs and famous shrines. Karuizawa, on the other hand, was a later discovery not yet visited by Japanese. When the missionary A.C. Shaw and Professor J. Dickson happened to stumble across the place in 1886, many of the lodging houses that had served as way stations on the Nakasendô route had fallen into decay. Shaw used the opportunity to buy a former lodging facility, move it to a quieter place on a hillside and thus start a process that was to transform Karuizawa into one of the best-known summer retreats in East Asia. As with Hakone twenty years earlier, foreigners soon began to buy old lodges through Japanese intermediaries, as they were not yet allowed to own land outside the settlement areas. In 1889, about 100 foreigners spent the summer in Karuizawa, which at that time took two days to reach from Tokyo. In 1893 a coach connected Yokohama directly with Karuizawa and two Western-style hotels opened in 1894 and 1899. After 1899, when foreigners were finally allowed to acquire land and choose where to live outside the settlement areas, the number of foreigners increased. In 1910 there were 134 foreign-owned second houses and twenty-five houses that were rented out to foreigners in Karuizawa (Satô and Saitô 2004: 10). Local inhabitants became involved in this new type of tourism at an early stage through services like laundries and shops specializing in Western food, such as milk and meat, and in land development for second houses. During the summer season, shopkeepers from Kantô and Kansai brought the newest fashions to the tourists who came to Karuizawa from different regions of Japan and East Asia.

In one respect, Karuizawa was very different in character to the Nikkô and Hakone areas. Possibly because it was 'discovered' by a Western missionary and a professor, it developed into a summer resort more popular among religious and intellectual circles than the general public. Regular meetings and conferences attracted missionaries from regional cities in Japan and from other areas of East Asia. Apart from exchanging information and religious experiences and knowledge, visitors enjoyed concerts, theatre, tennis and other sports. Until about 1900, this all happened in what was effectively an exclusive foreigners' enclave. Then Japanese diplomats and politicians with experience in Western countries gradually came to join this exclusive circle, looking for a lifestyle they had learnt to appreciate during periods abroad.

In 1918, Karuizawa's development entered a new stage when Tsutsumi Yasujiro, the founder of today's Seibu Enterprises, started acquiring land for development and built cottages, roads and utilities. At the same time, the resort's prestige was fortified by members of the imperial family, who bought residences in the area in the 1920s. However, though based on the land he bought in the 1920s and 1930s, Tsutsumi's main investments occurred after 1950, with his ski slopes and tennis, golf and skating facilities helping to boost the popularity of his large-scale cottage developments. He also was the main developer of the Hakone resort area (Havens 1994: 22–25).

Go to the Mountains!

The reinvention of Japanese mountains as sites for leisure and sporting activities shows some similarities to the process of the domestication of the European Alps during the eighteenth and nineteenth centuries, as Manzenreiter (2000) explains in detail. In contrast to the Alps, however, Japanese mountains are not as high, are more easily accessible, and are covered in forests up to 2,000 metres. Many of the peaks had been part of the religious system, places for prayer or pilgrimage, as explained above. Whereas the Alps in Europe became the target of explorers and climbers searching for virgin peaks, in Japan peaks that were already known were rediscovered and scientifically explored. The description below follows Manzenreiter's (2000) argument in its main points.

In 1860, the first Europeans climbed Mount Fuji, using traditional *yamabushi* as guides. To climb or at least view Mount Fuji soon became an indispensable part of every trip to Japan. Foreigners living in Japan, on the other hand, increasingly discovered the numerous mountains around 3,000 metres in height and recorded their experiences in the *Handbook for Travellers in Japan*, published since 1881 in several editions with slightly different titles. In 1896, Walter Weston, a British missionary, published *Mountaineering and Exploration in the Japanese Alps*. Although the term 'Japanese Alps' had been coined some years before, this book introduced the term and the area to a wider international public. The name refers only to the central mountain range. However, Japan's mountains in general were gradually reinterpreted as part of a modern vision of nature, as the European Alps had been a century before.

This process involved the natural sciences and literature, but also had political aspects, like nationalism. Geographical sciences became established in universities and academic societies, leading to the classification and analysis of landscapes. In literature, romanticism and the glorification of nature developed as responses to the rapid modernization that was promoted as national policy. The most famous example of the new interpretation of the landscape was the bestseller *Nihon fûkei ron* ('On the Japanese landscape'), published by Shiga Shigetaka in 1894. Although it describes all parts of the Japanese landscape, mountains as a symbol of Japanese nature form the centrepiece of this work. The book included a call for Japan's youth to go to the mountains, but also included many references and instructions from guidebooks published by foreigners. It not only served as an inspiration for the pioneers of Japanese mountaineering but also established mountains as the most representative part of the Japanese landscape, a fact that later was to influence the selection of sites for national parks.

The first Japanese alpine club or *sangakkai* independent of foreign groups was founded in Tokyo in 1905. Its members had close contact with Weston, who encouraged them to follow the British example and create an alpine club. The club's charter emphasizes that mountains form the cradle of civilization (Manzenreiter 2000: 69), thus giving its activities a higher purpose: to transfer knowledge about, and create access to, the mountains for a wider public. Its members included not only geographers, geologists and biologists, but also writers and ethnologists. Sufficient time and money and a high level of education became typical of mountaineers, as for participants in many other types of modern sports, in the early twentieth century.

Sangakkai soon spread to other regions in Japan, mainly the mountain areas, and to high schools and universities. By the beginning of the Shôwa period in 1926, almost all high schools and universities had established mountaineering clubs or *sangakubu*. Among the many types of sports clubs established in this era, mountaineering especially represented an ideal of independent, self-organized, risky and at the same time educational activity. As schools competed strongly in all fields, mountain climbing too became increasingly competitive.

Mountains also increasingly attracted recreational travellers, who followed tour descriptions in journals or guidebooks. For the pioneers of the *sangakkai*, the valley of Kamikôchi in Nagano Prefecture was an almost sacred place, a site that was seen as untouched before mountaineers entered its virgin forests. This, however, was a romantic idealization, as the area was already heavily used for forestry and cattle grazing. Romantic images nevertheless helped to develop Kamikôchi into a centre of mountaineering, as the beauty of its mountains and valleys and its quality as a sacred, hidden place were praised in guidebooks, especially from the 1920s onwards (Arayama 1998: 137). Mountain huts in the area started to serve customers from 1917 onwards, as did guide organizations. Both types of services spread to other areas. Local communities and railway companies combined their efforts to attract customers to the mountains. In the 1930s, recreational activities in the mountains were well established and diversified. Hiking and relatively easy access to famous peaks for the general public on the one hand, and risky, competitive activities like winter climbing by devoted student clubs on the other, were two traditions that characterized Japanese mountain climbing for years to come.

'Sea Bathing' and Sailing

In skiing and mountaineering, loanwords like *pikkeru*, *gerende*, *hyutte* and *shutokku* prove that certain technologies and facilities were necessary for their development and these were introduced from abroad, in this case from German-speaking areas. In contrast, sea bathing requires nothing more than a visit to the seashore and entering the sea – with or without clothes. This behaviour is nowadays known as *kaisuiyoku* (sea bathing), a term that was first used in 1881. In a journal published by the Ministry of Home Affairs, *kaisuiyoku* was promoted as a treatment for internal diseases and tuberculosis, similar to hot springs (Oguchi 1985: 26). Subsequent publications by several doctors helped to popularize sea bathing as a cure, either directly in the sea or in heated seawater on the shore. Bathing places were established, especially in areas with strong waves, which were believed to give stronger stimuli to the body. However, gradually the character of sea bathing changed, and like hot springs, bathing places increasingly offered enjoyment and amusement. When Hanshin Railways established the first beach in 1905 in the Kansai area close to the station of Uchide (Hyôgo Prefecture, Ashiya City), other private railway companies followed and, through offering amusement by the sea, managed to attract customers to their railways (Oguchi 1985: 33).

Unlike sea bathing, sailing requires expensive equipment. Together with summer resorts and mountaineering, the sport was brought to Japan by Western foreigners in the Meiji period (Sato 2003). Western-style sailing boats were first introduced in Nagasaki in the 1860s and later in Yokohama and Kobe, all of them ports open to foreigners. The first yachts were remodelled Japanese-style sailing boats or boats originally used for rescue and landing. The expansion of sailing concentrated on Yokohama, where a small wharf was taken over by foreigners with the first sailing boats, while the Yokohama Yacht Club was founded in 1886 in close connection with the Yokohama Amateur Rowing Club, founded in 1871. In 1909, this club had 151 members with 22 cruising yachts and 17 dinghies. Members consisted mainly of foreign diplomats, entrepreneurs and missionaries. As members of the foreign elite preferred to spend their summers in the cooler mountain areas of Nikkô, Hakone and Karuizawa, they took their hobby with them. Yacht clubs were founded at Lake Chûzenji near Nikkô (1906) and Lake Nojiri near Hakone (1921). Around Lake Chûzenji, members of the Tokyo Angling and Country Club also enjoyed fly fishing. This latter club also included wealthy Japanese who thus came into contact with sailing through social events at the clubs. In 1935, yachts that participated in races on Lake Chûzenji were restricted to one design built by a local shipwright.

The second houses of wealthy foreigners and Japanese soon spread south along the coast from Yokohama to Kamakura, Hayama and Zushi – places that nowadays still have the image of wealthy European-style resorts. In this area, small sailing boats were introduced, mainly to entertain children. When a new fishing port was built in Hayama in 1935, it had enough space to accommodate some yachts. As a result, local Japanese yacht owners founded Shônan Yacht Club which, with support from Yokohama Yacht Club, played a central role in the development of marine leisure in the area. Thus, sailing as a recreational activity closely connected to summer vacations and second houses spread from Yokohama to highland resorts and then back to the coast, and from foreign elites to the Japanese upper class.

Case Study: From Hot Water to Seawater in Shirahama

In some places, sea bathing developed as an extension to existing spas. The hot springs of Shirahama (Wakayama Prefecture) are well known as one of the three famous old spas of Japan, mentioned in records as early as AD 657. While having being known and used under different names throughout premodern times, from 1880 onwards Shirahama became an established curing place for the city dwellers of the Kansai area due to its convenient location and regular connections by ship to other parts of the country. In 1919, a development company was founded in cooperation between a local landowner and an entrepreneur from Osaka. The plan published by this company in 1921 was modelled after the modern resort created by German colonists in Qingdao in China before the First World War, including beach facilities, Western-style hotels, a music hall, indoor swimming pools, botanical gardens, an aquarium, a zoo, a library and an outdoor theatre – the whole range of Western cultural resort facilities. In reality, development concentrated on roads, parks, sports facilities and digging additional hot springs, thus adjusting to the needs of Japanese urban customers and the wishes of the local community. In 1923, the development company paid local villagers to give up their right to use the white sand of the beach for glass production. In 1929, the beach was officially opened, with changing rooms, hot showers, beach umbrellas, slides and diving boards. When the railway reached Shirahama in 1933, it was ready to be firmly integrated into the pleasure periphery of Kansai. Shirahama, literally meaning 'white beach', attracted many young visitors through its 'whiteness', consisting of the whiteness of its beach, of its modern concrete landscape, and of the young women's white skin, which successfully helped to create the image of a European-style beach resort (Kanda 2001).

Foreign Tourists, the Tourist Industry and the State

Of the many changes that occurred during the Meiji period, two developments had a strong influence on tourism in Japan: the expansion of steamship and rail routes, and the beginning of an influx of foreign tourists. Up to the Second World War, foreign tourism developed into an important source of foreign exchange revenue and thus increasingly attracted the attention of the state. Railway company investment in recreation and tourism facilities, a shift from Japanese-style inns (*ryokan*) to Western-style hotels, and the involvement of the state through the Ministry of Railroads were the consequences of this change.

At the beginning of the Meiji period, the travel restrictions of the preceding Edo period (Cooper et al. 2008; Graburn 1983) were lifted. In 1869 the Meiji administrators declared that passports were no longer necessary for domestic travel by Japanese citizens (Ashiba 1994: 31). They remained obligatory for foreigners, since they were a convenient means of controlling and monitoring the movement and duration of stay of foreigners in Japan. Nevertheless, it was recognized that the building of an infrastructure for domestic and international travel was a priority. By 1870, the world's four largest steamship companies had offices in Yokohama, as did Japan's largest marine transportation company, Mitsubishi Yusen (Shirahata 1996). With the opening of the Suez Canal in 1869 and the completion of the trans-American railway line, around-the-world travel by the rich became a reality. By the 1880s, travel time from London to Tokyo was thirty days via North America. *The Times* of London reported in 1887 that:

> The day cannot be far off when [Japan] will be brought within the reach of any vacation tourist able to spare the three or four months for exploiting a country that offers attractions of the highest order as a holiday resort. Japan, indeed has the enviable reputation of inspiring love at first sight in the heart of every comer. (*The Times*, 20 August 1887: 3)

The first Japanese railroad was completed in May 1872 between Tokyo (Shinagawa) and Yokohama, financed by a loan from Great Britain of one million pounds; three months later it was extended to Shinbashi, and was soon followed by the Kobe-Osaka-Kyoto line. The advent of rail triggered a boom in leisure travel as Yokohama became a popular destination for Tokyoites. In 1874 the number of passengers between Shinbashi and Yokohama was recorded at 1,438,417 (Yanagida 1957: 146). Also, the building of bridges that had been banned during the Edo period (1603 to 1868) was soon underway. Thus travellers in Japan were well served in the early Meiji period by government investment and policy. The Rikuun Kaisha (Land Transport Company) set up in Tokyo, with branches in major towns and villages, was the precursor of the domestic travel agent. This organization arranged the transport of travellers and luggage by pack horses and 'coolies' to carry luggage or pull the *jinrikisha*, a rickshaw pulled by humans (=*jin*). Reflecting a tradition dating back to the mid seventeenth century (Kanzaki 1991), by the early Meiji period most provinces had picture and guide books, 'illustrated by woodcuts of the most striking objects, and giving itineraries, names of *yadoya* [inns], and other local information' (Bird 1888: 71).

From the beginning of railway development, private railway companies had been involved. Voices proposing the consolidation of Japan's National Railway through mergers with private railway companies became stronger after the war with Russia in 1904/5, when the military needed a unified railway system to transport troops and material. In 1906, the Railway Nationalization Act was introduced and seventeen private companies were integrated into the National Railway. The activities of the remaining twenty companies were restricted to local and regional lines (Wakuda 1981).

The involvement of private railroad companies with tourism and recreation can be divided into three stages, each with a distinctive type of development (Aoki 1973; Havens 1994). In the nineteenth century, private railways based their routes on existing tourist attractions like shrines, temples and *onsen* to secure basic demand. Examples include railways linking the hot springs of Dôgo *onsen* to the city of Matsuyama or the Kotohira shrine to Takamatsu City, both situated in Shikoku. In the latter case, the section between the shrine and nearest town was even built first and the link to Takamatsu City some years later, showing the importance of tourist resources (Aoki 1973: 59).

The first twenty years of the new century saw the creation of regional or local railway empires with a combination of railway lines, department stores, hotels and cinemas at their urban terminal stations, housing developments along the lines, and recreational facilities and tourist attractions at the rural end of the line. Later, bus and taxi companies and travel agencies were added to the mix, turning private railway companies into major players in the tourist industry. The Hankyû Railway in the Kansai area, for example, pioneered this form of development when they gradually expanded recreational activities in Takarazuka *onsen* at the end of their Takarazuka line from 1914 onwards with the foundation of a revue theatre and leisure park. The former is still popular; the latter existed until 2003. Leisure parks and beaches were the most popular attractions for this type of development (Aoki 1973: 60).

The third phase coincided with the establishment of a national park system in 1931. Tourism to areas of outstanding natural beauty became popular and required the large-scale development of cottages, hotels and leisure facilities. In the Kantô area in the 1920s, the companies of Seibu and Tôkyû fought a development war over the Hakone area, a major tourist destination in close proximity to the capital region. The rivalry continued well into the 1950s (Havens 1994: 26). The Seibu group traces its origins to the combination of resort development and a private commuter railroad, and later developed into an extensive network of luxury hotels, ski, golf and vacation resorts in the 1980s (Havens 1994). Kinki Nihon Railway (Kintetsu), on the other hand, had a shaky start when construction costs for a tunnel between the plains of Osaka and Nara ballooned. Through mergers with other companies, though, it later established 500 kilometres of railway lines around the Kii Peninsula, connecting the metropolitan areas of Osaka and Nagoya with tourist destinations like Kyoto, Nara, Ise, Yoshino and the coastal area around Toba. It therefore played a decisive role in the tourism development of the Shima Peninsula, the region between Ise and Toba (Tanno 1998: 113). Networks established by private railway companies thus created the pleasure peripheries of metropolitan areas and formed the base for daytrips by urban residents until the increase of individual car ownership restricted the importance of railway recreation. As a consequence of railway development, by the start of the twentieth century, domestic and foreign tourists in Japan favoured Hakone, Miyanoshita, Kamakura and Karuizawa as summer destinations and Shuzenji on the Izu Peninsula (Ponting 1910: 325) during the winter. Miyanoshita was a weekend destination favoured by residents of Yokohama, while Karuizawa, a six-hour train journey from Tokyo by the turn of the century, was a popular escape for Tokyo residents during the hot summer months. While Hakone, 10 kilometres towards Fuji from Miyanoshita was difficult to reach, English-speaking 'coolies' could be hired by foreigners in Miyanoshita for 'three shillings a day' (Ponting 1910: 136) to assist.

The additional idea of attracting foreign tourists to Japan for the sake of promoting national interests was first proposed in the early 1890s (Ishimori

1989). A desire to correct existing unequal treaties may have been behind this proposal. There also was an intention to show visitors that Japan was a civilized country, as well as a recognition that foreign currency would contribute to reinforcing the nation's wealth and military strength. In March 1893 the Kihin-Kai (Welcome Society) was established to promote and support foreign travel in Japan (Shirahata 1996: 26–27). Overall, it appears that the establishment of the Welcome Society was viewed more as a diplomatic strategy than as an economic one. The main objectives of the Society were to: generate methods to assist *ryokan* owners upgrade their facilities; institute a travel guide system; plan listings of tourist attractions such as ruins, buildings and parks; and publish reliable travel information and maps. This was at a time when less than 10,000 foreigners were visiting Japan each year. The Kihin Kai was funded by donations from railways and international shipping companies, hotels, inns and department stores profiting from foreign tourists. However, in 1906, all the major private railway companies were nationalized in line with the Railway Nationalization Act, radically slashing the resources of Kihin-Kai and disrupting its operations.

The increase in foreign tourists led to diversification in Japan's lodging industry as Western-style hotels became the new standard after 1868. Traditional Japanese inns, *ryokan*, offered common baths and bathroom facilities for all guests, fixed meal times and no choice of menus. The rooms had tatami flooring and futon bedding that allowed for a flexible number of persons sleeping in one room, which were often separated only by sliding doors. In contrast, a hotel or *hoteru* would feature Western-style rooms with individual baths, privacy and European cuisine. This basic distinction between Western-style *hoteru* and Japanese-style *ryokan* still exists today, as accommodation facilities receive their operation license in one or other of these two categories. The first Western-style hotel opened in Yokohama in 1863, and was followed by one in Tokyo's foreign-settlement district Tsukiji in 1868 (Muraoka 1981). From the 1870s onwards, hotels began to spread around the country, first close to foreign settlements in Yokohama, Kobe (1868) and Nagasaki (1870), and in the destinations preferred by foreigners for their summer holidays like Nikkô (1872) and Hakone (1873), then in other resort areas like Beppu and Shizuoka. Some of the latter facilities developed from wealthy Japanese families providing lodging for visiting foreigners or from Japanese-style inns Westernizing their facilities. By 1914, nine hotels in Kobe were able to accommodate up to 500 guests, sufficient to accommodate visiting cruise ships. The famous Fujiya Hotel in Hakone had up to 19,000 guests per year by 1915. These facilities were also used by Japanese travellers; in fact, it is estimated that in the 1930s more than half of the guests were Japanese.

In 1907, the Hotel Development Law enabled the Railway Bureau, later the Ministry of Railroads, to build publicly owned and operated hotels to attract foreign tourists; however, only a very few facilities were actually developed. In

1930, the Ministry of Railroads established the Board of Tourist Industry, with the purpose of supporting the lodging industry, mainly through low-interest loans for hotel construction. As a consequence, although Japan was already heading towards war and little international tourism developed in the 1930s, fourteen international tourist hotels where constructed around the country, mainly in prime resort locations like Nikkô, Kamikôchi, Lake Biwa and Mount Aso (Sunamoto 2009: 203). By this time, Japan's accommodation facilities had started to meet international standards (Leheny 2003: 59). Support of the lodging industry continued after the Second World War, when a law to promote hotels and *ryokan* of a high international standard was introduced in 1949.

Lodging was not the only area where the state became involved in the tourism industry. In 1912, the Japan Tourist Bureau was established on the initiative of the Ministry of Railroads to promote foreign tourism (Shirahata 1996: 26–27). Later it became the Japan Travel Bureau (JTB), the leading travel agency in postwar Japan. At first, it set up offices overseas and created tourist offices around the country. To make up for budget restraints, the JTB started to sell tour coupons and tickets, taking the first step towards the role of a travel agency. The agency was very successful; the number of foreigners who used JTB services increased twenty fold from 1915 to 1936 (Leheny 2003: 61).

After the onset of the Great Depression in 1929, acquiring foreign currency through tourism became an even more important political goal. The Board of Tourist Industry mentioned above also took charge of tourism promotion, including the revision of guidebooks and distribution of posters, and overseas promotion offices were established in New York, Paris and London. Before and during this period, Japanese tourism authorities used different strategies to generate interest in Japan. American sporting teams had begun visiting Japan from the beginning of the twentieth century: the first visits were by baseball teams in December 1913. Another strategy used was to sponsor tours of key decision makers to Japan. In 1937, eight American high-school teachers were sponsored on a month's tour by the Board of Japanese Tourist Industries to 'acquaint themselves with Japan's social, cultural and economic achievements' (*New York Times*, 5 October 1937: 28). Since this time, the Ministry in charge of transport, nowadays the Ministry of Land, Infrastructure, Transport and Tourism (MLIT), has been responsible for tourism policies.

At the time, Japan's investment in inbound tourism promotion was widely acknowledged and admired. In 1928, the JTB reported that some 55,000 overseas visitors had spent US$25 million during the spring holiday season (*New York Times*, 15 April 1928: 32). The same report noted that this period was also marked by a nostalgic 'revival' of the *jinrikisha*, which cheap bicycles and automobiles were fast making obsolete, and the revival of native costumes (*New York Times*, 15 April 1928: 32). By 1936, spending by foreign visitors represented Japan's fourth largest source of foreign-exchange revenue after cotton, raw silk and silk products (Leheny 2003: 61). In fact Japan was well-placed geographically for travel in the early twentieth century. All steamships between Hong Kong and the Americas stopped at Kobe and Yokohama, and improvements in passenger ship construction saw the introduction of tourist class accommodation on Pacific liners by 1930. As late as June 1940, tourism between Japan and the US was still being promoted, this time with the maiden voyage to San Francisco of NYK Line's latest Pacific passenger liner, the *Nitta Maru* (*New York Times*, 9 June 1940: S10).

When the government started to lean towards nationalism and militarism in the 1930s, foreign tourism had to be reinterpreted. Leheny (2003) points out that articles in the Board of Tourist Industry's magazine increasingly emphasized the uniqueness of Japanese culture and hospitality, and finally even interpreted tourism as a means to promote Japan's war case among foreign visitors.

However, gathering war clouds from the early 1930s gradually had an impact on the tourist trade. From around 1931, the Japanese authorities classified numerous areas of the coastline as 'strategic zones' and forbade the taking of photographs. The *New York Times* noted 'every year scores of foreign tourists submit to detention, hours of questioning and confiscation of films because they have unwittingly used a camera in one of these zones' (*New York Times*, 16 December 1934: E2). Despite these restrictions, however, inbound tourism remained important and the same newspaper article reports on growing tension between Japanese 'merchants and hotels', who benefited from the international tourist trade, and the authorities, who were becoming increasingly paranoid about foreign spies. Many tourists complained to Japan's Foreign Office of the overzealous questioning of new arrivals in Japan, and the Foreign Ministry often came into conflict with the Ministry of Commerce and Industry, which was charged with improving the quality of tourist operations, and the government-funded Bureau of Tourist Industry, which promoted Japan overseas. This all came to a head in 1939 with the outbreak of the Second World War – the scheduled 1940 Tokyo Olympics had to be cancelled, and although international tourism in Asia was still being promoted by Japanese organizations as late as 1940, the following year saw the outbreak of war in the Pacific and an end to fully normal tourism to and from Japan for twenty-three years (see below). In 1943, the JTB was finally integrated into the war administration and mainly restricted to the organization of travel activities in the territories conquered by Japan.

Thus from the Meiji period to the Second World War some crucial patterns of the Japanese tourist industry and the way the state was involved in it had been established. The contradiction between promoting Japan's uniqueness as a tourism resource, while at the same time guaranteeing international standards in the tourist industry and restricting the number of foreigners in the country, was greatest in the nationalist phase before the Second World War; however, it continues as a thread in tourism policies even today.

The Making of Destinations: Cultural Heritage Designation and National Parks

When in the Meiji period travel for purely religious reasons lost its popularity, cultural and natural heritage came to incorporate traditional temples and shrines as destinations. This is especially true for temples, which suffered from the enforcement of Shinto as a state religion and the ensuing destruction of many important buildings or their incorporation into shrine precincts during this time. At the same time, the government engaged in different ways of creating a national identity, a process that continued from the Meiji period into the twentieth century. Following Western patterns of designating sites of cultural and natural importance as representing 'the nation', laws were introduced protecting cultural properties (1929) and national parks (1934). It is interesting to note that most current textbooks on tourism studies (e.g., Ashiba 1994) in Japan classify tourism resources according to the categories of these laws in their modern versions.

The idea of national parks was introduced to Japan at the beginning of the twentieth century. In 1911, the subject was debated for the first time in Parliament. If we consider that this was a year before the foundation of the JTB, it is possible to see a connection between the promotion of foreign tourism and the idea of national parks designed to present Japan's landscape to the world. In 1919, a law to protect historic landmarks, places of scenic beauty and natural monuments came into force together with urban planning law; a year later, the Ministry of Home Affairs ordered a preliminary investigation to prepare for a national park system. These movements therefore appear to be closely connected. However, due to the interruption caused by the great Kantô earthquake of 1923, it took until 1931 to complete the legislation on national parks. Tamura Tsuyoshi, a forestry expert who was the key person in the design of the law and the selection of sites, formulated five characteristics for national parks in 1918: that they should offer public park facilities; consist of great landscapes representing the country; be important for the economy of the whole country; contribute to the education, religion, moral stature of and research into the country; and be too difficult to manage on a regional basis (Arayama 1995). His ideas clearly include two nationalistic aspects of national parks, namely, that they represent the nation to the outside world, and that they contribute to national education. Japan's national parks were established to show off the country's beauty to the world while at the same time offering a clearly identifiable Japanese culture to Japanese people (Arayama 1995: 802).

When it became publicly known that the government was preparing a national park system, regions across the country competed to suggest sites, just as they tried to attract railway lines, as it was thought both would bring gains to regional economies from tourism. All in all, sixty sites were proposed to Parliament between 1920 and 1931, famous sites like Mount Fuji or Nikkô several times. To underscore the importance of candidate sites, historical and cultural reasons – like the fact that they belonged to the famous 'three Japanese landscapes' (*nihon sankei*) or had been favoured by members of the imperial family in the past – were cited. However, the twelve sites eventually chosen in 1932 show a peculiar concentration on mountains, gorges and forests, leaving out famous coastal landscapes except for the Seto Inland Sea. Reasons for this shift include the re-evaluation of mountain landscapes as a consequence of the Western-inspired interest in the Japanese landscape as explained above, and a belated romanticism towards areas that had so far been places of production like mining. In the end, it was not culturally loaded historical landscapes but sites of the nature appreciated by foreign visitors that became the newly designated symbols of the country. However, unlike America and Canada with their vast territories, in Japan with its intensive land-use patterns and predominantly private land ownership, the government could not create parks where it owned land, so the aim of creating parks was to preserve nature through mutual cooperation with landowners (Sutherland and Britton 1980: 7), a task not always easy to accomplish. Compared to European countries, which had to establish their national park systems under similar constraints, Japan's national parks law was accomplished quite early, preceded only by Sweden (1909), Switzerland (1914) and Slovenia (1924). Larger countries like Germany and France didn't succeed in this issue until well after the Second World War.

Another important feature of the protection system for cultural properties and natural parks that actually served to designate tourism resources was its hierarchy. Ranging from 'national treasures' (*kokuhô*) and 'national parks' down to cultural properties and parks designated by municipalities, this system helped to grade sites for the tourist market.

Summary: Centre and Periphery in the History of Japanese Tourism

This overview of the history of tourism in Japan brings to light several lines of continuity which are still felt today. Graburn (1983: 58) notes that the continuity of modes of non-work-related travel – from pilgrimage to sightseeing – is obvious, summarizing these as 'to pray, play and pay'. Interestingly, this discussion has shown that many of these phenomena in fact have extensive historic roots. The fundamental contours of the tour and the beach holiday of today are found in the pilgrimage and the *onsen* long-term stay of yesterday, even though the latter has disappeared almost completely due to changes in the world of work. In this, both central and peripheral regions are found as travel destinations. But the bulk of visitor flows, however, is clearly directed toward the religious, cultural, economic, political and transport centres such as Ise, Kyoto, Osaka, Edo and the Tôkaidô. These destinations continue to enjoy social recognition. In that sense, tourism in

Japan represents not a movement away from the known to the discovery of the 'other', but serves instead to affirm the existing order (Graburn 1983: 61).

Journeys to the periphery, on the other hand, have a clearly defined purpose, in which fulfilment of overcoming the element of adversity is in fact significant. For example, the dangers involved in pilgrimages to Shikoku or climbing holy mountains gave these experiences their special religious meaning. Other peripheral destinations involved the *onsen*, although as visitor numbers grew these turned into central tourist locations, for example Arima in Hyôgo and Beppu in Kyûshû. The way they were and are visited in groups for purposes of recreation also makes them less peripheral. However, it also took the influence of international tourism to turn the periphery into a stage for leisure activities. Here too, tourist centres with a range of different functions like Karuizawa and Hakone developed quickly, their most important location factor – apart from their natural environment – being their relative closeness to the capital. Historically speaking, Japanese domestic tourism thus demonstrates a strong centralist tendency, standing in contradiction to a European emphasis on the periphery. Historical developments also created the conditions under which several different types of tourist town could arise. These historically rooted types represent the nuclei of the most important tourist regions.

Religious tourism created the *monzen machi*, towns connected to the temples and shrines, where the visitor's needs for board and lodging, entertainment and souvenirs are satisfied. Ise (Mie) and Nikkô (Tochigi) are two of the most famous examples of this type. Similarly structured tourist towns also sprang up near non-religious sites such as palaces, castles and *onsen*. The *onsen* resorts with their hot springs provided for longer stays and assisted in the creation of 'entertainment zones'. Here a range of different types of establishment developed to cater to different social classes of user, creating contrasts which are still reflected today in the various standards of accommodation. The resorts with the greatest number of overnight stays almost all fall into this category, such as Atami (Shizuoka), Beppu (Ôita), Arima (Hyôgo) and Shirahama (Wakayama). However, the former post stations along the great old overland roads have lost their importance since the building of railways and modern roads along other routes, although some have regained tourist significance as places with historically valuable architecture and today belong to the type of tourist town that draws visitors by virtue of their historical image and traditional arts and crafts. Finally, the mountain tourism that began during the early decades of the twentieth century brought the idea of 'summer holidays' to Japan. These days, sport plays a growing role in recreation in the mountains and at the seaside. In principle these four types and their derivatives form – individually or in combination – the foundations of most existing tourist regions in the country.

3

THE RULES OF THE GAME

POLICY, PLANS AND INSTITUTIONS FOR TOURISM

The role of the state in the development and promotion of tourism is an important topic of discussion in many countries (Hall 2000; Cooper and Flehr 2006), but there is much disagreement on its nature and powers, and of the relevance of the policies it espouses. Reviewing earlier writings, Hall (2000: 10–15) argued that tourism policy making is first and foremost a political activity, influenced by the economic, social and cultural characteristics of a particular society, and by the formal structures of government and other features of its national and local political system. This policy-making process may be seen as one of action and reaction over time within the societal context of the state as the 'institutional fabric' by which collective choices are made, implemented and enforced in a society (Buhrs 2000: 27). More specifically, in many countries the continued expansion of the tourism industry has raised interest in the formal and informal policy processes through which tourism-development decisions are made – within the industry and within the institutional fabric of state and international policy making (Hall 2000; Dredge 2001; Sorensen 2002; Tosun and Timothy 2003; Treuren and Lane 2003). State involvement in tourism policy and development may take the form of national, regional and local plans, direct investment in and control over a major project, joint ventures with private businesses, tax breaks for investment and other business concessions, and/or infrastructure provision. At the local level, legislative and regulatory recognition of local community requirements for environmental protection and control of land use is available as a tool to direct tourism investment, and/or protect local ecosystems and communities from tourism.

The principal methods of state involvement are thus tourism promotion, regulatory frameworks authorized by legislation (standards and procedures for development control), state-sponsored industry planning and research, development incentives and subsidies, and government-supported networks of information pro-viders to tourists, of which local and regional tourism bureaus are an example. As Treuren and Lane (2003: 2) note, this regulatory and facilitative role in relation to tourism development can occur at a variety of levels: in Japan it is exercised at prefectural (regional) and local government levels, overseen by the national government. These distinctions are important because, at the state (national) or prefectural (regional) level, the concerns of planning are usually of a more general nature and involve maintaining and/or increasing the long-term viability of the socio-economic system, attempting to ameliorate particular economic and social failures, and ensuring electoral survival for politicians (Soshiroda 2005), rather than local land-use control. By contrast, at the local level, regulatory frameworks are more important, even if they are usually given legitimacy by and interpreted within a wider context by higher levels of government. Since major tourism policy developments up to 1945 have been outlined in Chapter 2, our analysis in this chapter will start with the period after the Second World War.

The New Era: Tourism Policies after the Second World War

The Early Period until 1964

For two years following Japan's defeat in August 1945, travel into and out of the country was strictly regulated by the Occupation forces; no foreign business travellers were allowed entry until August 1947, and inbound pleasure travel was forbidden until December 1947, when American tourists travelling to the Far East on board the liner *President Monroe* were allowed to disembark at Yokohama for twenty-four hours. While a tour of Tokyo was not allowed during this first postwar visit, these tourists visited Kamakura and the US Army base in Yokohama (*New York Times*, 30 December 1947: 4). The first tour that included Tokyo occurred in February 1948 when passengers aboard the same ship, the *President Monroe*, were permitted a one-week package excursion in Japan (*New York Times*, 24 June 1948: 11). In June 1948, the Occupation authorities announced that a single seven-day conducted tour each week for a maximum of twenty-four persons would be allowed for American visitors to Japan.

Throughout the immediate postwar era, or at least until Japanese manufac-turers began to successfully export overseas, the inbound tourism industry was regarded as a major foreign-exchange earner, as it had been before the war, and the Japanese government invested substantially in the development of tourism infrastructure. There was insufficient hotel accommodation for even the limited number of Westerners allowed in by the mid 1950s, and such was the importance of inbound tourism at the time that a Japanese government delegation on a visit to the US in June 1956 announced a five-year tourism plan (*New York Times*, 12

June 1956: 3). However, the growth of domestic tourism was hampered by the fact that the Occupation authorities refused to allow Japanese airlines to operate until February 1951, and only then if they were able to charter planes and pilots from foreign companies. However, by 1958 Japan had eighty scheduled domestic air services linking twenty-one principal cities, though roughly 20 per cent of air passengers were foreigners, mostly Americans (*New York Times*, 21 July 1958: 40).

Shortly before this, July 1947 saw the commencement of Northwest Airlines services to Tokyo, followed two months later by Pan American services. By the end of 1947, foreign business representatives had begun travelling to Japan. In 1948, Nihon Tourist, the predecessor to the major travel agency Kinki Nippon Tourist, and Hankyu Tourist were established. From the outset, both companies, as well as the newly renamed JTB, targeted inbound group travel. For their regulation, the government passed the Travel Intermediary Law in 1952 to ensure fair and ethical trading; and in 1953, as a result of the demand for inbound travel, the International Air Transport Association (IATA) gave approval to seven Japanese travel firms to operate as travel agencies. At this time, the overwhelming bulk of travel company business involved arranging domestic tours for foreigners visiting or staying in Japan – usually US military personnel. The only Japanese allowed to travel overseas were government officials, government-sponsored students studying abroad, and migrants. Leisure and business travel was strictly one-way traffic in the early postwar years. It was not until January 1950 that the Occupation authorities allowed Japanese to travel abroad for business purposes.

Other than business travellers, the first overseas group tours by the Japanese were thus comprised of sporting teams, the first of which was of Japanese athletes attending the first Asian Games in New Delhi in 1951. In 1952 Japan participated in the Oslo winter Olympics and the Helsinki summer Olympics. At this time, under the Passport Law of 1952, Japanese citizens began to be issued passports valid for one overseas trip, though a failure to take the trip within six months of issuance rendered them invalid. In February 1954 Japan Air Lines (JAL) began flights to San Francisco, which was hailed by an official as 'the biggest single step' that had been taken since 1945 to improve Japan's economic performance (*New York Times*, 4 February 1954: 40).

The major breakthrough came on 26 May 1959, however, when the International Olympic Committee announced that Tokyo would host the 1964 Olympic Games, and Japan's staging of the Olympics marked the country's re-emergence into international society. To take advantage of this event, in 1963, immediately prior to the Olympics, the Basic Law on Tourism (*Kanko Kihonhô*) was promulgated. This law set the scene for a liberalization of economic policies on travel as well as emphasizing the importance of the new Japanese state abroad. Thus, as a result of Japan's rapid economic growth and its emerging political position as an industrialized country, the previous restrictive regulations were set to be eased, letting Japanese people travel overseas freely.

The Period from 1964 to the 1990s

In keeping with its higher economic and political status, the government decided to liberalize the outbound travel market. From 1 April 1964, all Japanese became free to travel overseas. Nevertheless, travel liberalization after the Olympic Games did not just focus on outbound tourism: it was intended to promote equal treatment for both inbound and outbound travellers. However, the strength of Japan's currency, the yen, at the time made outbound tourism attractive economically for the Japanese, while internal regulation of tourism industries and less competitive domestic transportation systems kept prices high in Japan for both domestic and inbound tourists.

The Establishment and Organization of the Japan National Tourism Organization

The Japan National Tourist Organization (JNTO), also established by law in April 1964, is a statutory organization currently under the supervision of the Ministry of Land, Infrastructure, Transport and Tourism (MLIT), and is tasked with promoting inbound travellers to Japan and deepening their understanding of Japanese history, culture, tradition, customs and people. Towards this end, JNTO engages in a diverse range of inbound-tourism promotion overseas: marketing and promotion at international conventions, expansion of international interchange through grassroots exchange programmes, and support for overseas visitors through tourist information centres. Under the direction of a president and executive vice-presidents, the head office has six departments that correspond with the above activities. JNTO also has fourteen overseas offices and two tourist information centres (TICs) in Japan. Some 73 per cent of its total budget is provided by way of subsidy from MLIT, and the remaining amount is obtained from contributions or co-sponsorship by local government and the private sector. In 2003, JNTO was subject to organizational reform when it was transformed into an independent administrative corporation in order to increase the transparency of its management, the efficiency of its business administration and accountability for its performance.

In the early 1970s Japan's economic planners also realized that the state had an important role to play in shaping the country. It was decided that the society that was envisaged would benefit from an increase in, and appropriate use of, leisure time, and thus the state should not simply support official tourism organizations like JNTO (Leheny 2003). In 1972, the Ministry of International Trade and Industry (MITI) established the Leisure Development Industrial Office (*Yoka Kaihatsu Sangyôshitsu*) within its Industrial Policy Division to coordinate policy legislation and implementation in the field of leisure development. Specific recommendations by the Ministry included the need for a two-day weekend, the promotion of community sports, and the construction of large-scale recreation facilities, regional public inns, culture centres and city parks that would become important features of the burgeoning domestic leisure environment.

When the trend for increasing outbound travel became obvious in the early 1970s, MITI and the Economic Planning Agency decided that facilities for Japanese outbound tourists should also be built overseas. Such facilities were said to be needed because Japanese tourists had been found to be unprepared for the era of mass international tourism, and that therefore a 'mental gap' existed between the tourists and their required behaviour while overseas. This gap required the government not only to provide information to Japanese citizens on how they ought to behave while overseas, but also to Japanese firms and foreign countries in order to smooth the development of Japanese-style resorts overseas (Leheny 2003). According to MITI's Leisure Development Industrial Office (MITI 1974), it was necessary for the Japanese government to formulate a policy stance that would enable its people and firms to take advantage of the new 'global' leisure environment. More specifically, the government should be involved in designing 'international-level' leisure environments and networks both at home and abroad, thus establishing Japan as a first-class leisure country and aiding developing markets to create world-class environments that the Japanese might enjoy.

Since that time the government has been directly and consistently involved in promoting overseas tourism to Japanese holidaymakers. This has involved creating overseas tourist sites and environments in which Japanese tourists can feel safe, comfortable and relaxed. The International Tourism Development Institute of Japan was established in 1987, for example, to create master plans and feasibility studies for tourism development around the world and provide technical guidance on attracting foreign tourists to destination countries (in particular, Japanese tourists). But it also has a role as an agency in carrying out tourism-related research for the Japan International Cooperation Agency (JICA)'s overall development surveys, and in training visitors from the developing world in the processes of tourism development. As a result, the number of tourism-related overseas aid projects rose dramatically after it was established.

Leheny (2003) considers that these programmes were aimed at conveying two messages: to the Japanese, 'you should get out more'; and to other countries, 'you need to adapt to make yourselves more attractive to Japanese visitors'. By encouraging outbound tourism, the government could on the one hand reduce the country's trade surplus (heavily criticized at the time), and on the other, it could get Japanese people to go and have fun overseas and encourage foreign countries to become more friendly towards the Japanese. One of the most significant policies to emerge as a result of these influences came from the then Ministry of Transport (later the Ministry of Land, Infrastructure and Transport, MLIT), when it instituted the 'Ten Million' programme, formulated in September 1987, to double the number of tourists travelling overseas annually within five years from five million in 1986 to ten million by 1991. The target was actually reached in 1990 – one year early. The overall purpose was displayed in the MLIT's own assessment of the plan:

> With improvements in income levels and the growth of free time, the spread of the package tour, etc., the number of Japanese outbound tourists is definitely growing. Especially with the appreciation of the yen and the relatively cheap prices, there was a big jump, to 5.52 million travellers in 1986, the first time this number has exceeded 5 million. Even so, if examined as a percentage of the population, by 1986 only 4% of Japanese travel abroad annually, compared with the other advanced countries at 39% of U.K. citizens, 34% of the West Germans, 16% of French, and 12% of Americans, meaning that it is definitely a low level for us. Even when compared with another Pacific country, Australia, we travel abroad less than half their rate of 10%. Drawing up the promotion of outbound travel would increase international mutual understanding and would mean the cultivation of our people's sense of the international. It would furthermore promote the economies of other countries, result in an improved balance of payments between our country and others, and will definitely help our country secure a stable existence in an international society with greater interdependence. For this reason, the Ministry of Transport, in cooperation with other relevant ministries and agencies, has created the Overseas Trip Doubling Program and aims within five years to bring the number of Japanese outbound travellers to the level of at least ten million. This will bring Japanese travellers, as a percentage of the country's population, to about the same level as that of Australia. (MLIT 1994: 1)

According to Leheny (2003), the 'Ten Million' programme is one of the most remarkable of Japan's leisure initiatives to date. Although many governments have highly liberal rules regarding outbound travel, only the Japanese government has established a clear policy advocating more trips overseas. By combining the perceived requirement that Japanese citizens travel abroad in numbers more similar to those of other developed countries, but with an emphasis on the uniqueness of the Japanese national character, this policy and its related foreign-aid programmes made a simple but powerful link: the Japanese would behave 'normally' when their 'special' needs were recognized and catered for by the global tourism environment. So if the world were to recognize and to cater to Japan's uniqueness, Japan would become like any other advanced industrial nation (Leheny 2003).

Also at this time, the Ministry of Transport, in an effort to promote domestic travel, began promoting measures to develop new resorts, such as comprehensive health resorts and family travel villages, in accordance with the Resort Law described in Chapter 5. In addition, it promoted a variety of steps to build model zones for international tourism and international-exchange villas, and to promote plans for international convention cities from the standpoint of encouraging visits to Japan by foreign tourists. Moreover, the ministry gave elaborate guidance and supervision to travel agents from the standpoint of protecting the travelling public.

From 1997 Onwards: An Emphasis on Inbound Tourism Policies

By 1997 thoughts had once again turned to the inbound tourist as a means of developing a tourism culture in Japan, after the importance of outbound tourism as a promoter of things Japanese had begun to wane. The background to this was the recognition that two-way international tourism enhances mutual understanding between people from different nations and cultures. In order for Japan to fulfil its long-cherished role of fostering long-standing friendship and trust among nations, it was thought highly important that visits to Japan should be facilitated in order that the world might gain a better understanding of the Japanese at home. At about this time the number of outbound tourists was around seventeen million, while inbound tourists totalled between four and five million, only one quarter of outbound flows. In terms of visitor arrivals, this situation meant that Japan was ranked well below its neighbours and many other developed countries around the world, and that such a substantial imbalance between outbound and inbound tourism was also unfavourable to the development of tourism in Japan.

The 'Welcome Plan 21', 1997

Arising out of the recognition of this fact, the 'Welcome Plan 21', a programme to double the number of incoming visitors to Japan, was set up in 1997, along with the enactment of a law to promote inbound international tourism. The government had decided to take all possible measures to increase the number of incoming visitors to eight million by 2007. Policy measures under this law and plan included: developing international tourism theme areas (targeting areas suitable for foreign tourist promotion such as the Fuji-Hakone-Izu area and the Seto Inland Sea); drawing up foreign tourism promotion programmes (by local governments); introducing preferential taxation for accommodation investment; promoting more inexpensive tourism; introducing communal tickets exclusively for foreign tourists (the Welcome Card); promoting discounted fares exclusively for foreign tourists (such as the Japan Rail pass); providing information concerning budget travel; providing and upgrading tourist information systems; improving services at TICs to accommodate the needs of foreign tourists; the upgrading of the Japan National Tourism Organization (JNTO) website; the upgrading of visitor reception capabilities; introducing special interpreter/tourist guide licenses for local areas; and developing overseas campaigns by JNTO.

The Inbound Campaign of JNTO, 2001

For many years JNTO had been actively developing strategic overseas promotional activities in cooperation with Japanese embassies, local governments, tourist industries and foreign national tourist organizations in target markets. Following the impetus generated by the 1997 policies, in 2001 the organization began to develop much stronger public relations activities for the purpose of inbound market development. In reorienting its promotional campaigns, JNTO strategically varied the appeal points in its knowledge of respective international market characteristics. These included: TV advertisements in Korea, China and Hong Kong; advertisements in influential newspapers and magazines in Korea, China, Hong Kong, North America and the United Kingdom, which directly appealed to 150 million consumers in total; invitations to foreign press and travel agents to visit Japan (familiarization); and seminars for inbound market development for local providers.

In addition JNTO extensively upgraded its website in 2001, providing the latest tourist information about Japan in ten languages. The organization also produced a 'Visit Japan' promotional video on the occasion of the 2002 football World Cup, held in Japan. The then Minister of Land, Infrastructure and Transport, Chikage Ōgi, appeared in the video in person, introducing the tourist attractions of Japan and inviting foreign travellers to visit the country. The video was shown in the cabins of incoming international JAL flights and in eight airport terminals nationwide until the end of 2002.

The East Asian Sphere for Tourism (EAST) Plan, 2001

The Fourteenth General Assembly of the World Tourism Organization (UNWTO) was jointly held in Seoul and Osaka from 24 September to 1 October 2001. The General Assembly attracted the attention of the international community as a whole because it was the first large-scale international conference on international travel after the 9/11 terrorist attacks in the United States. The General Assembly was co-hosted by Japan and Korea for the first time in history, and attracted delegates from more than 120 countries and regions and the presence of 61 tourism ministers. As part of UNWTO discussions on the promotion of international tourism, an EAST Plan was agreed between the tourism ministers of Japan and South Korea in September 2001. This plan aimed to increase tourism exchange within the broader context of East Asia. The two countries were to make efforts to double their bilateral tourism flow from three million to six million by 2006. Moreover, both countries for the first time considered Japan and South Korea as a single destination and sought also to increase the number of inbound visitors from third countries, from six million to ten million, by the same target year.

The China–Japan Mutual Visit Year, 2002

The year following the UNWTO meeting was also the thirtieth anniversary of the re-establishment of diplomatic relations between Japan and China after the Second World War. For this, MLIT and the China National Tourism Administration organized a large-scale mutual tourism exchange programme whereby 5,000 Chinese visitors from across the country came to Japan in May, attended a commemorative ceremony in Tokyo, and travelled all over Japan afterwards in separate groups to deepen mutual understanding and friendship. In September that year, 10,000 Japanese tourists visited China in return, participating in a commemorative ceremony in Beijing and grassroots exchange programmes. This type of exchange was increasingly being seen by Japanese policy makers as offering good opportunities to promote Japanese culture, people and other tourist attractions to the Chinese and other potential markets.

Bilateral Consultations on the Expansion of Tourism in the Early Twenty-first Century

A memorandum of understanding on the expansion of bilateral tourism exchange between Japan and the USA was also agreed in April 2002. This aimed at creating a non-binding tourism expansion promotional initiative to assist tourism to recover promptly from the 2001 9/11 event in New York, and expand visitor levels to both countries by approximately 20 per cent by 2006 from the 2001 level. In order to achieve this goal, a Tourism Expansion Council, co-chaired and coordinated by the Minister of Land, Infrastructure and Transport for Japan and the Secretary of Commerce for the United States was established. Japan also engaged in bilateral consultation on tourism expansion with the South Korea, China, Canada, Australia and Germany, having discussions on the expansion of tourism flows in both directions and other imminent issues of mutual interest. Policy makers in Japan noted at the time that they intended to use such consultations as a strategic framework to promote foreign visitors to Japan.

The 'Yōkoso! Japan' Campaign, 2003

In February 2002, just before the football World Cup was held, Prime Minister Koizumi announced in a policy speech that Japan would once again commit to increasing inbound tourism and revitalizing local regions (JNTO 2005b: 428), a culmination of previous policies. The incremental policy evolution seen before this commitment set the groundwork for a sweeping revision of inbound policy. Since then the promotion of tourism has been a pillar of Japan's internal development policy under a succession of prime ministers. In his policy speech in 2003, Prime Minister Koizumi set the goal of attracting ten million foreign tourists to Japan by the year 2010. The prime minister established and presided over a national tourism promotion council, which published a report on basic strategy for inbound tourism promotion. Based on the report, the government gathered all cabinet ministers at a conference for tourism promotion, which then devised a tourism promotion action plan. This plan, which essentially comprised of related policy measures already determined by the concerned ministries and agencies, was pushed forward under the leadership of the vice-minister in charge of the promotion of tourism at the Ministry of Land, Infrastructure and Transport.

To achieve this goal, a new 'Visit Japan' campaign joint effort with local government and the private sector started in the fiscal year 2003, with 'Yōkoso! Japan' (Welcome! Japan) as its catchphrase. The campaign focused on increasing visitor numbers from South Korea, Taiwan, the United States, China, Hong Kong, the United Kingdom, Germany and France. For the first time, the prime minister (along with the minister of Land, Infrastructure and Transportation in charge of tourism promotion) appeared in videos and invited people to visit Japan. In May 2004 this approach was strengthened by the establishment of a tourism promotion strategy panel under the conference of cabinet ministers to place the wisdom of key figures in the private sector at the disposal of the government. Presided over by the chief cabinet secretary, the panel deliberated on effective and comprehensive methods for promoting tourism, and in November 2004 presented its recommendations with respect to more specific steps to be taken by the private sector and local regions, including suggestions in relation to the World Expo 2005 at Nagoya in Aichi Prefecture.

Post 2007

These policies began to make a significant impact, with inbound tourism rising to some eight million by 2007. However, this was short-lived as the worldwide conditions for tourism were dramatically affected by the global financial crisis, which came to a head in 2008.

The 'Visit World Campaign', 2008

In an attempt to offset the resulting decline in both inbound and outbound tourism, the Japan Association of Travel Agents (JATA) launched the Visit World Campaign (VWC) to revitalize the Japanese market. The objectives of this campaign were: to increase the number of Japanese outbound travellers to twenty million by 2010; and to review their current business model with a view to building a stronger business relationship between Japanese tour operators and travel agencies and their overseas travel business partners. This campaign brought together JATA, the newly renamed Ministry of Land, Infrastructure, Transport and Tourism (MLIT) and related government ministries, tourism offices, airlines, airport authorities and other concerned parties as members of the VWC '20 million travellers' promotion special committee, and established a VWC promotion office at JATA. These two bodies were tasked with stimulating outbound travel, including greater numbers from Japan's regions outside Tokyo and Osaka. The campaign also prioritized government efforts by concentrating on stimulating three target markets: the youth market of people in their 20s and 30s; the senior market; and the family travel market. It also sought to promote nine major destinations (South Korea, Hong Kong, Thailand, Taiwan, Guam, Australia, the US mainland and Hawaii, and France) and three new destinations (China, Vietnam and Macao) for travel agents and the government to focus on (JATA 2008). On the outbound side, this policy remained the major government focus despite increased efforts to sell Japan as an inbound destination in the face of the earthquake and tsunami (and the associated nuclear disaster at Fukushima) that occurred in March 2011.

The Framework of Tourism Policy in Modern Japan

It goes without saying that in most countries a large number of laws and ordinances connect directly to tourism or influence it indirectly. A study compiled by Japan's tourism Association, the NKK (NKK yearly a 1994) found more than fifty laws had been passed between 1927 and 1992 in Japan on a wide variety of tourism-related subjects (some examples are given in Table 3.1). These laws covered accommodation standards, basic community control of tourism, the development of resorts and many other matters. Often they were designed to promote investment as well as to control standards; for example, in exchange for improving their facilities, accommodation establishments could receive tax breaks, loans and the quality label 'registered international tourist hotel' under the *Kokusai kankô hoteru seibi hô*, a law to promote higher standards in hotels and *ryokan*, with a special emphasis on their use by foreigners. At the same time as these policy changes were being brought into effect by legal means, the organization of the national tourism administration in Japan went through a series of changes. The following discussion details those made after 2001.

The Establishment of the Ministry of Land, Infrastructure and Transport

The policies and administration connected to tourism described in previous sections became the bureaucratic task of the then newly established Ministry of Transport in 1949. These arrangements endured until January 2001, when four governmental agencies including the Ministry of Transport and the Ministry of Construction were integrated, and the new Ministry of Land, Infrastructure and Transport (MLIT) established. Tourism promotion and development were

Table 3.1: A selection of laws relating to tourism promulgated since the Second World War.

Date	Name	Description
1949	Act on Development of Hotels for Inbound Tourists	This law established a system of registration and standards for hotels and *ryokan*
1952	Travel Agency Act	A law to regulate the activities of travel agents
1963	Basic Law on Tourism (replaced in 2007)	This law has been dubbed the 'constitution of tourism' and for over half a century formed the basis of tourism policies in Japan. The law led to the constitution of the council on tourism policies, which works across the boundaries of ministries and agencies, and to the publication of an annual white papers on tourism
1987	Law for the Development of Comprehensive Resort Areas (Resort Law)	As described above and in Chapter 5, this law led to massive investment in regional resorts, golf clubs and theme parks
1992	Act on the Promotion of Tourism and Specific Regional Industries through Traditional Festivals and Events	This law aimed to facilitate festivals that promote traditional arts and customs. The law answered criticism of the Resort Law with its heavy emphasis on facility development and tried to promote the soft skills of regions and localities
1992	Act on Promotion of Green Tourism	Promoted by the Ministry of Agriculture
1994	Act on Promotion of Inbound Tourism by Facilitating Solicitation and Implementation of International Conferences	Japan seen as a hub of international conferences in the Asia Pacific Region
1997	Act on Promotion of Inbound Tourism through Enhancing Travel Convenience of Foreign Tourists	This law was designed to allow for the increased use of foreign languages in transport hubs, for the limited deregulation of banking practices and for the promotion of inbound tourism
2006	Guide-interpreter Law (Amendment)	Easing regulations for interpreter-guides
2007	Tourism Nation Promotion Law	Replaces the Basic Law on Tourism
2008	Law to Promote Visits and Stays by Tourists through the Development of Tourism Spheres	Tourism area development plans by municipalities or prefectures, exceptions to relevant laws required for the implementation of tourism area development projects
2008	Act on Promotion of Ecotourism	Promoted by the Ministry of the Environment

Note: Translation of the names of national laws is not consistent. Where possible, the translation provided by the governing agency was used; in all other cases, translations from the online dictionary *hônabi* (Law Navigation, http://waei.hounavi.jp/) or from English publications have been used.

Source: Compiled by the authors.

expected to be a major field in which overlapping specialisms in this administrative integration could be fully realized, since tourism is closely related to transport policy (air, land and maritime), the provision of infrastructure, regional development policy, the need to build communities with diversity and a higher quality of life, and the goals of the organization. Within this structure a Department of Tourism was set up under the policy bureau of MLIT, responsible for tourism policy and policy coordination on behalf of the government of Japan. Under the direction of a director-general of tourism, three divisions were initially organized: the tourism planning division, responsible for the total coordination of tourism policy, research and planning, promotion of inbound tourism, and international affairs; the regional development division, responsible for regional development through tourism promotion, the provision of tourism-related facilities, the sustainable development of tourism, and registered hotels and *ryokan*; and the travel promotion division, responsible for the supervision of travel agents, the development of tourism industries, the promotion of tourism demand by Japanese citizens, and consumer protection.

In addition, a tourism division was set up in each of the ten regional transport bureaux of MLIT nationwide, functioning as a coordinating and correspondence agency with local governments and tourism-related industries. The total budget of the Department of Tourism when established in 2001 was ¥3.773 billion (US$30 million), of which ¥2.659 billion (US$21 million) was the subsidy to the pre-existing JNTO. This figure does not include infrastructure development funds available within MLIT programmes nor tourism-related budgets of other ministries. Further development has seen the addition of one further division, for international tourism promotion, and an office for a counsellor for tourism policy (Figure 3.1).

Enhancing the Attractiveness of the Country and its Local Regions

In the early twenty-first century, the government saw that it was also important to create better conditions for receiving Japanese and foreign tourists in regional areas. Consequently, programs such as the 'Tourism Exchange Space Model Projects' and the 'Tourism Plus 1 Strategy' (MLIT 2002a) were developed to help create local communities with their own characteristics that attract tourists. These and other tourism-promotion programmes can be seen as direct descendants of the raft of earlier regional funding programmes, and were in fact blended with other MLIT programmes for special zones for structural reform and for urban and local renewal. In the fiscal year of 2005, a new project called the 'Tourism Renaissance' was begun as an offshoot of these programs in order to support the private sector's tourism-promotion efforts, basic research, local brand development, human resource cultivation and information transmission. The government also started urban and local development tourism projects on

Minister of Land, Infrastructure and Transport

Deputy Vice-Minister for Tourism Policy
· Oversees the tourism policy of the Ministry of Land, Infrastructure and Transport.

Counsellor for Tourism Policy
· Participates in planning for important matters related to tourism within the jurisdiction of the Ministry of Land, Infrastructure and Transport.

Tourism Planning Division
· Matters related to the promotion of tourism
· Financial matters related to tourism
· Matters related to tax coordination for tourism
· Matters related to annual reports to be published on tourism status and measures in accordance with the provisions of the Basic Law on Tourism
· Matters related to general affairs of Tourism Committee, Council of Transport Policy

International Tourism Promotion Division
Senior Officer for Convention Promotion
Director for International Tourism Relations
· Matters related to the promotion of visits by foreign tourists
· Matters related to communication and international cooperation with tourism-related international agencies, foreign governments and others
· Matters related to the Japan National Tourist Organization

Regional Development Division
Tourism-Based Community Development Office
Senior Planning Office for Tourism Industries
· Matters related to the improvement of tourist sites and facilities
· Matters related to the promotion of tourism that contributes to regional development
· Matters related to the registration of hotels and inns
· Matters related to the development, improvement and coordination of tourism industries (excluding tour operator/agency and guide industries)

Travel Promotion Division
Senior Officer for Travel Consumer Affairs
· Matters related to the facilitation, promotion and development of tourism
· Matters related to the development, improvement and coordination of tour operator/agency and guide industries

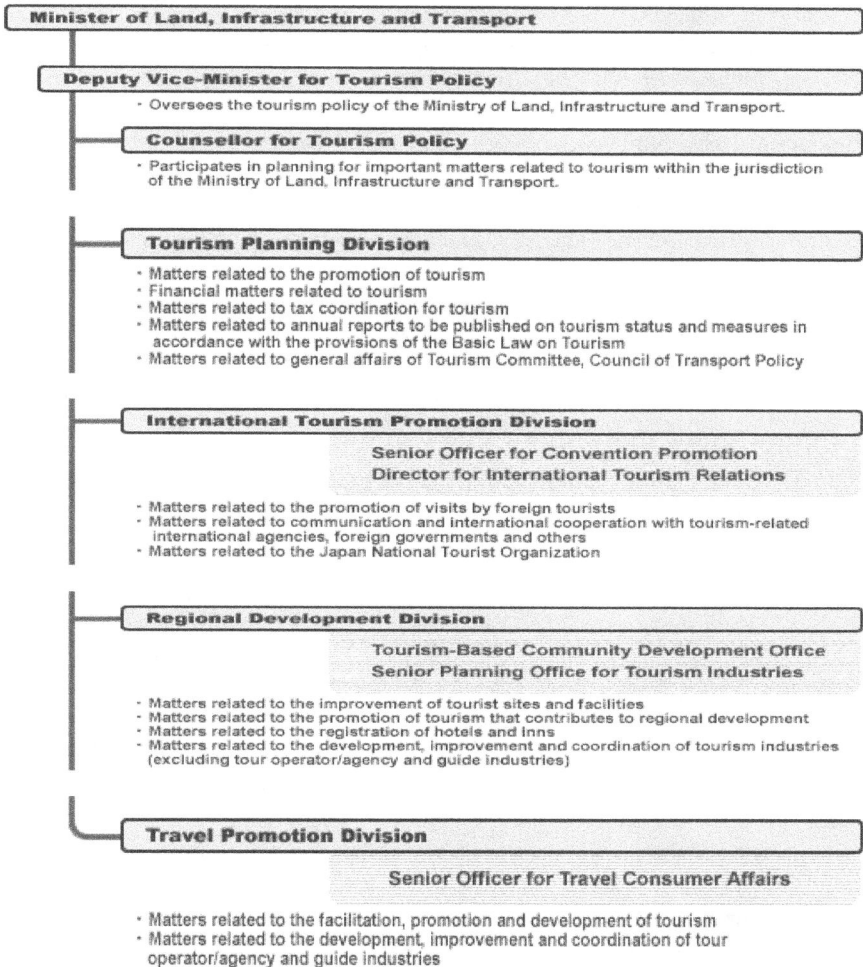

Figure 3.1: Organizational structure of the national tourism policy system up to 2007.
Source: MLIT (2007).

the basis of the Laws on Landscape and Greenery Conservation enacted in 2004.

In response to such efforts by the government, tourism promotion at the regional and local level in Japan has recently gained momentum. The ten regional transport bureaux of MLIT have played a central role, but prefectural and municipal governments have also restructured their administrations to place a stronger emphasis on tourism. In Kyûshû, a public and private sector partnership established the Kyûshû Region Strategy Panel, comprising the prefectural governors, the Kyûshû-Yamaguchi Economic Federation and Federation of Chambers of Commerce and Industry on the island. This panel published the 'Kyûshû Tourism Strategy' in October 2004. Further north, the city of Kobe appointed a director-general for tourism in April 2004 to oversee all aspects of tourism on a cross-functional basis. Similarly, the cities of Ise and Futami in Mie Prefecture are actively engaged in 'tourism charisma' and 'tourism exchange space model' projects. In the same way, residents of Matsuyama City in Ehime Prefecture (Shikoku Island), the home of the famous Dôgo *onsen*, have participated in tourism promotion linked with urban renewal and structural reform zone programmes. These forms of tourist promotion efforts and associated information signs for tourists are rapidly spreading to all parts of Japan. However, clear differences exist between prefectures and municipalities actively engaging in tourism policies, especially inbound promotion, and others that are less enthusiastic about tourism.

The Tourism Nation Promotion Basic Plan of 2007 and the Establishment of the Ministry of Land, Infrastructure, Transport and Tourism

In the midst of the international financial crisis and the persistently high value of the yen, the Japanese government has continued to give emphasis to tourism. In 2007, the Tourism Nation Promotion Basic Law, which clearly identified tourism as an important cornerstone of Japan's national policy in the twenty-first century, came into effect, replacing the Basic Law of 1963. Based on this legislation, the Tourism Nation Promotion Basic Plan was promulgated by the cabinet on 29 June. This plan sets out basic principles related to measures for materializing a tourism nation and specifies a number of targets, as well as government measures and other actions necessary to achieve those targets. The targets include: increasing the number of foreign travellers to Japan to ten million; increasing the number of Japanese tourists travelling overseas to twenty million; increasing the value of tourism consumption to ¥30 trillion; increasing the number of overnight stays per person in connection with domestic travel to four nights per year: and increasing the number of international conferences held in Japan each year by at least 50 per cent. In future, based on this plan, the government has committed itself to make concerted efforts to implement measures to promote Japan as a tourism nation in a comprehensive and systematic manner through the concurrently reorganized and expanded Ministry of Land, Infrastructure, Transport and *Tourism* (MLIT).

The Japan Tourism Agency

Securing the provision of quality services that harness the characteristics of tourist locations through collaboration between local public bodies, tourist businesses and other stakeholders has thus been the central focus of the tourism policy framework of Japan since 2007. As a policy direction, this is undoubtedly an important one for a country that has all the facilities to develop strong inbound tourism but has in the past often lacked the political will to overcome the politics of exclusion (Cooper et al. 2007) in relation to international visitors. It is well recognized by the government that local education on the value of inbound tourism is critically important if the 2007 plan is to succeed.

In order to achieve these desired changes, the Japan Tourism Agency (JTA) was established on 1 October 2008 as an external agency of MLIT. The upgrading of the former tourism department to an agency is an important step in several ways. First, tourism will become much more visible, as the commissioner leading the agency will represent the importance of tourism on official occasions and will also be on a more equal standing with other ministers internally, and with other tourism ministers at the international level. Second, the agency will not only coordinate policies and projects on tourism within MLIT, but can also comment on policy and give advice to other Japanese ministries. One recent example of this expanded role involved the relaxing of visa restrictions for Chinese tourists. One of the agency's first successful moves was to convince the Ministry of Justice to allow not only Chinese groups but also individual tourists into the country under certain conditions. The new visa regulations came into force on 1 July 2009 and are already resulting in more Chinese inbound tourists to Japan.

The JTA has a workforce of about one hundred people, only one third of which are permanent staff (JTA, personal communication). The other two thirds are either on loan from regional agencies, from other public and private institutions, or rotate on a career course inside MLIT. The JTA has a very small budget: in 2009, ¥4.25 billion were earmarked from the MLIT budget, of which ¥3.3 billion were to be spent on the 'Visit Japan' campaign. However, if budgets on tourism policies and projects of all ministries are combined, the overall tourism budget reached ¥218 billion in the 2009 fiscal year (approximately US$2.3 billion). Future tasks of the JTA include research on the effective use of individual paid holidays, on the travel behaviour of the younger generation, and on the promotion of regional cooperation in designated tourism areas to answer to the needs of the domestic as well as the international market. Common standards for tourism surveys across the countries were introduced from 2010 in order to gather reliable data on flows, lodging and the consumption patterns of tourists.

Policies and Systems Supporting and Regulating Tourism Development

Local Tourism Development: The Development Control System in Japan

The fundamental state policies that govern local planning processes relating to tourism development in Japan are the National Land Use Planning Law of 1974 (as amended), the Construction Standards Law of 1950 (as amended), the City Planning Law of 1968 (as amended), and regional and state planning policy, as set out in the series of national development plans outlined below (Callies 1994). These, together with related laws covering the protection of the environment and cultural heritage, and local planning ordinances, function as a multi-layered system to promote and control urban and regional development.

This system had its genesis in the rehabilitation of the urban fabric of Japan following the Second World War (Sorensen 2002). In 1951, comprehensive national development legislation was enacted and a national land-planning system created. Between the mid 1950s and mid 1960s, the area development plans developed under this legislation played a major role in the spectacular economic development of Japan. However, investment was concentrated in infrastructure in the larger cities, and as a result the country's population was further concentrated in the so-called Pacific Belt Zone, from Tokyo to Fukuoka. During this period, the national government realized it was necessary to think in more comprehensive terms about the whole country, and in 1962 the first comprehensive National Development Plan was drawn up, to bring about balanced development across all regions. This plan has been renewed five times, but with a focus on different themes each time, such as 'new industrial cities', 'integrated residence policy' and 'integrated interaction policy', which were framed according to the perceived needs of the moment. The theme of the fifth plan, developed in 1998 but focusing on the period from 2000 to 2015, is 'grand design for the twenty-first century', and it is noteworthy that tourism plays an important role in this plan (Regional Planning and Coordination Division, MLIT 2004).

The group of laws and plans that affect tourism land-use planning and management in Japan mirror this approach and are divided into four basic types:

Group A: The Laws of Higher Authorities

The laws promulgated by government and administered through such ministries as the Ministry of Economy, Trade and Industry and MLIT involve those that directly determine national and local planning parameters, including national highways, construction standards and major land-use projects, including those of tourism. This can be illustrated by two examples. First, the alignment of roads ultimately approved in city planning ordinances to serve tourism developments controlled under the City Planning Law of 1968 (as amended) are decided according to the requirements of national road planning under the Roads Law, of 1952 (as amended). Secondly, while national land-use planning law broadly determines the national distribution of particular types of land usage, the Law for the Development of Comprehensive Resort Areas of 1987 provided the finance and development control parameters for major local tourist and leisure related investment in association with it.

Apart from laws on planning and land use, there are laws on the protection of the environment and cultural heritage, for example the Natural Parks Law and the Law for the Protection of Cultural Properties, which also affect tourism development. However, since they are controlled by different government authorities they do not form a unified system with existing urban planning policies.

Group B: National Development Plans and Projects

These include the policy frameworks and mechanisms through which public infrastructure investment is achieved on an integrated basis under the national planning system. It should be noted that there is a hierarchy of plans in Japan that can and have impacted on tourism development policy. This system is topped by national development plans, followed by prefectural and municipal development plans, and is detailed finally in urban planning policies and regulations. National development plans form the outline for regional policies that are concretized in laws and ordinances; for example, in the National Development Plan of 1962, tourism was seen to have a role as an economic sector that could support regional development. The necessity of preserving space for leisure in urban areas and natural and cultural heritage as tourist attractions was also emphasized in this plan. On the other hand the plan of 1969 coincided with economic expansion and the first leisure boom in the country. It promoted tourism development in natural areas, a concept taken up by then Prime Minister Tanaka Kakuei's blueprint for a better Japan, *Nihon kaizenron*, in 1972. Tanaka's blueprint, although only a personal vision, led to an investment boom in peripheral areas, where land prices shot up in expectation of resort and infrastructure development.

The fourth National Development Plan of 1987 laid the groundwork for the Resort Law, implemented in 1987 (Rimmer 1992). This plan identified rural areas as a space for exchange between rural and urban citizens and as the setting for facilities that can satisfy increased needs for leisure activities. While each of these plans was ultimately connected to laws and projects for tourism development, their biggest influence on the structure of tourism was in the promotion of transport networks, a central theme running through all the plans. The plans governed the development of high-speed transport routes – like *shinkansen* lines, regional airports, and highways, bridges and tunnels connecting the four main islands – and have had an immense influence on the flow of tourists to, from and across Japan.

Besides the national development plans, other plans have influenced tourism development. Since 1962, comprehensive development plans and basic plans for public investment have been promulgated every few years, with attached gross investment amounts. The 1994 New Basic Plan for Public Investment, for example, proposed a gross investment of ¥630 trillion (US$6 trillion at the time) for the years 1995 to 2004 on public infrastructure, and provided detailed planning and location guidelines for the intended investment. These plans in effect mobilized local government through subsidy premiums for public works, preferential locally allocated tax grants and the like, because in such developments there is a local need for central government assistance, which is very difficult to reject. However, such assistance comes at a price, generally distorting the local financial base, and is now being seriously questioned (Hebbert 1994).

Group C: Related Local Adjustments

This framework ensures that the 'proper' development of local planning laws and ordinances is achieved by synchronizing city plans and lower-level ordinances with the higher-level laws of Group A. Of particular importance is the adjustment of urban land use under the City Planning Law to protect agricultural land use (for example, the Chûbu Region Development Law, 1966), or land for industrial development (such as the Key Facilities Siting Law, 1988). Formally, the jurisdiction of local planning is decided by classifying areas of agricultural land use and urban/industrial land use under the national land-planning legal framework. This is determined locally by interactive adjustment of land use, based on altering higher land values to protect agricultural and other land of lesser value wherever necessary, but otherwise ensuring that there is sufficient land for those uses deemed important at the higher level. In this vein, the Resort Law was a higher-level law requiring the favourable treatment of major tourism development proposals under local laws.

Group D: Individual Local Laws and Regulations

Separate individual laws regulate city or prefecture land-use plans, for example, in land-use zoning, urban development projects and urban facilities (Callies 1994: 61–62). After the collapse of the bubble economy in the 1990s (Sorensen 2002: 288), this level of planning became popular and included significant public participation in plan formulation, as also occurred elsewhere, in Australia for example. The techniques adopted include master planning of new areas, district planning, community-based planning (machizukuri) ordinances, and historical preservation controls (Okata 1999; Hohn 2000). Community-based planning ordinances are significant because they allow residents to be involved in the incremental improvement of their own communities (Sorensen 2002: 269–72), and unlike earlier approaches, which were fragmented among competing jurisdictions, were comprehensive in nature. Finally, the introduction of the Landscape Act in 2004 and the Act on the Promotion of Ecotourism in 2008 for the first time created a legal basis for municipalities and prefectures to introduce stricter regulations on development, buildings and access than provided for in national laws in designated areas.

The Landscape Act aims to create 'good landscapes . . . produced by the harmony between the nature, history and culture of the area and people's lifestyles and economic and other activities' (MLIT 2010). It is hoped that the preservation and creation of locally diverse landscapes will also promote tourism. Emphasis is put on shared responsibilities between national and local government, local businesses and local residents. Local governments can designate 'landscape districts', in which building regulations stricter than those operating at the national level can be applied. On the basis of this law, Kyoto City introduced comprehensive tourism control regulations in 2007. The Law for the Promotion of Ecotourism requires the establishment of eco-tourism promotion districts as a first step. Within these districts, it allows for the designation of resources vital to eco-tourism, which can be protected through access restriction or rules. Such resource conservation policies as the protection of sea turtle breeding grounds and of restricted car access to mountain trails on Yakushima Island (see Chapter 8) are promoted within this context.

This system of laws and regulations reflects the hierarchical nature of Japanese society, where most resources in urbanization and planning are consistently directed to national economic development before local and regional community wishes are taken into account (Sorensen 2002: 5–9). This has several implications: until very recently it has led to a predilection for major projects as the preferred solution to local developmental needs, 'producer-first' policies, and a disregard for any local protest that has occurred. At the local level, the result has often been poor local environmental management, and a relative lack of discussion and protest over centrally imposed decisions, which is indicative of a weak civil society (Sorensen 2002: 8–9). As a consequence, the local city planning and development control regulations (and restrictions on private property rights) that should protect public welfare did not evolve out of local societal movements (as they did in Europe or Australia, for example) but have been imposed by central authorities in ideal-typical form whenever such controls appeared to be necessary (Sorensen 2002: 338–39).

The top-down imposition of plans and regulations and the dominance of national over local goals and priorities has, however, allowed national ministries to concentrate planning expertise, keep a tight control over local spending, and focus available resources more effectively on key national goals such as regional development through tourism. The downside has been a lack of effective minimum standards at a local level, poor public environmental investment, and little local experimentation or innovation in urban planning terms. Another feature of the top-down system has been the use of 'model' large-scale development projects, rather than regulation, to achieve and control land development activity (Cooper and Flehr 2006). These features of the Japanese land-use planning system have influenced overall urbanization patterns. Traditional statutory planning is generally orientated towards physical control in urban areas alone. Rural and resort development, which is one of the main concerns of planning in other countries, is normally beyond the scope of statutory planning in Japan, and is influenced by such factors as agricultural protection policies and legislative arrangements that allow prefectural governors in conjunction with central government to designate land as one of two types of planning area. These are 'urban promotion areas', in which development is encouraged, and 'urban control areas', where in theory development is restricted but where in practice exemptions are frequently allowed (Shapira 1994: 4). In contrast to other planning systems that emphasize comprehensive socio-economic development as part of the rationale for land-use controls, physical planning and control remains the mainstay of Japanese planning. Such urban projects as land readjustment, urban redevelopment, major tourism projects and the provision of urban facilities have received prominence and special treatment, but their wider socio-economic ramifications have generally been facilitated by specific enabling laws, for example the Resort Law, rather than being controlled solely through urban planning law.

Independent of the urban development control system, the management of tourism resources has been promoted through the protection of natural and cultural heritage. Environmental control largely falls under the jurisdiction of the Ministry of the Environment, whereas cultural property is managed by the Agency for Cultural Affairs. National parks were introduced in 1934 (see Chapter 2) and the Natural Parks Law now provides for national, quasi-national and prefectural nature parks. The current Law on Protection of Cultural Properties dates from 1950, but has been constantly expanded to include tangible, intangible and folk-cultural properties, as well as groups of traditional buildings and cultural landscapes (see Chapters 4 and 7), in a hierarchy of national treasures, important cultural properties, 'normal' properties, and finally prefectural municipal properties. These designations serve as important markers for the evaluation of tourism resources (Yamamura 1995: 65; Funck 1999a: 131–38). While some of this legislation has been influenced by 'Western' concepts like the national park idea, the category of 'monuments', including historic sites, sites of scenic beauty and natural monuments, was introduced in 1919 as a unique system to protect sites that combine natural beauty and human influence. It has been expanded to accommodate the increasing need of protecting industrial and modern heritage (ACA 2009).

While this legislation has been successful in protecting and preserving islands of natural and cultural heritage that form the core of today's tourism system, it has not been sufficient to integrate them into a wider concept of development control, partly due to the lack of cooperation between different government agencies at the vertical and horizontal levels. However, this may be changing and, as noted above, recent community-based planning projects indicate a trend to perceive the environment not merely as physical surroundings but also as representing a unique way of life which should be subject to local control, especially if it is to be subject to pressures from tourism.

Summary and Conclusions

This chapter has outlined why and how the role of the state in the development and promotion of tourism is an important topic of discussion in Japan. In it we have taken a close look at how tourism policy in Japan has developed since the Second World War. We have outlined the principal methods of state involvement in Japan in respect of tourism promotion, regulatory frameworks authorized by legislation (standards and procedures for development control), state-sponsored industry planning and research, incentive schemes and subsidies for development, and government-supported networks of information providers to tourists. The economic development policies espoused by Japan generally assume that any transfer of capital and technology overseas (in this case to support outbound tourists) must be connected to a strategy for upgrading economic sectors at home (in the present case supporting inbound and domestic tourists). While our review shows that this has not been the preferred model in relation to international tourism for many years (Japan concentrated almost exclusively on outbound tourism from the 1950s to 1997), it is precisely the model we now see in the Tourism Nation Promotion Basic Plan of 2007. As a result, in the future we expect to see a much more balanced promotion of tourism in policy terms and actions that more fully integrates inbound tourism with domestic and outbound tourism.

4

DOMESTIC TOURISM AND ITS SOCIAL BACKGROUND

In this chapter the analysis shifts to domestic tourism, tracing changing travel flows and travel patterns through the economic ups and downs of the postwar era. While the domestic market has long been characterized as having strong cultural signifiers and well-established forms of mass tourism, recent years have seen a diversification within it that is closely connected to social changes. We also analyse the multifaceted social relations which have characterized local tourism, be it within destinations or between hosts and guests.

Population Structure and Distribution

Japan has undergone extreme changes in population distribution and structure during the postwar years. From a largely rural society it developed into a modern country famous for its megacities, technological advances and wealth. However, the economic miracle has now given way to the fastest ageing rate among developed nations and a stagnant economy. These changes form the background to the development of destination structures and the domestic tourism market. In the 1950s, Japan's population structure was still in the expanding phase with a typical triangular population pyramid. However, the number of births started to decline after the postwar baby boom (1947 to 1949) and then again and more rapidly after the second baby boom (1971 to 1974). The total fertility rate, defined as the average number of children that would be born per woman if all women lived to the end of their childbearing years and bore children according to a given fertility rate at each age, decreased from 4.32 in 1949 to 2.13 in 1970 and further to 1.26 in 2005, but has since recovered to 1.39 in 2011. On the other hand, since the Second Word War, average life expectancy has drastically increased in Japan:

JAPAN'S POPULATION CHANGES

Children   Working age   Retired

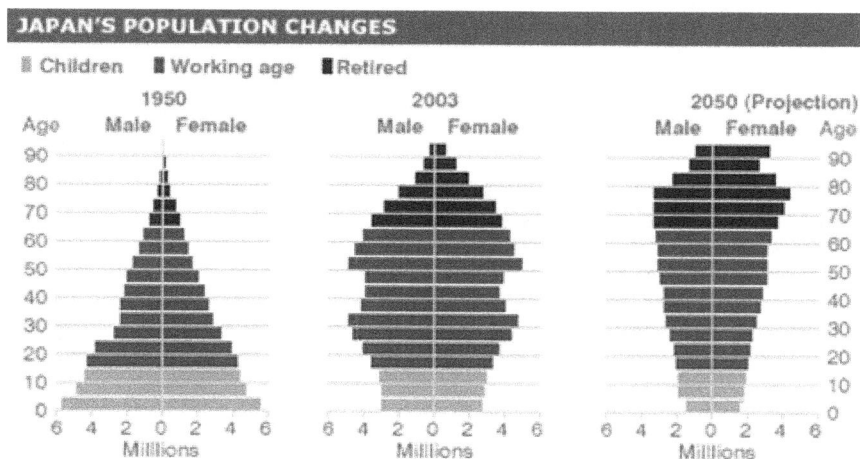

Figure 4.1: The changing profile of the Japanese population, 1950 to 2050.

Source: Buckley (2004).

in 2003, it was 78.36 years for males and 85.33 years for females. Comparing the percentage of the population over the age of 65 in developed countries, Japan ranked low until the 1980s, climbed to the middle ranks in the 1990s and has since reached the highest rank in the twenty-first century (JCO 2005). For overall trends we present a series of remarkable population pyramids for the period 1950 to 2050 (Figure 4.1; see Buckley 2004), the purpose being to demonstrate that Japan will need large supplies of immigrant labour for the foreseeable future if the economic effects of the *kôrei shakai* or aged society are to be warded off.

What these pyramids illustrate dramatically for Japan is something we are all aware of: the rapidly changing life expectancy and declining birth rates of a number of developed and developing countries over the last half century (for a summary of recent work in Japan, see Knight and Traphagen 2003, and for the newest trends, see Coulmas et al. 2008). By the late twentieth century, the birth rate in Japan and most of the other industrialized countries (apart from countries of immigration such as the US) had fallen so low that any population growth still happening was due to immigration and people living longer. Japanese women with a life expectancy of well over 80 are the longevity champions of the world, so much so that they have been able to stave off the effects of declining fertility on the total population size for some time. The impact of this probably ran out around the end of the last decade as the population peaked in 2006 at 128 million, and is now declining: by 2050 it will be closer to Second World War levels, at around 90 million (Table 4.1). Less apocalyptically and more practically, the percentage of the population over 65, which stood at around 10 per cent in 1985,

Table 4.1: Forecasts of Japanese population changes (in 1000s).

Year	Total	0-19 years	20-64 years	65-74 years	75 +
2006	127,770	23,859	77,307	14,438	12,166
2010	127,176	22,542	75,223	15,190	14,222
2015	125,430	20,823	70,826	17,329	16,452
2020	122,735	18,810	68,026	17,162	18,737
2025	119,270	16,925	65,991	14,687	21,667
2030	115,224	15,502	63,052	14,011	22,659
2035	110,679	14,486	58,945	14,897	22,352
2040	105,695	13,560	53,608	16,382	22,145
2045	100,443	12,584	49,452	15,937	22,471
2050	95,152	11,552	45,959	13,912	23,728
2055	89,930	10,566	42,901	12,597	23,866

Source: IPSS (2006).

is due to climb to 26 per cent in 2025, an increase in actual numbers from 12.5 to 31.5 million (Traphagen 2000: 11).

These changes are well illustrated in Figure 4.1. The first population pyramid, for 1950, shows the kind of pattern typical of developing countries, with high fertility, steady mortality, and few people in the older age groups. The second shows the dramatic fertility decline of the postwar period, with the pyramid on the way to becoming inverted. The middle age groups form the largest population, while the population of children is already in steep decline. The postwar baby boomers are also clearly visible: the birth rate actually halved between 1947 and 1957 (Knight and Traphagen 2003). But the projection for 2050 is perhaps the most interesting. The population pyramid has become inverted, with the decline in fertility continuing steadily, and with most people surviving into their eighties. Indeed one of the most remarkable features is that the residual category of women above 90 will then be so large that it becomes an extrusion, suggesting that the graph ought to be continued upwards for those aged over 100 and even over 110 to cover this cohort in future. But this is not the only problem: the number of those under 20 years old will decline to less than half, the number of retirees (over 65 years) will rise to 36 million from its current level of 26 million, and the working age population (20 to 64) will decline by 44.5 per cent. As a result, the population dependency ratio is projected to decrease from a high of 2.3 in 1990 to 1.4 in 2030 (NIPSS 2002). While the same dependency ratio existed in 1950, the difference in 2030 will be that the populations of the elderly and children have reversed positions. As a result, today Japan is not only well into the low stationary phase of population development but it is also is seen by other developed countries as a model case of a shrinking population.

However, to offset this gloomy forecast, the 'mature', 'older' or 'senior' tourism market in developed countries, as in some rapidly developing economies like China or Taiwan, is of growing interest to service providers. Escalating numbers of ageing consumers with relatively large financial resources, time flexibility, more independence, increasing levels of educational attainment and better overall health are known to travel more frequently, for longer distances and to stay for longer periods at destinations. Furthermore, a tendency to favour packaged travel has been observed in older tourists, which makes this market segment even more attractive to the tourism industry. However, it has been repeatedly pointed out that this large emerging market is not yet well understood. Japan, given its fast changing population structure, may constitute an ideal case study for examining the seniors market (Funck 2008). An ageing population also affects the structure of destinations. As buildings fall empty, traditional methods of maintenance are forgotten, and inhabitants lack the strength and energy to keep up cultural activities, the material and cultural heritage of an area will suffer (Cooper and Eades 2007). The ageing of whole communities, for example, in remote areas or in designated protected historic districts also inhibits the introduction of modern resource management due to lack of interest and human resources (Moeran 1997).

In the tourism industry, small-scale family-run businesses, which offer a large proportion of the services available, face difficulties in securing business successors or service personnel, and ageing demographics at tourist destinations also affect the ability of destinations to adjust to new, more diverse patterns of demand, to offer new or trendy forms of recreational activities, and to cope with the increasing influx of foreign tourists (Funck 2008). Processes of population change and ageing proceed irregularly in different parts of the country (You and Leary 2000). The concentration of population, wealth and power in the Tokyo Metropolitan Area is notorious, as is the Pacific Belt Zone of major cities extending to Fukuoka in the west and Sendai to the north. Witherick and Carr show very clearly the unbalanced regional structure of the country: 'Japan continues to be characterized by a two-class spatial society, of the "haves" and "have nots", of the core and the periphery' (Witherick and Carr 1993: 172).

During the bubble economy of the late 1980s it was assumed that economic growth had finally spread throughout the country and a better balance had been achieved through rising incomes, also due in part to the continuous development of high-speed transport links like highways, *shinkansen* express trains and regional airports. However, the ensuing economic downturn and the changing population dynamics of recent years have shown that the dual regional structure never really disappeared. In 1998, the introduction to the Fifth Comprehensive National Development Plan by the Japanese government described the existing regional structure as follows:

So far, Japan has been structured in a way that has led to an over-concentration of population and function in the Pacific belt, and control emanating from the single pole that is Tokyo. This structure reflects the historical development of the country's economy in this century, in catching up with Europe and the United States within the shortest possible period. Japan's current high economic standard is a result of focusing everything on quantitative growth in the economy. At the same time, however, the country has grown around the single pole, Tokyo, and with a single national population axis that is called the Pacific belt. This structure is at the root of numerous problems including the lack of vitality in rural communities, the lack of comfortable living in large cities, the destruction of the natural environment, the loss of much of Japan's beautiful scenery, and the country's vulnerability to local disasters. (MLIT 1998)

In the twenty-first century the result of this is that peripheral rural areas not only lose population but might fall empty in the long run, and even regional cities feel the pressure of competition for a decreasing younger population segment and workforce.

As can be seen in Figure 4.2, population continues to concentrate in and around the ever expanding metropolitan areas. Within each prefecture, the city housing the prefectural government or, in a few cases the largest city, creates its own core and periphery system. This population distribution has manifold impacts on the

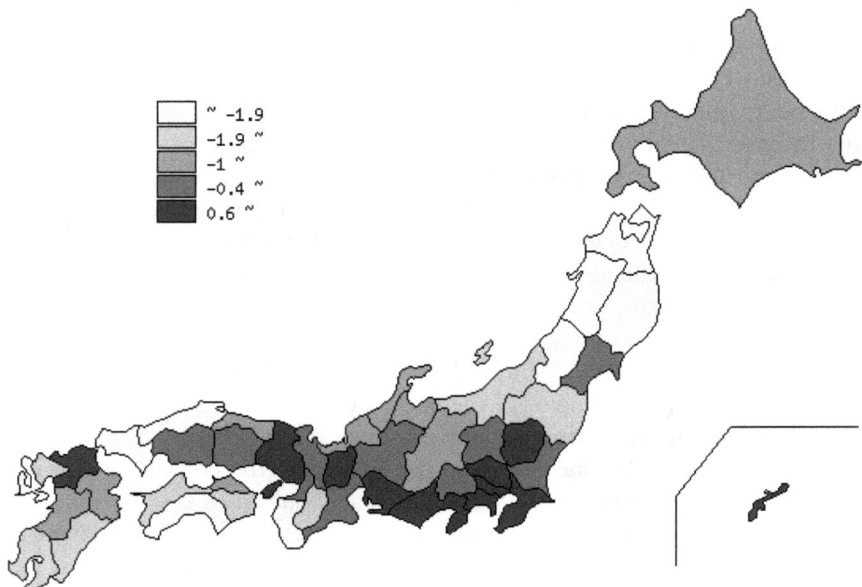

Figure 4.2: Population change by prefecture, 2000 to 2005.

Source: MIAC (2000, 2005).

domestic (and inbound) tourism markets. Given the fact, explained in detail below, that most domestic trips last only one or two nights, 'pleasure peripheries' with a stable tourism industry can only develop in areas that lie two to four hours from urban centres. While time–distance ratios can be continuously reduced through the development of high-speed transport systems, leading to a constant shift and expansion of the border between destinations for overnight stay and for day trips, the cost has in fact increased, as all high-speed means of transport are distinctly more expensive than their former, slower counterparts. Thus, typical travel patterns during phases of economic downturn are increasingly the so-called *an-kin-tan* (cheap-close-short) type and have put peripheral regions in an even more marginal position in the tourism market since the 1990s. Theme parks developed during the bubble economy in peripheral regions of Japan, for example, have suffered severely due to access problems from major population centres, whereas the Disney theme park in Chiba Prefecture near Tokyo has a constant source of visitors from the ever-expanding Tokyo metropolitan area as well as from overseas visitors arriving through nearby Narita airport.

The Social Background

Possibilities for travel are influenced by a variety of social factors that control the time and budget of individuals. Some of them, like working hours and holidays, are easier to identify as they occur in the public realm, while those in the private sphere like the gender division of leisure or family restrictions are more difficult to analyse. Since the 1970s, Japan has been criticized for long working hours, especially during the years when it accumulated a large surplus in foreign trade. Whereas leisure policies in the 1970s were advocated as a precondition for the development of a stronger service industry, in the 1980s the Japanese government tried to address diplomatic pressure by the EU and USA through formulating a leisure policy that aimed at shorter working hours, a five-day working week and more leisure opportunities (Leheny 2003: 114). Ensuing changes in the labour laws in 1988 led to a decrease in scheduled, contract-based working hours. However, in 2003, Japanese were still working 1,975 hours per year, about the same as Americans (1,929) and British workers (1,888), but more than employees in continental Europe (less than 1,600 hours in France and Germany). In 2004, working hours had in fact increased for the third consecutive year, due to more non-scheduled work. Since 1992, officially registered non-scheduled work has amounted to about 10 hours per month on average (MHLW 2006).

In 1985, before the government embarked on a policy to actively reduce working hours, 76.5 per cent of employees in companies with more than thirty employees worked under some kind of system that allowed them two days off per week; this percentage had increased to 96 per cent in 1996, but has since declined again to around 90 per cent in 2010. However, only 56.1 per cent enjoy a consistent five-day week; the rest have to work six days every other or every third week. The average number of individual paid holidays in 2008 was 18 days, up from 15.2 in 1985, but only 47.4 per cent of these were actually taken, down from 55.2 per cent in 1995. Apart from their individual days off though, Japanese workers enjoy 14 national holidays and many employees also have about four days of special summer holidays (MHLW yearly a). The number of national holidays has increased constantly with additions like the Day of the Sea in July. Since 2000, four of these holidays have been shifted to Mondays to create a three-day weekend, and domestic tourism depends heavily on these national holidays. In the annual survey on tourism published by the NKK (Japan Tourism Association), 75 per cent of respondents in 2004 did not use their individual paid holidays for domestic trips, and this percentage hasn't changed over the last fifteen years (NKK 2005: 64). The reliance on national holidays rather than individual paid leave has severe consequences for the domestic tourism industry and individual destinations, as it leads to an increased concentration of visitors.

Finally, in considering working hours and leisure we should not neglect the fact that about 47 per cent of the labour force work in small companies with less than thirty employees and often have to endure much stricter working conditions. For example, small companies or self-employed persons mostly work on national holidays. Unpaid overtime, not registered in any surveys, is also common in private companies as well as public services. In addition, people work past retirement age more commonly than in many other countries. According to the population census in 2005, half of all men and one quarter of all women between the ages of 65 and 69 were still part of the labour force (Funck 2008).

The connection between work and travel is thus manifold, as work certainly restricts time for travelling. On the other hand, it provides the necessary financial background and creates opportunities for business trips, company recreational trips or combinations of business and recreational trips. The employment and business structure of Japan may not favour individual leisure travel over long periods, but it certainly creates many requirements to travel in connection with work. Company recreational trips are a regular feature, even in small companies. The highly centralized structure of companies and bureaucracies necessitates frequent travel between the centre and the regional 'outposts', especially since Japanese business culture values face-to-face encounters more highly than written or even telephone contacts. The transfer of employees throughout the country also separates families and thus increases weekend travel. Travel in connection with work therefore forms an important segment of the travel and tourism market, and influences the structure of the tourism industry.

The second major social factor that affects travel is the restrictions resulting from household and family structures. In Japan, care for children and the elderly is mainly carried out by women. Compared to 16 per cent of men, about one quarter of women in their 40s and 50s cite 'not being able to leave the house' as a reason for not travelling (NKK 2009:118). Children also experience their own time restrictions that indirectly bind the whole family. School activities on weekends and prep schools for different types of entrance examinations, but also club activities at school leave little free time and often require the attendance of parents too. On the other hand, Japan's high life expectancy, combined with low birth rates and a social policy that emphasizes care for the elderly at home, is resulting in a situation where care for the elderly might soon become a bigger social phenomenon than child care. In respect of tourism in Japan then, time generally is a much stronger constraint than money and is the most often cited reason for not travelling, even for those in their teens or twenties (NKK 2009: 118). Limited time budgets are therefore an important factor in Japanese domestic tourism.

Travel Life Cycles and Market Segmentation

It is a truism that opportunities to travel change during a person's life and ulti-mately combine into personal travel biographies. However, it can also be argued that there are collective travel life cycles that most members of a society or a segment of its population experience. March introduced the 'Japanese travel life cycle' as a useful classificatory scheme for the Japanese outbound market, as it fitted Japanese society at the time with its 'highly organized and group-oriented patterns of travel that have emerged over the past one hundred years' (March 2000: 185). He distinguished between family trips, school excursions, language trips, graduation holidays, honeymoons, overseas weddings, in-company trips and silver trips, the latter referring to older travellers after retirement. Japan's biggest travel agent, the Japan Travel Bureau (JTB), also uses age, marital status and working status to classify Japanese outbound travellers (JTB 2001, 2003). In an analysis of the national tourism market, JTB considers type of travel companion as the most important factor influencing travel behaviour, but adds the existence of children and their age as an additional, life-stage-dependent element (Nihon Kôtsû Kôsha 2006: 12). Certainly, Japanese ways of travel have come a long way, from the time when 'finally everybody can go out' and enjoy mass tourism on the package tours that became important during the 1960s (Yasumura 2001: 127), to the present, where the expression 'one person ten colours' (Nihon Kôtsû Kôsha 2006: 11) is used in market analysis to symbolize the variety of travel behaviour, not between people but within one single person. However, opportunities to travel still depend on life stages and social patterns and it is therefore useful to examine and expand on the idea of the 'travel life cycle' suggested by March (2000).

Most Japanese have their first travel experience as part of a family trip. Family trips have developed into one of the most important and highly differentiated market segments in the country, as elsewhere. In the 1960s, cheap Japanese-style inns called *minshuku* developed in the mountains and along the coast. Different types of public lodgings, the Japanese version of 'social tourism' (Yasumura 2001: 142), also offered cheap accommodation in attractive natural surroundings to families from the cities. Nowadays, family trips abroad are common and 'family' has been expanded to include adult children and their parents, or three generations travelling together.

Market Segmentation: School Trips

The next important segment is the first official opportunity people get to travel, and Japanese children experience this as the school trip (*shûgaku ryokô*). School excursions date back to the late nineteenth century, when they were introduced as a means of physical and spiritual training for Japan's youth (Oedewald 2009: 116). Most Japanese experience three trips during their school life, one each in elementary, junior and senior high school. These trips form part of their education for adult life, and accordingly the aims of school trips emphasize learning to act in groups, fostering lasting ties among students, and creating good memories of school life, rather than integrated learning and fieldwork linked to the study of history, geography and society (NSRK 2005). Since the 1980s, sports like skiing have also become popular. In the 1990s promoting international exchanges through trips abroad was added as a new aim, mainly in senior high schools. Popular domestic destinations are Kyoto, Nara and Hiroshima for elementary school children, the Tokyo area for junior high, and Hokkaidô and Okinawa for senior high school students. Visits to historic sites, temples and shrines are the most popular activities. Sites connected to peace education like Hiroshima, Nagasaki and Okinawa offer serious education, while visits to theme parks provide entertainment (NSRK 2005).

School trips have undergone three major changes in the last 20 years. Permission to use air travel has increased the range of possible destinations and was a precondition for the second change, an increase in trips abroad. The third change occurred with the introduction of integrated learning in the curriculum, which led to an increasing emphasis on experience in trips which were previously oriented around sightseeing. School trip regulations are the responsibility of the prefectural or, in the case of independent cities, municipal education boards, and therefore vary widely across the country. However, these rules only apply to public schools. For private schools, especially those that emphasize quality of service over quality of education, interesting or even extravagant school trips form an important part of the image that attracts their 'customers', the pupils and their parents. Private school trips by airplane began in 1969, and trips abroad started in 1972. Public schools had to wait until Fukuoka Prefecture allowed flights to Okinawa in 1978, and Kumamoto Prefecture was the first to permit trips to Korea in 1987 (NSRK 2007: 111–15). When the national government in 1987 embarked on its 'Ten Million' programme to increase the number of outbound travellers as a means to counter international criticism of Japan's high trade surplus, school trips became part of the target (Leheny 2003: 151). The Ministry of Education had no choice but to change its educational directives and to declare in 1988 that trips by airplane and to foreign countries were 'not forbidden'. In 1992, 70 per cent of prefectures and cities permitted travel by plane, and all did so by 2005. The number of educational boards allowing trips abroad increased from 14 in 1990 to 32 in 1995, 49 in 2000 and almost all by 2005 (NSRK 2007). However, permission is subject to restrictions concerning cost, length and destination.

As can be seen from the regions that first gave the permissions for overseas trips, educational boards in the west of Japan are much more enthusiastic about foreign travel than their eastern counterparts. In the Kansai area and to the west of it, 8 to 12 per cent of public and 32 to 39 per cent of private senior high schools went on international school trips in 2010, compared with 6 per cent and 23 per cent in the Kantô area, which includes the capital (ZSRK 2010). This runs counter to the general trend in international travel, where inhabitants of the metropolitan capital area show higher travel intensity than the rest of the country. International school trips also differ from general outbound trips concerning their destination. When trips abroad gained popularity in the 1980s, travellers favoured Western destinations like the USA or Europe. It was not until the 1990s that trips to nearby Asian states increased. The opposite pattern can be seen with school trips, which first went to cheap, nearby South Korea and China and only recently expanded to North America, Australia and Oceania, and Europe. In general then, school trips follow many traditional patterns of domestic tourism: visits to famous and recognized sites, buying presents, and travelling in groups with some form of guidance (Oedewald 2009: 124). They also help to establish this kind of travel as normal in later life.

University life includes the possibility to experience new ways of travel. While backpacking among students is less popular than, say, in Europe, many young Japanese now set out on individual trips on their own or with friends. Trips connected to university education include language trips abroad, often part of a university programme, trips included in club activities, and seminar trips conducted with their advisor and other students from the same seminar. Graduation trips, on the other hand, are again left to individual taste. Club trips (*gasshuku*) organized by students themselves, mainly for intensive sports training or to participate in sporting events, are an important opportunity to experience travel organization. A whole sector of cheap accommodation and sports facilities in rural areas of Japan now caters to this particular activity. Although many students do not join clubs, student orientation camps, seminar trips and other study trips offer similar experiences. By the time they leave university, most students have thus

72 • JAPANESE TOURISM

learned not only how to organize a trip for themselves, but also how to plan, decide and move in a group.

Adult Trips

The stage of life between the end of education and setting up a family, characterized by a certain degree of economic and social freedom, has been expanding in Japan due to the increasingly older age of marriage. The average age for marriage changed from 25.9 to 29.8 (men) and from 23.1 to 28 (women) between 1950 and 2005 (MHLW yearly b), and many do not marry until their 40s. During this phase such freedoms mean that travel activities are plenty and varied. Although travel as a non-married couple is also common, trips with colleges or friends, or business colleagues, in small groups often of the same sex, are a far more distinctive feature (Nihon Kôtsû Kôsha 2006: 15).

Working life is accompanied by company trips, although according to surveys conducted since 1988, the percentage of companies using incentive trips decreased from a peak of 99.3 per cent in 1992 to 39.5 per cent in 2004 (SRI 1999, 2004). The most important reason given for abolishing trips is a change in the attitude of employees, followed by a lower budget for social and welfare costs. However, compared to 1988, when only 8.6 percent of companies had ever conducted a trip abroad, in 2004 this had increased to 46 per cent. While 62.7 per cent of companies paid for more than 50 per cent of their worker's travel expenses at the peak of the bubble economy in 1990, this decreased to 49.1 per cent in 1999 during the recession but had recovered to 71.1 per cent by 2004. In general, smaller companies cover a larger part of the expenses. Trips are usually short, two days for domestic and three to four days for international trips, and are conducted mainly around weekends and/or national holidays. To make the trips more attractive, companies conduct questionnaires among employees about the destination, allow for participation in free groups rather than by department, offer different routes to choose from, and include some free time or start the trips at the destination; as a result, the participation rate in 2004 was 70.1 per cent.

Favourite domestic destinations include Hokkaido, Shizuoka, Nagano and Okinawa, and Hong Kong/Macao, Guam, Seoul and Taiwan for international trips. With general travel patterns shifting from group tours to individual travel, the Sanro Research Institute concludes that the balance between individual and company will have to be carefully considered on company trips in future (SRI 2004). In addition, the traditional bus trip, where talking, singing, drinking and playing games on the bus were probably more important than the destination, will have to be replaced by trips that attract employees to spend their money and free time with their company if this form of travel is to continue. A special kind of these work-related group tours are the trips organized by agricultural cooperatives for their members. As questionnaires conducted among cooperative members show, a 'group tour as regular event' is the most common occasion for a trip for many of them (ZNKK 1997), but its nature is changing.

Family life starts with one of the most expensive trips, the honeymoon. Legend has it that the first Japanese honeymoon was undertaken in 1866 by Sakamoto Ryôma, a popular hero of the Meiji Restoration. He took his newly wed wife with him to Kagoshima where he went to heal his wounds from an assassination attempt. Popular honeymoon destinations in Japan after 1945 were Shirahama Spa south of Osaka, the Izu Peninsula, and Miyazaki in Kyûshû, all located by the sea and with a distinctive 'southern' image (Kanda 2001). Miyazaki even established itself as 'Japan's Hawaii', though it was soon replaced by the 'real' Hawaii. According to data from JTB, the three most popular honeymoon destinations booked through the company changed from southern Kyûshu (Miyazaki), the southern Kinki area (Shirahama) and southern Izu in 1970 to include Hawaii for the first time in 1978. Since 1985, foreign destinations have topped the list, namely Hawaii, Europe and Oceania (mainly Australia and New Zealand). Couples spend about ¥500,000 for a trip abroad and half that amount for a national destination (JTB 2000).

After having married and settled down with their family, residents find a variety of local organizations to join. Traditional neighbourhood organizations organize festivals, garbage disposal and clean-up days. These are still very common even in the urban context (Hohn 2000: 517). Children's, women's and seniors' associations are also organized at a local level. Many of these organizations offer regular trips for their members, from one-day shopping excursions to travel abroad. These trips are mainly joined by older members of the community, especially those living alone or with their children but without a spouse.

After retirement, neighbours and friends thus become increasingly important as travel companions. The percentage of over 60s travelling with neighbours is twice as high as the average, and the percentage of those choosing friends as travel companions is 10 per cent higher than average (Figure 4.3). Travel intensity is higher than the general average for those in their late 50s and early 60s, but then declines (MIAC 2001), as health problems become the major reason for not travelling for those in their 70s (NKK 2009: 118).

Travel Flows and Patterns

After discussing the social background of domestic tourism, we now turn to travel flows, travel patterns and travel behaviour. However, in this context a background note on data availability is necessary.

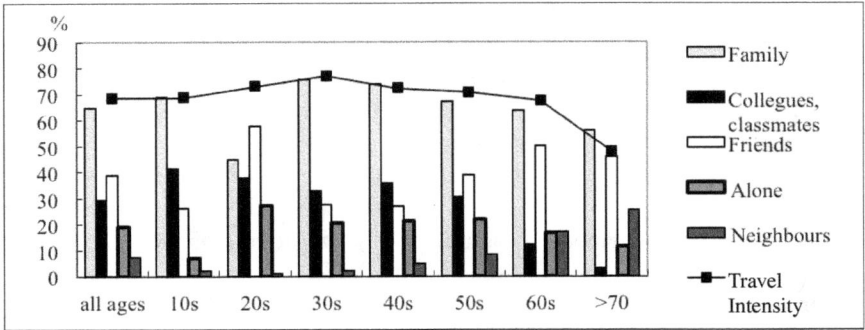

Figure 4.3: Travel intensity and travel companions by age, 2001.
Source: MIAC (2001).

A Note on Tourism Statistics

As has been noted frequently (Funck 1994, 1999a), there exist even today no reliable tourism statistics in Japan. Each prefecture is free to choose their methods for counting tourists, and thus results cannot easily be compared across prefectures. Most prefectures gather their data through the municipalities; some also use material provided by transport agencies or conduct their own investigations. But neither the definition of tourist used nor the methods of investigations are explained. All prefectures give aggregate numbers, which means a person visiting different facilities is counted at each facility and so it is actually not the number of persons visiting the prefecture which is being reported but the total number of visits to sites. Most prefectures use the calendar year to enumerate visitors, but some use the fiscal year from April to March. Given these restrictions, regional statistics can only be compared within each prefecture or, when given, for singular attractions. Data provided by the prefectural administrations is summarized in two yearly publications: NKK's 'Zenkoku kankô dôkô', and Seikatsu Jôhô Sentâ's 'Databook of Tourists and Tourists Resorts in Japan'.

Apart from statistics collected at the local and regional level, most countries conduct regular sample surveys on tourism. NKK conducted such a survey every second year from 1964 and have done so every year since 1999 (this being the 'Kankô no jittai to shikô'). Questions cover domestic overnight trips, domestic holiday overnight trips, domestic excursion holiday trips (one day) and overseas trips. The number in samples has varied; the survey presently covers 4,500 persons over 15 years old from over 200 places, selected by two-step layered random selection, and about 3,300 valid answers are collected each time. From this sample, only the data on travel intensity and on the number of trips are calculated for the whole population. The survey is publicly available and contains a summary, tables for the year, basic tables for the whole period since 1964, and the original questionnaire. This survey is a major source for analysing long-term changes in travel flows and patterns.

In accordance with a stronger emphasis on tourism policy since 2003, the Ministry of Land, Industry and Transport (MLIT) has strengthened collection of tourism statistics as a necessary base. In 2003, a survey on consumption trends in travel and tourism (*ryokô kankô dôkô chôsa*) was introduced. Another recent addition to the tourism statistics has been the 'overnight-trip statistics survey' (*shukuhaku ryokô tôkei chôsa*), conducted for the first time in 2007 (MLIT 2008). This is an annual survey and conducted under national uniform standards in all prefectures. The survey is used to collect time-series data such as the number of guests staying in all hotels, inns and simple guesthouses with ten or more employees. Under the newly established Tourism Agency, the government also started a unified system of nationwide data collection based on common rules created in 2009. The development of a survey covering the economic effects of tourism in destinations is also in progress (MLIT 2012). For data on the origin of tourists, the 'Survey on Time Use and Leisure Activities' (MIAC 1996, 2001, 2006a) outlines travel intensity by prefecture and is conducted every five years.

Travel Flows

Due to the limited availability of data, travel flows can be analysed only very broadly. First, the departure point should be considered. All surveys show higher travel intensity for major metropolitan areas compared to rural parts of the country. In 2001, 72.4 per cent of metropolitan area inhabitants travelled in Japan and 15.7 per cent abroad, compared to 57.3 per cent and 7.6 per cent for those living in small towns (MIAC 2001). However, domestic travel intensity exceeds 70 per cent only in the Kantô and Kansai conurbations. As Figure 4.4 shows, not only is population concentrated in the urban core areas, but urban residents also travel more. As a consequence, given the average domestic trip length of around two days, this creates a kind of 'pleasure periphery' around the major metropolitan areas. As mentioned above, the limits of these peripheries have been constantly pushed outwards by changes in transport infrastructure.

Second, data on region of departure and destination collected in the surveys of the NKK since 1964 show a strong consistency of travel flows between regions. While 79.5 per cent of all respondents cross prefectural boundaries (NKK 2005: 19), many trips stay within the wider region. In particular, the most peripheral areas – Hokkaido, Tôhoku and Kyûshû – show strong independence as tourist regions, as more than 60 per cent of trips are conducted within the region. Kansai, including major tourist attractions like the historic cities of Kyoto and Nara and the coastlines of the Pacific Ocean and Sea of Japan, also shows a high percentage of intra-regional travel. Kansai inhabitants rarely visit the regions east

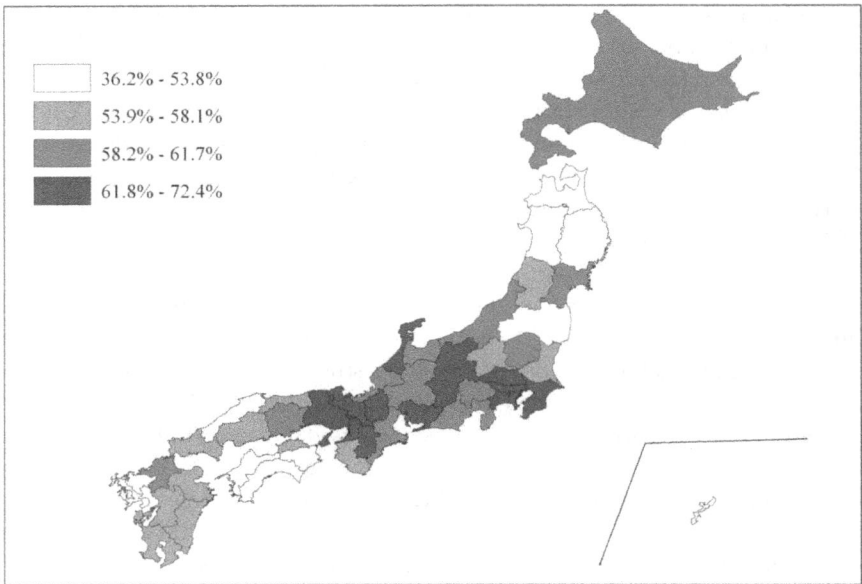

36.2% - 53.8%

53.9% - 58.1%

58.2% - 61.7%

61.8% - 72.4%

Figure 4.4: Travel intensity (domestic, overnight) by prefecture, 2006.
Source: MIAC (2006a).

of Kantô, and Kantô residents seldom travel further west than the Chûbu region. Shikoku, the smallest regional unit, is the only area where travel to an outside region, namely Kansai, is more frequent than inside Shikoku. In all prefectures, trips to neighbouring prefectures account for the highest number of trips crossing prefectural borders. Destinations of trips by train and by plane show a wider distribution.

Third, the 'overnight-trip statistics survey' conducted in 2007 finally allowed for the analysis of destination patterns, although only by prefecture and not by tourist destination area. Figure 4.5 identifies three types of regions in Japan with high numbers of overnight stays: prefectures containing large conurbation core areas; regions easily reached for a one-night trip from the three metropolitan areas of Kanto, Kansai and Nagoya; and the national pleasure periphery consisting of Hokkaido and Okinawa. The only exception is Kumamoto Prefecture in western Kyûshû, which in this year might still be an effect of the partial opening of the Kyûshû *shinkansen* in 2004. The survey also differentiates accommodation facilities according to the percentage of visitors staying for holiday or sightseeing purposes as opposed to business. Overnight stays in facilities with more than 50 per cent holiday/sightseeing visitors show a very similar pattern, but with smaller numbers in urban core areas, and with larger numbers in prefectures with famous

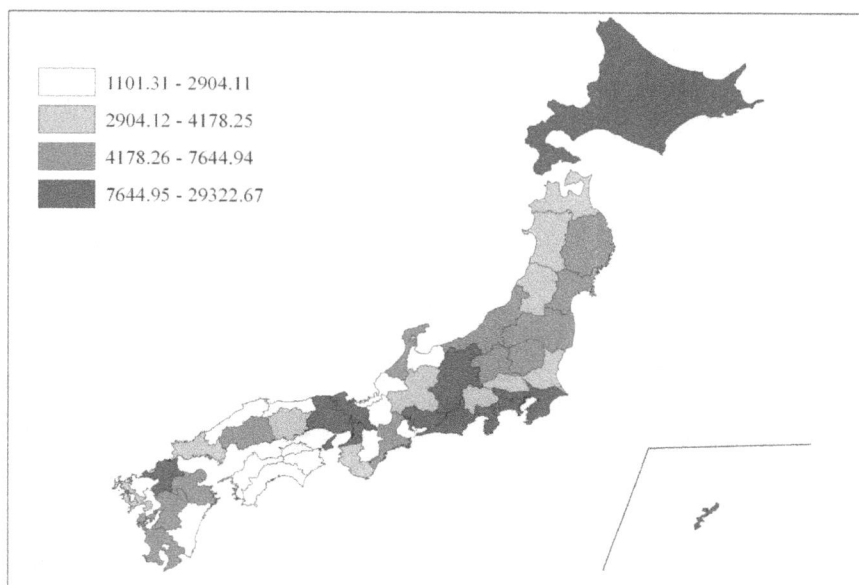

Figure 4.5: Number of nights stayed in accommodation facilities by prefecture, 2007
(Japanese visitors only, in 1000s).

Source: MLIT (2008).

onsen like Ôita in Kyûshû and Ishikawa on the Sea of Japan coast. Generally, eastern Japan has more overnight stays than the western part of the country; Shikoku and the Chûgoku region of the western end of Honshû are especially weak destinations. Population patterns therefore strongly influence the distribution of overnight stays, as could be expected considering the short duration of domestic trips.

Travel Patterns

Major changes in Japanese domestic travel patterns have been pointed out. According to the White Paper on leisure (YKS 1994), postwar tourism can be separated into ten-year phases. In the first phase, starting in 1963, mass tourism spread as a consequence of high economic growth. The construction of the *shinkansen* railways and the deregulation of trips abroad in 1964 increased domestic and foreign travel, while the Olympic Games held in Tokyo the same year raised interest in sport. This first growth period came to a halt with the oil shock in 1973. In the following ten years, *an-kin-tan*, or 'cheap-close-short', became the keyword for travel. Easy-to-afford urban recreation like culture classes and wellness activities were popular. The opening of Tokyo Disneyland in 1983 started the third phase, dubbed the 'decade of the leisure industry'. In the surveys conducted regularly by the government during this phase, for the first time Japanese adults cited leisure as their biggest concern in life rather than work or family. From 1987 the bubble economy fuelled demand in the leisure and tourism market. The Resort Law, passed in 1987 (see Chapter 5), aimed to create resort facilities all over the country. When the yen started to rise after the Plaza Agreement in 1985, trips abroad became affordable and the number of travellers to foreign countries soon passed the ten million mark. When the bubble burst in 1991, once again tourism markets felt the effect of the resultant economic uncertainty. Although travel intensity did not decrease, the number, length and cost of trips was reduced. Rather than visit theme parks and resorts, many people began to meet with friends, watch TV and rest. But as the yen was still strong against the US dollar, longer trips were increasingly aimed at destinations abroad in the 1990s. Domestic travel destinations, especially theme parks developed during the bubble economy, saw a decrease in visitors and sales. When the ten-year cycle of the economy eventually showed some recovery, around 2003, the tourism market swung back into a positive mood. However, the rise of terrorism, the second Iraq war and scares over SARS and avian flu and so forth kept many safety-conscious Japanese travellers inside the country. From 2007 onwards, when the first baby-boom generation started to retire, a further upswing was expected but this has been dampened to date by the financial and economic crisis that began in the autumn of 2008.

Within these trends however, recent market analyses emphasize the high diversity of the Japanese tourism market and attempts by domestic destinations and tourism industries to cope with this (Nihon Kôtsû Kôsha 2006). Considering this pattern of diversification, Graburn's claim that 'the Japanese have a low sense of cultural self-confidence, and they usually only travel in groups or at least visit well-known "culturally approved" attractions' (Graburn 1995: 48) doesn't hold true anymore. Throughout these ups and downs, some changes in travel patterns have emerged. Group travel, especially with companies, schools, or neighbourhood, agricultural and other associations, has been replaced by individual travel with families and friends (Figure 4.6). Women, who showed an almost 10 percent lower travel intensity than men in the 1960s, travelled equally frequently in the 1990s, and the tourism industry has had to adjust facilities accordingly. Accommodation suppliers found that they needed to diversify, as the traditional Japanese *ryokan* and even Japanese-style family inns, *minshuku*, lost popularity to hotels, Western-style pensions and camp sites. Modes of transport shifted from train and tour buses to cars and, from the late 1980s, to planes. Only the length of domestic trips and the fact that residents of metropolitan areas travel more than their rural counterparts remained basically unchanged over the years.

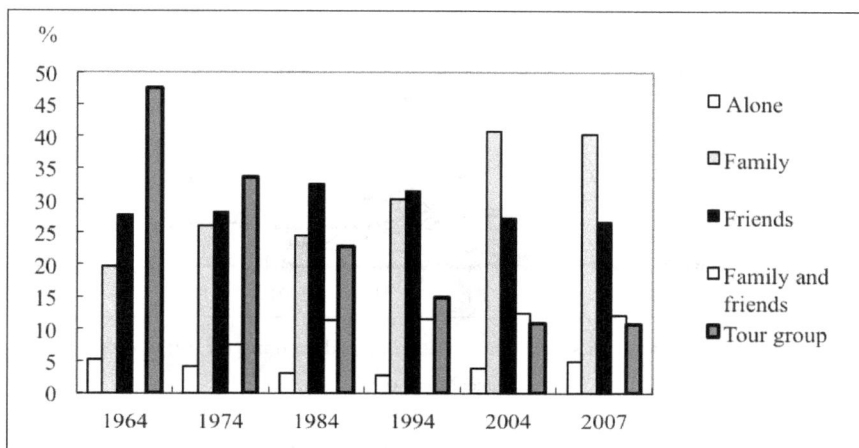

Figure 4.6: Changes in travel companions, 1964 to 2007.

Source: NKK (yearly b).

Changes in Modes of Transport

The shift in modes of transport from trains and buses to private cars and planes is a common feature of postwar mass tourism development in developed countries, and the pattern in Japan is no exception. It should be noted, however, that trains and buses, especially tour buses, are still an important feature of Japanese domestic tourism. The latter have a strong competitive advantage, as they provide fast connections between spread-out and difficult-to-reach locations and are much cheaper than planes and trains, which offer few discount possibilities. The railway system remains one of the most extensive, most reliable and quickest systems in the world today.

Changes in the mode of transport used are not restricted to tourism. Figure 4.7 shows changes in general transport modes that also have influenced tourism flows. Due to the increased importance of private cars as a mode of transport in tourism, the construction of highways has a very strong influence on the development – and abandonment – of destinations. Motorways were extended from 286 kilometres in 1985 to 2,494 kilometres in 1995 and 3,965 km in 2005. Each extension, especially those connected with the metropolitan areas, put new locations on the map and deprived others of overnight visitors. On the other hand, while airplanes are an important transport mode, especially to the national pleasure peripheries of Hokkaido and Okinawa, the construction of small regional airports all around the country has done little to attract new tourists. Most of these airports feature only one regular flight per day to Tokyo, and charter flights are uncommon in domestic tourism. Only in the twenty-first century have these airports seen their

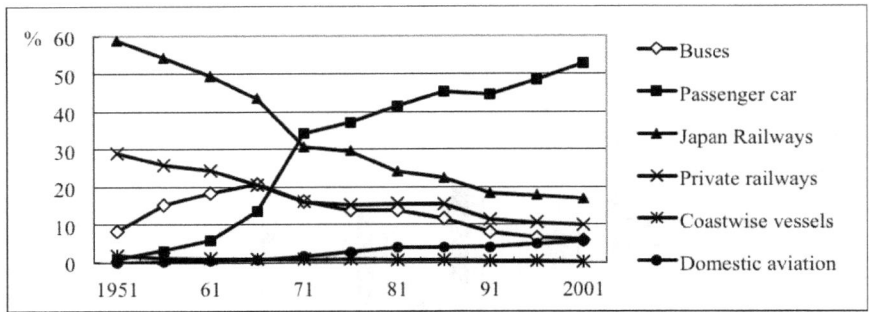

Figure 4.7: Domestic passenger transportation by mode of transport, 1951 to 2001.

Source: MIAC (n.y.).

role in tourism increase, as they have become the target of charter flights to and from nearby Asian countries.

The Diversification of Activities and Motivations

As mentioned in Chapter 2, many forms of outdoor recreation and ways of spending leisure time and holidays were introduced or influenced by Westerners coming to Japan from the late nineteenth century on. On the other hand, recreational activities and tourism after 1945, while following some trends common to industrialized nations worldwide, developed in close connection with the national policy context (Chapter 3), so that by the end of the twentieth century Japan had developed a very distinctive domestic tourism market catering almost exclusively to the Japanese tourist (Figure 4.8).

Pattern analysis shows that traditional sightseeing activities, like looking at nature and landscapes or visiting temples and shrines, have been declining. Visits to hot springs are the only traditional pastime that has actually increased in popularity. On the other hand, tourist activities organized around facilities, like theme parks, museums and urban facilities, have gained in popularity. Less visible in the statistics, the rural areas have experienced a re-evaluation as nostalgic places worth a visit (Moon 2002). This diversification of tourist activities from the 1960s to the late 1990s can be divided into trends in outdoor activities, increased interest in newly developed tourist facilities, and the rediscovery of heritage.

Trends in Outdoor Activities

Outdoor activities connected to natural resources like mountains and the sea or to the availability of wide open spaces mainly happen outside everyday environments, especially in a country with large metropolitan areas like Japan. Therefore,

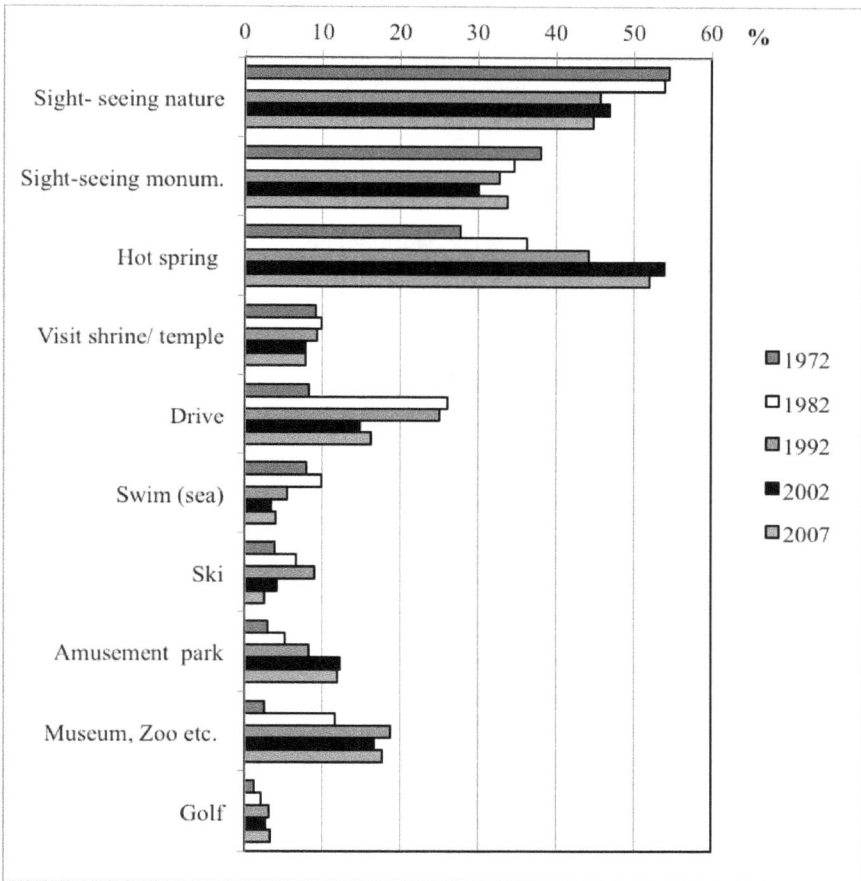

Figure 4.8: Changes in major activities at destinations, 1972 to 2007.
Source: NKK (yearly b).

it is difficult to distinguish between leisure and tourism and it can be argued that they both occur in the tourism space. We look at trends in skiing, golf and marine leisure sectors in this section. According to Kureha (2002), skiing experienced three growth periods: in the 1930s as a competitive sport for student clubs and as a leisure activity for wealthy people, as a mass tourism activity in the 1960s, and as a fashionable leisure activity for urbanites in the 1980s. In the 1960s, small ski areas were developed by local capital on former common land in villages close to railway lines. Their number increased from 71 in 1960 to 417 in 1980 (Kureha 1995). These ski slopes formed the heart of small clusters of *minshuku* and other facilities. They provided income during the winter season, where traditionally many farmers had to relocate temporarily to urban areas to find work. The development of ski slopes and resorts occurred in two different patterns: as part of a local revitalization strategy (Moon 1989) or as large-scale development through large investors like the Seibu Group (Havens 1994). Skiing was popular mainly among students and young male company workers in metropolitan areas. From the 1980s, skiing increased in popularity and national developers started to invest in large-scale ski resorts. They used national forest land and redesigned it for recreational purposes, as the forest industry had declined due to increased timber imports. The chosen locations were concentrated near highway interchanges and in areas without outstanding landscapes, so that development was not restricted by protective regulations like the Natural Park Law. During the bubble economy, skiing spread as a hobby for families, but also as a fashion among young women.

As many skiers in Japan visit the slopes only once or twice a year, rental gear is very important. Large ski resorts therefore offer a wide range of services: rooms to rest for skiers who arrive on night buses, rental gear, changing rooms, hot springs to soak in after skiing, restaurants, and accommodation adjacent to the slopes. With the introduction of snow cannons, ski slopes also spread to locations in western Japan. However, recent climatic change has threatened the survival of many ski resorts situated in the borderland areas of snow security. In addition, as in all ski resorts around the world, the arrival of snowboards has changed the age structure and behaviour of visitors. Japan's ski resorts have had to fight a much more fatal change: an absolute decrease in skiers that has only partly been substituted by the increased popularity of snowboarding, as can be seen in Figure 4.9. During the economic recession of the late 1990s, skiers left the slopes. Many ski resorts had to close or scale down, and some were taken over by foreign investors (Kureha 2009: 44). Like many other declining tourist activities in Japan, however, foreign tourists are filling the gap. Australians who enjoy ski holidays during their

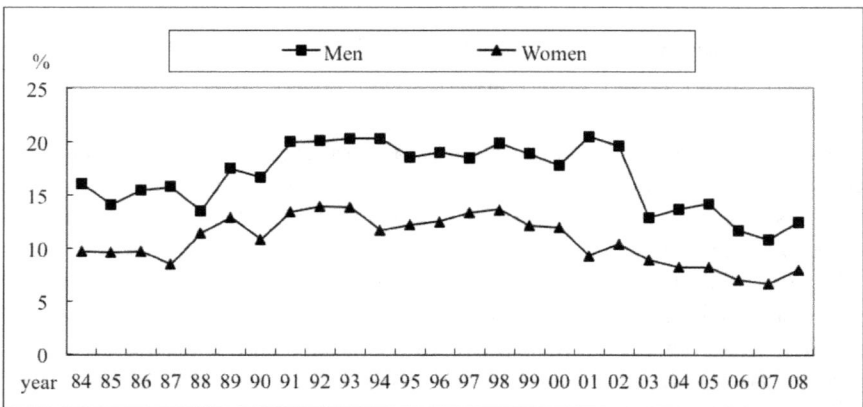

Figure 4.9: Changes in skiing participation by sex, 1984 to 2008.

Source: YKS (yearly).

own summer, and Koreans and Chinese who don't have sufficient slopes in their own countries, have become the target groups for many ski destinations (Fukuda 2008).

In contrast to winter sports, marine leisure has spread less spectacularly than might be expected in an island nation with about 16,000 kilometres of coastline, an attractive landscape with varied coastal forms, almost 4,000 islands, rich fishing grounds fed by cold and warm sea currents, and a warm and, in most areas, sunny climate (Funck 2006). The main reason lies in the many conflicts that surround access to the sea and its resources. Industrial and urban development along the coast and a strong fishing industry combined with traditional property rights compete with coastal tourism and marine leisure for the use of coast and sea. Mooring space for pleasure boats therefore is scarce and expensive. Time constraints also restrict marine leisure activities, especially when involving any form of boat, as it requires at least half a day to reach the shore, set up equipment and launch a vessel. Additionally, the swimming season in Japan has been traditionally fixed between the beginning of the school holidays in July and the *Obon* festival (a festival to honour the spirits of the dead) around 15 August. The start of the season is marked by a ceremony to pray for safety during the summer (Figure 4.10).

Although the mild climate would allow for a much longer season, the tendency to restrict marine leisure activities to the summer is still strong and participation is concentrated on public holidays and Sundays in the summer season. Participation rates for marine leisure are highest for swimming (21.8 per cent) and fishing (15.5 per cent) (SJS 2002). Diving, sailing and surfing participation rates each hover around the 1 per cent level. Rates have been declining in swimming, fishing and sailing, but rising in surfing and diving. Data on the number of registered pleasure boats (NKSKK 2003) offer some information about trends in marine leisure. The number of registered pleasure boats increased until 2000 and has surpassed the number of professional fishing boats. However, it has been slightly declining since. Significantly, the number of personal water craft (PWC) increased tenfold from 1987 to 2000. In contrast, the number of sailing yachts has been in decline since 1991. There are 4.4 pleasure boats registered per 1,000 people. While this number is difficult to compare due to different registration systems, it is said to be much lower than in other developed countries, with about 150 boats per 1,000 people in Scandinavia and 60 in the US (NKSKK 2003).

Types of and participation rates for marine leisure activities vary regionally according to climate, coastal conditions, marine resources and access from conurbations. The number of pleasure boats is highest along the pacific coast south of the Tokyo Metropolitan Area (Kanagawa and Shizuoka prefectures), in conurbations situated close to large bays where PWCs are especially popular (Aichi, Osaka and Hyôgo prefectures) and in the sheltered Seto Inland Sea area (Hiroshima and Ehime prefectures). Here the number of pleasure boats per capita

Figure 4.10: Sea-opening ceremony (photo courtesy of Carolin Funck).

is especially high, as fishing around the many small islands is a popular pastime. The most famous spots for diving and surfing are situated in southern Kyûshû and on Okinawa, as these locations have the necessary wave heights and rich wild life these activities rely on. Whale watching has become popular on the Ogasawara Islands stretching south from Tokyo and in former whale-hunting communities in Kôchi and Wakayama prefectures. Sea-kayaking participants searching for wilderness experiences choose locations in parts of Hokkaido and on Okinawa, but also along the Izu Peninsula stretching into the Pacific (Shizuoka Prefecture).

Apart from Japan's distant location from major pleasure boat markets, immigration regulations also inhibit visits by foreign private boats. Foreign sailors have to register at each harbour they visit and give detailed information on their planned route. These and other international tourists looking for spots to dive, surf or sunbathe find plenty of cheap and attractive locations in nearby Southeast Asia, and as Japanese tourists are following this trend, there is little prospect that marine leisure other than swimming and fishing will develop into a major tourism market segment in Japan.

Golf, on the other hand, is probably the only outdoor activity really closely connected to the image of Japan internationally (notwithstanding its baseball players being in demand in the American leagues). As early as the late 1950s, Japanese golfers winning international tournaments induced a small boom for golf as an elite sport. During the general leisure boom up to 1973, golf spread to other social classes. With the economic upturn of the 1980s, managers making deals while playing golf became the symbol of corporate Japan. More than any other leisure activity then, golf is connected to the ups and downs of the economy. During the bubble economy, companies paid for golf outings to entertain clients, and memberships in golf clubs were traded like stocks. Most golf courses in Japan are situated in mountain areas and require large development investment for forest clearance, landscaping and access roads. These were financed in part by membership admission fees, in theory to be paid back when members leave the club, that were returnable at the earliest after ten years and therefore could be used for investment by developers during this period. Members, on the other hand, could sell their membership. With prices constantly rising during the bubble years, golf club membership thus became a form of real-estate speculation. In consequence, many golf clubs went bankrupt after the real-estate bubble burst, and while golf still remains a company sport, lower fees and new management styles introduced by foreign investors have made it a more affordable activity that also attracts tourists from South Korea and Taiwan.

Skiing, golf, sailing and other outdoor leisure-sport activities became popular first during the rapid economic growth period prior to 1973 and then during the bubble economy in the late 1980s, when there was sufficient money and more leisure time available. In the 1980s facilities were developed to cater to the affluent urban customer and created an image of luxury and fashion. This image – and reality – of expensive pastimes contributed to the decrease in outdoor recreation during the recession, when the fashion for leisure and sport faded away (Kureha 2002). The tendency to spend leisure time in virtual spaces is also a widely observed international phenomenon, fuelled by the increase in internet participation amongst youth – up 15 per cent between 2001 and 2006 – and this has also led to a shift from outdoors to indoors. Nevertheless, winter sports and marine leisure constantly see the introduction of new tools for play, like snowboards, snowmobiles, wakeboards or new diving equipment. However, these don't connect to an overall increase in participation numbers, but rather replace old modes of leisure. As a result of these factors, although the variety of outdoor activities increased, from 1996 to 2006 participation in golf decreased from 13.8 to 8.9 per cent, in skiing from 14.0 to 7.3 per cent, in fishing from 16.9 to 10.0 per cent, and in other marine sports like sailing the decline was not even counted any more (MIAC 1996, 2001, 2006a). In a yearly publication on participation data in leisure activities, a review of the years 1998 to 2008 summarizes these trends as a 'squeeze' in the number of leisure activities individuals engage in. It proposes the idea of 'selected investment leisure', where individuals have moved from the stage of sampling different activities to the selection of one or two favourites in which they invest more time and money. However, the fact that leisure participation is decreasing especially among young people is seen as a serious threat to the domestic tourism market (SKSH 2008). This especially impacts on time- and money-intensive activities like outdoor sports. In a market survey by the leading travel agency JTB (Nihon Kôtsû Kôsha 2007: 72), trips connected to outdoor activities like skiing, camping, golf and fishing don't figure very high on the list of trips respondents would like to make. In 2006, skiing scored highest among outdoor activities with 12.4 per cent, down 5 per cent from four years earlier and much less than the most popular *onsen* trip, selected by 51.3 per cent.

The Attraction of New Facilities and 'Miniature Cities'

The increase in facility-based activities observed in Figure 4.8 has therefore to be interpreted in the context of development booms in the late 1960s and 1980s respectively. The latter period saw the construction of museums and theme parks in almost every town and village across the country. Even hot springs changed their character from natural *onsen* to multi-purpose recreational facilities called *kuâhausu* (Kurhaus) or *supâ* (spa) that relied on ever deeper and more costly artificial drilling for hot mineral waters (Erfurt-Cooper and Cooper 2009). The economic aspects of this trend and the connection of tourist facilities like theme parks to regional and local development are discussed in Chapter 5, but here the emphasis is on the multi-functional structure of these facilities and their ability to evoke the image of a 'miniature city'.

Figure 4.11: Miroku no Sato theme park (photo courtesy of Carolin Funck).

The Japanese fascination with theme parks has attracted the attention of Western scholars for quite a while and has led to speculation that European tourists too will develop a taste for compact small worlds to enjoy themselves in. Fichtner and Michna (1987) see the Japanese tendency to spend leisure time in groups and their high interest in technical entertainment equipment as the main reasons for the large number of amusement and theme parks in Japan. Takada (1995: 122) emphasizes that theme parks represent a 'miniature city', making it possible to grasp a stable view of the city where the actual city has grown too large to be comprehensible. He then connects the popularity of theme parks to the failure of Japanese urban planning to establish comprehensible and visually structured cities. While this conclusion can be contested, European historic cities are often described in Japan as theme parks of the past, thus adding to the idea of theme parks as small, comprehensible worlds in Japanese eyes. The reconstruction of the city landscape of the 1950s as seen in Figure 4.11 may also serve as an example where nostalgia for the good old times of the economic miracle provide grandparents, parents and children with an opportunity to communicate their personal history in an enjoyable and easily understandable setting. Hendry (2009: 138) argues that Japanese theme parks provide travel in time as well as in space, and thus distinguish themselves from the mainly ride-based attractions found in America.

Clammer (1997: 140) sees theme parks as an attempt to create the different and exotic in a convenient setting and in combination with educational functions. Most recently, Hendry (2009) compares them to museums, emphasizing the effort of theme parks to recreate the original and their ability to provide interaction, experience and entertainment – a capacity now in high demand among traditional museums trying to attract visitors. Whereas amusement parks look back on a long tradition as part of suburban development by private railway companies, theme parks made their debut in 1983 with the opening of Tokyo Disneyland (TDL) in Chiba Prefecture on the outskirts of the Tokyo metropolitan area. Up to now this is the only theme park that has survived and even expanded despite economic downturns and changes in tastes and fashion (Cooper et al. 2007). As Raz (2002) explains, Disneyland's concept concentrates on control, cleanliness and family entertainment. Adjusted to Japanese needs and run by a Japanese company, TDL perfectly fits the trend for leisure to be spent increasingly with family members. Although theme parks might be seen as a contrast to unstructured metropolitan areas, the daily experience of urban Japan is a clean environment with a punctually running, well-organized system of urban transport. TDL's high levels of cleanliness, punctuality and control therefore meet the basic expectations of Japanese consumers.

Other theme parks around Japan have struggled to survive, as have traditional amusement parks. Takarazuka Family Land, one of the best known and longest established suburban attractions in Japan, collapsed in 2003 after more than ninety years in operation after a decline in visitor numbers. Furthermore, a lack of investment in facilities caused fatal accidents that tarnished the image of amusement parks. In the 1990s, large-scale shopping centres replaced amusement and theme parks as urban attractions. The deregulation of restrictions on shopping centre development and in urban planning regulations (Fujii et al. 2007) allowed for large-scale developments in areas formerly occupied by transport or industrial facilities. A visit to a new development area nowadays forms an essential component of a Tokyo tour, be it for domestic or international tourists. Bus tours in Tokyo include combinations of established attractions like Ginza, Asakusa, Tokyo Tower and the Imperial Palace with the newly developed Odaiba waterfront area, the metropolitan government high-rise complex in Shinjuku and commercial developments like Shiodome and Roppongi Hills (Tanno 2004: 27). In smaller cities around the country, shopping centres including restaurants and cinemas have become the local choice for spending an afternoon with the family.

The Rediscovery of Heritage

The rediscovery of the past by tourists and its designation as heritage worth protecting started with laws on the protection of burial mounds, shrines and temples in the nineteenth century. More comprehensive protection began in 1950 with the Law for the Protection of Cultural Properties and proceeded through interactive processes between local initiatives, tourism promotion campaigns, national legislation and public interest. In the context of high economic growth until 1973, development projects like the Kyoto Tower Hotel and the Nara Prefecture office threatened the integrity of former capital cities. In 1966, Parliament delegates from the historic capitals of Nara, Kamakura and Kyoto took the initiative in the first law to protect building ensembles and their surroundings, the Special Action Law for the Preservation of Historic Environments in Ancient Capitals. Movements to protect districts of historic buildings sprang up all around the country as part of social movements against the deterioration of the environment. As a result, in 1975, a new heritage category was introduced for the protection of cultural property. Municipalities could now designate districts in towns or villages that had thrived in the past as ports, post-station towns, castle towns or centres of production for goods no longer demanded by modern society. On the basis of sufficient scientific investigation these could then be recognized at the national level as 'important preservation districts for groups of historic buildings'. By 2009, eighty-three such districts in eighty-three cities, towns and villages had been classified and received financial assistance for their preservation (ACA 2009).

While some of these districts are so remote that even devoted tourists hardly ever visit them, many have now developed the character of open-air museums full of souvenir shops, restaurants and small-scale accommodation facilities in old buildings. With electric lines buried underground, stone pavements, vending machines hidden in wooden frames and other historic street furniture promoted through national preservation projects, these districts can be easily distinguished from their non-protected colleagues. They are firmly built into the tour circuit and group tour buses unload their participants to spend an hour or two strolling around. Those adjacent to larger urban areas are pleasant destinations for day-trippers. However, as most visitors leave to go home or to their hotels, usually the whole town closes down at around 5 PM. Though many of these places must have enjoyed a thriving nightlife at the time they were flourishing and were once crowded with people, they now operate like a museum that shuts its doors in the evening. The fact that many of the historic houses stand empty as people find them too inconvenient to live in further strengthens the impression of walking through a history theme park.

The designation of these preservation districts coincided with a campaign by the Japan National Railways in 1970 called 'Discover Japan'. This campaign is widely quoted as being a trigger for tourism to historic towns and rural areas, as the railway brought people back to the countryside and to a nostalgic past (Robertson 1995). Places like Hida Takayama in Gifu Prefecture, once an important administrative and production centre in central Japan but by the 1970s just a little old town tucked away in the foothills of the Japanese Alps, were put on the tourist map for the first time. However, this campaign focused on individual towns, often dubbed as 'little Kyoto's' to emphasize their historic value. It took until the 1980s for the wave of nostalgia to target the rural areas and the villages scattered around. Robertson (1995) and Moon (2002) describe in detail the process of re-evaluation of rural heritage and the political movements to establish rural villages as the *furusato* or old hometown for the whole nation. Rural life, perceived as backwards during the postwar growth period, became the symbol of 'real' Japan, where tradition and community ties were still strong. In terms of culture, it served as the 'other' for Japanese. Just as Europeans searched for their 'other' in Third World literature, music and culture, in Japan, the discovery was of the traditional life of the countryside. This could be described as a dual process of construction: tourists create identity, and urban tourists in cooperation with rural communities constructed the countryside (Clammer 1997: 145, 150). The establishment of a Furusato Information Centre in 1985 and the '100 million yen project for the creation of home towns' (*furusato sôsei ichiokuen jigyô*), an amount of money that was distributed to every municipality across Japan in combination with extended possibilities for further loans in 1988/89, helped to establish the concept of *furusato*: the idea that every Japanese person had a nostalgic home place somewhere, and that rural areas were ready to provide this home to people who had lost their roots in the process of urbanization. While this can be seen as an attempt to strengthen a common cultural genealogy as a form of Japanese identity (Robertson 1995: 101), it also served the practical purpose of attracting city dwellers to depopulated areas as tourists, but maybe in the long run as inhabitants or regular visitors. Through these processes, nostalgia acted as a strong tourist motivation. Destinations, attractions and facilities adapted themselves to the expectations of urban visitors. However, national preservation strategies for historic towns and the promotion of common, supposedly traditional features of rural areas ignored distinctions and differences between localities, and thus deprived them of their potential to appeal to tourists individually.

The system of protection for cultural properties has developed further in recent years, reflecting the increased interest in rural areas. As a result of an amendment to the Law for the Protection of Cultural Properties in 2005, 'cultural landscapes' were established as cultural properties, defined as 'landscapes formed by people's lives or work in a given region and the climate of the region in question such that they are indispensable for understanding the lives and work of the Japanese people'. Tourism is one perspective behind this change, as protected landscapes will enhance the attractiveness of communities (ACA 2010).

Case Study: Asuka Village

The place that best illustrates changes in heritage and nostalgia tourism during the 1970s and 1980s is probably Asuka village in Nara Prefecture, site of the national capital between AD 592 and 709. The history, emperors, nobles and palaces of Asuka are depicted in semi-historical chronicles from the eighth century, called *Kojiki* and *Nihon shoki*, while its landscape was celebrated in the *Manyôshû*, a poetry collection from the same period. Since the 1950s, archaeological excavations have shed much light on this period, which marks the beginning of a structured state and the introduction of Buddhism to Japan. However, the heritage of Asuka remains situated on the borderline between historic facts backed by archaeological evidence and the realm of legends, leaving it open to all kinds of interpretation.

In the late nineteenth century, Asuka was already labelled the 'home town of the Japanese heart' (Fawcett 1996: 64); it was still promoted using this phrase on the home page of the Asuka Preservation Foundation in 2008. In 1970, after several years of debate between local, regional and national interests, parts of the Asuka area were included in the Special Action Law for the Preservation of Historic Environments in Ancient Capitals. As the area was slowly integrated into the commuter belt of Osaka, thus offering opportunities for real-estate speculation, local interests opposed restrictions on the sale and development of land (Fawcett 1995). Villagers also feared the negative side-effects of tourism. These fears soon materialized when the discovery of spectacular murals in the Takamatsuzuka tomb in 1972 put Asuka in the national limelight, and started a boom in tourism to archaeological sites. The Ministry of Construction promoted conservation together with tourism through the establishment of a tourism office, the Asuka National Historical Museum and the Asuka Historical National Government Park. This was a new category of urban park specially created for Asuka in 1974 to preserve and make use of its nationally important cultural heritage. Pressure by villagers and Nara Prefecture for greater consideration of local interests finally led to the introduction of the Special Action Law regarding the Preservation of the Historical Environment and the Lifestyle Environment of Asuka Mura in 1980. On the basis of this law, substantial funds were paid by the national government not only for archaeological site surveys but also for the support of buildings, agriculture and forestry and for roads and other infrastructure. As a result, sites in Asuka are connected by wide, comfortable roads and a network of small paths for hikers and cyclists, connecting burial mounds and other historic sites (Figure 4.12).

Visible heritage in Asuka includes not only temples, large carved stone figures, tombs and the excavated sites of palaces, but also a small-scale, traditional agricultural landscape that has disappeared in most parts of the country. Signposts abound and detailed signboards explain stories from the old chronicles and cite old poems. However, little of the scientific discussion raised by excavation is reflected in these. A tourist without some knowledge of these books can certainly enjoy cycling or walking through a pleasant, well-preserved rural area but will not receive much historic information. In some cases, excavations became necessary

Figure 4.12: Tourists take a picture in front of Ishibutai burial mound, Asuka
(photo courtesy of T. Asano).

to clear the ground for the construction of tourism facilities and infrastructure, although archaeologists would have preferred to leave relics and sites undisturbed and underground as long as possible.

The murals of Takamatsuzuka tomb illustrate the conflicts between national and local interests, scientific preservation and tourism. The murals were reconstructed for visitors in an identical artificial tomb adjacent to the original, which was then sealed off. This project was financed by donations and sales of a special postage stamp, thus showing the high level of national interest in Asuka. The decision to leave the originals on site inside the closed tomb rather than transfer them to a national museum where they could be constantly monitored and conserved was influenced by strong local interest in the valuable heritage site, although it ran counter to scientific experience in preserving murals. It was feared that, had the murals been shown in a museum in Tokyo, people would no longer visit Asuka to see the reproductions. However, as had been predicted by specialists, in 2007 the original murals were so heavily damaged by mould that they had to be removed for restoration. A restricted number of visitors could register then during two short periods in 2008 to see the originals, an event that was taken up by national television and newspapers.

Although tourist numbers increased rapidly during the 1970s, tourism infrastructure consisted mainly of government-run facilities and there was little input from the private sector apart from bicycle rental. Restaurants and accommodation facilities are scarce, with small-scale facilities offering accommodation for only about 300 persons (NCS 2008). Unlike other historic towns, where preservation efforts started as a local movement, Asuka was the target of national attention. It seems that government attempts to create a showcase conservation project and increase tourist interest in a historical site perceived as genuinely Japanese was not mirrored by local interest in tourism as an economic activity. Tourist numbers peaked at about 1,800,000 in the early 1980s, declined during the bubble period and since then have fluctuated around 700,000. The abandonment of farming activities in favour of working in tourism and hospitality since Asuka became famous has threatened the local traditional agricultural landscape. Small-scale plots, part-time farming and an ageing workforce in agriculture are common problems throughout Japan. In Asuka they were even more serious, as landscape preservation regulations prevented the redeployment of arable land to facilitate more effective forms of agriculture (Uyama and Urade 2002). In the late 1990s the village started to investigate the possibilities of rural tourism and in 1998 it created a foundation to promote projects like rice-terrace ownership or direct sales of local products that actively involved urban residents (Shimoura et al. 2006). The thematic shift in heritage tourism from an interest in historic townscapes in the 1970s to an emphasis on agricultural landscapes in the 1990s is clearly visible here; however, the former produced much higher visitor numbers.

Adapting the Product

This chapter so far has outlined changes in tourism in the postwar period. Trends and changes in tourism develop through interaction of demand and supply. How have industries and locations adapted to or influenced these processes? The case study of Miyazaki Prefecture will illustrate the long-term development, from the 1950s to 2000.

Case Study: Miyazaki

Miyazaki Prefecture is a good illustration of the adaptation of Japanese tourist destinations to changing demands from the 1950s onwards and the problems they have encountered. Located in southern Kyûshû, tourism development has concentrated on its eastern shoreline, called the Nichinan Coast, where tourists can enjoy a mild, sunny climate and sub-tropical vegetation. As early tourist attractions, a cactus park and a children's amusement park were developed in the late 1930s and established a sub-tropical image for the region. In the 1950s, the area around Aoshima, a small islet with peculiar washboard rock formations, became a Mecca for honeymooners. At its peak it was visited by one third of newly wed couples (Takano 1994). Large white hotels and palm trees lined the coast to create the only Western-style coastal resort in Japan at the time, an imitation of Hawaii. However, since restrictions to travel abroad were abolished in 1964, a Hawaii in Japan was no longer needed: the real Hawaii became the dominant honeymoon destination for Japanese.

Visitor numbers from outside the prefecture peaked at 5,000,000 in 1974 and subsequently declined. Plans for a Nichinan Coast sub-tropical-belt park were designed by the Prefecture in the late 1970s to counter this decline. These formed the basis for Miyazaki Prefecture's plans under the Resort Law of 1987, so the Prefecture was able to apply for recognition as a resort development area under this new law as early as 1988, one of the first three prefectures to do so. Due to their early applications, the first three prefectures to receive funding completed large parts of their projects before the economic bubble burst and other resort plans were shelved. In Miyazaki, a project called Seagaia formed the core of the plan and was developed in a public–private partnership by Miyazaki Prefecture, Miyazaki City and the Phoenix Group, a company that already ran a golf course, amusement park, hotel and convention facility at the site. Seagaia was located in a large pine forest behind the coastline, about fifteen minutes by bus from Miyazaki airport. It comprised a large indoor water park with an artificial beach, a wave machine and a sliding roof called Ocean Dome, a golf course, a hotel, cottages, a convention facility and a shopping mall – a perfect example of the taste for artificially perfected environments prevailing at the time. The real coast just a few hundred metres away is too dangerous for swimming because of strong currents and high waves, although surfing is possible. Development costs for the large 135 hectare area equalled those of Tokyo Disneyland. The target number of visitors was set at 2.5 million for Ocean Dome and 5.5 million for the whole resort (Takano 1994). Ocean Dome, the golf course and the cottages opened in 1993, and the remaining facilities in 1994. Consequently, visitor numbers to Miyazaki from outside the Prefecture climbed to 5.7 million in 1996, but then went into decline again, falling to 4.4 million in 2006.

Renewed investment could not save Seagaia from going bankrupt in 2001; it was then bought by Ripplewood Holdings of the USA. However, even foreign management could not market the concept of indoor coastal tourism in Japan; Ocean Dome finally closed in 2008, having received only ten million visitors in fifteen years (PSR 2008). It was replaced by a Thai tropical spa facility, a Japanese spa and an activity centre, which offers sports, kids programmes and excursions in the area. The Prefecture created a small beach in an artificial bay along the real coast near Seagaia to offer space for swimming and surfing in 2001, thus realizing a project included in the resort development plan thirteen years before. While these efforts did not help to revive tourism from outside the Prefecture, visitor numbers to attractions from within have constantly increased over the years, so Miyazaki has been downscaled from a national to a regional destination.

In 2007, Miyazaki finally adapted successfully to current trends. It elected a TV personality for governor who made the Prefecture famous again and put a new tourist attraction on the map: the prefectural government office! However, as he left Miyazaki after one term in office to follow a career in national politics, even personality tourism has failed to rejuvenate Miyazaki as a tourist destination.

Summary and Conclusions

This chapter has provided an outline of domestic tourism from the 1950s to the present and has pointed out trends of further change. We have identified the restricted time budget as the strongest component influencing domestic tourism. Okamoto (2001: 280) points out that the failure to legally guarantee employees the right to take holidays of more than two consecutive days has created a very unbalanced domestic market relying on two-day trips, weekends and holidays. The ups and downs of the economy are another important factor that not only influences consumers' willingness to spend money on trips but also investment in tourism facilities. Two investment booms from the late 1960s to 1973 and during the bubble economy of the late 1980s have influenced the way Japanese tourists enjoy their travel. However, both periods have left a legacy of buildings and facilities that have not adjusted well to the changing needs of society and are fast approaching the end of their life cycles. As a third factor, a shift in society from an emphasis on organizations like companies and schools as the main framework for social networks and leisure activities to families and friends has forced mass-tourism destinations to rejuvenate their facilities and services. Coupled with the extension of high-speed transport networks, this has opened up the market for new destinations to find a niche. However, a declining and ageing population will induce further changes.

Finally, the cultural re-evaluation of things Japanese, supported by efforts to reinvent a common Japanese heritage and by the growing number of foreign tourists, has affected the appearance of destinations and facilities. Innovations range from national chains selling traditional crackers in tourist destinations to high-end *ryokan* offering rooms with individual European-style baths and antique Japanese furniture. Some of the trends identified in this chapter will be taken up in Chapters 7 and 8, where inbound tourism as a growth sector and new forms of tourism like eco-tourism will be examined in more detail.

5

THE TRAVELLING YEN

This chapter explores in more depth the economic dimensions of Japanese tourism. The structure of the tourism industry and how it intertwines with regional economies, tourism as a tool for regional development, and tourism as an economic strategy in the context of deindustrialization and an ageing society are its foci. The interface of tourism and leisure industries in urban areas is also examined. It should be noted at the outset that the issues discussed here relate to one of the Asia Pacific region's most developed economies, one that, until recently, did not focus on inbound tourism to any great extent. The economy has simply not needed inbound tourists in a macro-economic sense until the recent past, though regional and local economies have benefited when they have visited, as we will show.

Within Japan itself, the role of national economic development policies in spreading growth and reversing decline through promoting domestic tourism has been of much greater importance than that of developing facilities for inbound tourists (Cooper and Flehr 2006). Moreover, outbound tourism has not been seen as a drain on the national economy, to be offset by attracting visitors from abroad as in other countries. In economic terms, it has been used as a counterbalance to the very high income obtained from exports of manufactured goods, and as a means of exposing Japan to other cultures, located safely offshore. In this chapter the role and impact of government boosterism (Hall 2003) in the development of domestic tourism facilities and attractions is illustrated by reference to developments attributable to the Resort Law of 1987 (see also Chapter 3) and its antecedents and successors; to Space World, a major redevelopment project on the western island of Kyûshû; and, to the local government areas of Beppu and Yufuin, also on Kyûshû. From these case studies it can be observed that government and private sector agencies seeking to develop and market land for tourism in Japan have used the term 'tourist attraction' to justify an essentially public–private form of commercial land development; a situation which illustrates the lengths to which governments in the twentieth and twenty-first centuries go to secure rights for developers in the tourism industry (Mason and Leberman 2000: 97–100). It is also apparent that while the contents and policies of local development plans have to be taken into account, decisions with respect to major facilities in Japan are commonly not taken by local communities (as in Australia); instead, it is common for the national government to directly finance private development, so that the developers receive certainty of investment support through government backing (Cooper and Flehr 2006).

Having set the scene, it must be acknowledged that while there has been some change at the national level in terms of policy towards inbound tourism since 2007, the government still retains finger printing and photographing procedures at airports for foreign travellers. The effect of all these policies over the long term can be gauged from a World Economic Forum report on the international tourism industry: this gave Japan an overall ranking of 23 among 130 destinations based on high marks for its transport and cultural infrastructure, but noted that its position was badly affected by a ranking of 128 for its 'affinity', or how well visitors can connect with the culture (Blanke and Mia 2007). The tourism policies of Japan were more fully described in Chapter 3, but their impact on regional and local economies are discussed more fully in this chapter. Also covered are the state of the accommodation sector, internal transport and its impact on tourism, the effect of holidays such as Golden Week, and the most important issues in tourism promotion and marketing.

Background: The Tourism Markets of Japan

Following the Meiji Restoration and the building of a national railroad network across Japan, tourism became a more affordable prospect for domestic citizens, and visitors from foreign countries could enter Japan legally. As early as 1887, government officials recognized the need for an organized system of attracting foreign tourists. The government established a committee (the *Kihinkai*), which aimed to coordinate the various players in the tourism industry, was established that year with the then Prime Minister Ito Hirobumi's blessing (Asamizu 2005 6–7). Another major milestone in the development of the early tourism industry in Japan was the 1907 passage of the Hotel Development Law, as a result of which the Ministry of Railways began to construct publicly owned hotels throughout Japan. Since those times there have been many national, regional and local policy measures aimed at using or bolstering the position of tourism in the economy. These measures were discussed earlier in Chapter 3.

The Ministry of Land, Infrastructure and Transport (MLIT) has been the Ministry responsible for tourism since the 1970s: it has surveyed the industry regularly, and in 2009 it determined that the direct impact of tourism consumption

Table 5.1: Numbers of tourists and the value of tourism in Japan, 1970s to the present.

Measure	1970s	1980s	1990s	2000s
Domestic Trips (Estimated)	100 million	150 million	250 million	325 million
Inbound	0.8 million	1.3–3.2 million	4–4.7 million	5-9.15 million
Outbound	0.8–4 million	4–11 million	10-17 million	15-18 million
Economic Value of Domestic Travel (First estimated in 2004)	N/A	N/A	N/A	¥20-23 trillion
Economic Value of Inbound travel (First estimated in 2004)	N/A	N/A	N/A	¥1-1.5 trillion
Economic Value of Outbound Travel (First estimated in 2004)	N/A	N/A	N/A	¥1.7-1.8 trillion
Total Value of Tourism Activity*	N/A	N/A	N/A	¥50-54 trillion
Employment	N/A	N/A	N/A	3.9-4.4 million

Note: * Includes estimates of indirect and induced economic activity.

Source: UNWTO: World rankings for international tourist arrivals 6(2) and previous volumes; JNTO various; Ministry of Land, Infrastructure, Transport and Tourism, various.

in Japan (including inbound tourism) had reached about ¥22.1 trillion from 325 million trips (Table 5.1). At this level the industry was estimated to have generated direct employment of 2.1 million jobs or 2.9 per cent of total employment. The value-added portion of this tourism consumption was estimated to have been approximately ¥11 trillion or up to 2 per cent of nominal GDP in 2009. From this activity, the total direct and induced production effect produced by tourism was estimated to be ¥48 trillion – equivalent to about 5.2 per cent of total domestic production. This level of activity supports in the region of 4.1 million jobs or 6.3 per cent of total domestic employment. Table 5.1 relates the number of tourists to the value of tourism from the 1970s to the present.

Tourism's Contribution to the Economy

Tourism's overall contribution of approximately 5.2 per cent of nominal GDP compares with agriculture (1.6 per cent), industrial manufacturing (25.3 per cent) and total services of 73.1 per cent (MLIT 2012). On an individual industry basis, the contribution of tourism to the overall Japanese economy is equal to or more than that from such leading industries as automobile and electronics production. This can be shown by comparing the tourism industry's share of GDP in 2000

(2.2 per cent) with the automobile industry (2.3 per cent), telecommunications (2.0 per cent), electronics (1.9 per cent), and agriculture (1.5 per cent). Tourism's share of total employment was 2.9 per cent in 2000, compared with government employees (3.2 per cent), electronics (3.0 per cent), finance/insurance (3.0 per cent) and the food industry (2.3 per cent). By 2009, tourism's contribution had more than doubled while the others had remained static at the 2000 level. As the tourism market continues to grow steadily and the relative age of the population increases, it is expected to become even more of a leading industry in Japan in the twenty-first century (MLIT 2012).

The direct contribution of the Japanese tourism industry to the national economy, however, is relatively small compared to the situation in other countries. According to a survey by MLIT in 2000, for example, the direct contribution of tourism to GDP in Australia amounted to 4.5 per cent, followed by Chile (3.8 per cent), New Zealand (3.4 per cent) and Canada (2.4 per cent), while in the United States and Japan it stood at 2.2 per cent. In particular, the ratio of tourism consumption by foreign visitors to overall tourism consumption has also been markedly lower in Japan compared with that of other countries. In 2000, the ratio was only 6.2 per cent in Japan, whereas it was as high as 35.6 per cent in France, 30.0 per cent in Canada, 22.0 per cent in Australia and 20.9 per cent in the United States respectively. This fact of course indicates the disparity between inbound and outbound tourism in the Japanese market.

Breaking the contribution of tourism down regionally, it can be seen from Table 5.2 that the Tokyo metropolitan area benefits most from tourism, with an average of some 37 million visitor nights per year in the 2000s, followed by Hokkaidô at 25 million and Osaka with 16 million. These three prefectures accounted for 25.2 per cent of total visitor nights. Tokyo as the national capital region attracts many business travellers, while Hokkaidô has skiing, volcanoes and the frontier environment. Osaka is the second largest metropolitan area and is adjacent to Kyoto, the former imperial capital and a magnet for tourism. Important regional centres like Fukuoka and Hiroshima attract some visitors, at least as transport hubs, but most of the prefectures attract only small numbers of visitors to a small range of *onsen*, heritage or environmental attractions. If tourism intensity is calculated as the number of visitor nights relative to population, however, a different pattern becomes visible. Here, Okinawa, Hokkaidô, Nagano and Yamanashi (the site of Mount Fuji) all rank high as important destinations in the Japanese pleasure periphery.

The Domestic Tourism Market

The travel patterns shown in Table 5.2 are, as outlined in Chapter 4, mainly the product of domestic tourism. Japan's domestic tourism occurs in three major

Table 5.2: Number of visitor nights by prefecture and population, 2007.

Prefecture	No. of Visitor Nights	No. of Nights /Population	Prefecture	No. of Visitor Nights	No. of Nights /Population
Tokyo	37,183,240	2.4	Iwate	4,275,660	3.0
Hokkaidō	24,922,660	4.1	Yamanashi	4,128,690	4.3
Osaka	16,002,890	1.6	Okayama	3,722,160	1.9
Chiba	14,795,600	2.2	Yamagata	3,669,850	3.0
Shizuoka	13,424,430	3.4	Gifu	3,574,780	1.6
Okinawa	11,933,650	8.4	Wakayama	3,292,400	3.0
Kanagawa	10,583,010	1.1	Akita	3,187,370	2.8
Nagano	10,569,930	4.7	Saitama	3,166,930	0.4
Aichi	10,494,440	1.3	Aomori	3,152,600	2.1
Kyoto	9,614,710	3.4	Ibaraki	3,150,140	1.0
Hyōgo	8,792,470	1.5	Yamaguchi	3,124,310	2.1
Fukuoka	8,481,820	1.6	Shiga	2,873,150	2.0
Fukushima	7,516,240	3.5	Miyazaki	2,625,350	2.2
Miyagi	7,324,290	3.1	Toyama	2,570,380	2.2
Tochigi	6,966,530	3.4	Ehime	2,440,320	1.6
Gunma	6,364,380	3.1	Saga	2,235,810	2.5
Niigata	6,302,230	2.6	Kagawa	2,136,000	2.0
Mie	5,503,260	2.8	Fukui	1,958,170	2.4
Kumamoto	5,347,790	2.8	Tottori	1,952,330	3.2
Hiroshima	5,339,720	2.7	Kōchi	1,837,280	2.3
Kagoshima	4,799,330	2.7	Shimane	1,789,930	2.4
Ōita	4,749,470	2.7	Tokushima	1,241,500	1.5
Ishikawa	4,625,590	2.7	Nara	1,152,420	0.8
Nagasaki	4,486,550	2.6	Total	394,220,000	2.48

Source: MLIT (2008).

waves: the winter holidays at New Year, Golden Week (29 April to 5 May), and the summer holidays in July and August. From the early 1990s, domestic travel has stagnated owing to the prolonged economic recession and reduced personal consumption; per capita volume of travel activities has declined almost continuously since 1998. Based on a visitor preference survey conducted by MLIT each year, the Japanese went on an average of 2.26 overnight trips in 2001 (an 11.7 per cent decrease from 2000), and stayed an average of 4.31 nights away from home on those trips (a decrease of 16.8 per cent from 2000). In 2010 the per capita number of trips is estimated to have been 1.56, a decrease of 32 per cent since 2001. The number of overnight stays per capita was estimated at 2.39 in 2010; a decrease of 43 per cent since 2001. This is a larger decline than in other developed nations, reflecting the length of the economic recession in Japan after the collapse of the bubble economy (Shiratsuka 2003). Factors behind this decrease are thought to include a decline in the average number of holidays taken and an increasing emphasis on day trip leisure activities such as eating out, visiting local shrines and *onsen*, and other less time-consuming activities. The short-break leisure pattern is encouraged by the proliferation of one-day national holidays, many of which turn into long weekends. Therefore, the one-day or half-day visit is the staple of the Japanese domestic tourist industry for good economic and lifestyle reasons. However, it should be noted that the strong tendency to make domestic overnight trips on public holidays rather than using individual paid holidays creates a serious problem of concentration for the domestic market. The gaps between weekends and holidays have to be filled by retired citizens and inbound tourists.

According to the results of an overnight-trip statistics survey in 2011 (MLIT 2012), the total number of overnight stays in Japan between January and December 2010 was 394.2 million bed-nights overall, of which Japanese tourists contributed 376.7 million (95.6 per cent). In terms of individual months, August was the busiest with 46.3 million bed-nights (11.7 per cent), while April was the quietest with 24.9 million (6.3 per cent). One salient feature of these results is that Japan's tourism flows are actually quite even across most months of the year, which reflects two factors: the first is that the reduction in length of overnight stays described above has been compensated for by an increase in short breaks and day trips; and the second is that there is no real distortion effect from seasonal inbound or outbound travel. Moreover, the high number of single day 'national' holidays distributed throughout the year tends to even out the season of the trips taken by the Japanese population, especially to urban destinations. However, this overall pattern is influenced by local characteristics of tourist destinations. Seasonal patterns vary for each destination, and resorts where tourism depends on the natural environment show a much stronger seasonal contrast.

The Inbound Tourism Market

Following the gradual increase of foreign arrivals to Japan throughout the 1960s, the number of inbound travellers jumped sharply to 854,419, an increase of 40.4 per cent over the previous year, when Japan hosted the World Expo (Osaka) in 1970. The 1970s were also the period that marked the beginning of a shift in the Japanese inbound market, from Western visitors to Asian visitors. The rapid economic development experienced by Asian countries was the dominant factor in this shift. In 1990 the number of total inbound visitors to Japan exceeded three million (3.24 million) for the first time. Even though during the 1990s the number of inbound visitors fluctuated depending on the economic conditions of Asian countries, the value of the yen, and even the great Hanshin Awaji (Kobe) earthquake in 1995, as a basic trend the inbound market expanded throughout the period. In 1997 foreign visitor arrivals surpassed four million for the first time in history (4.2 million), a 9.9 per cent increase over the previous year (MLIT 2007).

Between 1999 and 2001, the number of inbound visitors to Japan reached a record high over three consecutive years. In 1999 the number of incoming visitors amounted to 4.4 million, 8.1 per cent up from the previous year, and reached 4.8 million in 2000 (a 7.2 per cent increase). This pattern can be attributed to the recovery of the inbound markets of South Korea and South-east Asia, and the favourable and steady expansion of the Taiwanese and US markets. In 2001 the number of inbound visitors increased slightly to 4.8 million in spite of the impact of terrorist incidents in the United States on global travel. Of all the inbound visitors in 2001, 57 per cent were tourists and 40 per cent came for business and/or other purposes.

As a result of further liberalization in visa requirements and the 'Visit Japan' campaign in 2003, the number of foreign travellers to Japan by 2007 had increased to 8,347,000, 13.8 per cent more than in 2006, and a new all-time record. In 2008, however, numbers remained static, but this in itself was a good result given the prevailing economic conditions in the latter half of the year. After a drop in 2009, the numbers recovered in 2010 (see Table 5.3), only to be hit by the natural and nuclear disasters of 11 March 2011 and the subsequent impact of territorial disputes with China and South Korea (total inbound only 6,219,000 in 2011, contributing 17.6 million bed-nights). However, despite a 62.5 per cent decrease for April 2011 when compared to 2010, the numbers in November 2011 were only 13.1 per cent below the pre-financial crisis levels (JNTO yearly a) and are expected to bounce back further in 2012.

In terms of year-on-year changes in the country or region of origin, visitors from South Korea maintained a very high growth rate during this period, rising by 22.8 per cent to 2.6 million to occupy top position for the ninth year in succession in 2006. Below South Korea came Taiwan with 1.39 million, China with 940,000, the US with 820,000 and Hong Kong with 430,000. However, by 2010

Table 5.3: Number of visitors from major markets, 2010 and 2011.

Source	2010	Percentage	2011	Percentage
Asia	6,528,000	75.8	4,724,000	76.0
North America	906,000	10.5	685,000	11.0
Europe	853,000	9.9	569,000	9.2
Oceania	261,000	3.0	189,000	3.0
Others	63,000	0.7	52,000	0.8
Total	8,610,000	100.0	6,219,000	100.0

Note: the official statistics do not make a distinction between total visitors and 'pure' tourists. JNTO estimates that in 2008, strictly defined tourists made up some 72 percent of the total number of visitors.

Source: MLITT White Paper (2012).

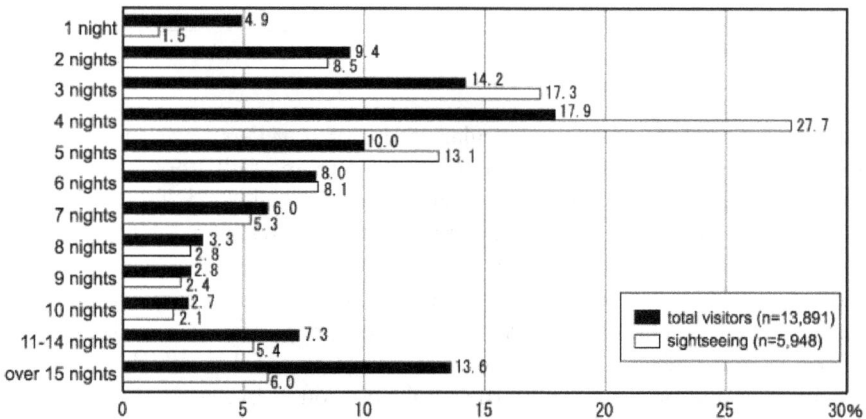

Figure 5.1: Average length of stay of overseas visitors to Japan, 2008.

Source: JNTO (2009).

China dominated the inbound tourism market with 1,415,000, reflecting its overall dominance of the East Asian region. In terms of economic impact, Figure 5.1 shows that international visitor stays in Japan have a modal value of around four nights, with a second concentration at 11 nights and above. This pattern of fairly short visits will be discussed in Chapter 7.

The Outbound Tourism Market

Outbound tourism has been a significant factor for both the Japanese tourism industry and the rest of the world since the 1970s (see Chapter 6). While favoured

Table 5.4: Breakdown of Japanese overseas travellers by age and sex, 1997 and 2007.

Age Group	Male		Female		Total	
	1997	2007	1997	2007	1997	2007
0-9	2.9	2.8	2.9	3.6	2.7	3.2
10-19	4.3	3.8	6.5	6.1	5.3	4.8
20-29	18.6	11.2	36.8	23.0	26.9	16.3
30-39	21.6	21.5	16.3	20.8	19.2	21.2
40-49	22.0	22.8	11.9	13.0	17.4	18.6
50-59	18.2	20.4	13.8	15.7	16.2	18.4
60+	12.8	17.3	11.8	17.7	12.3	17.5
Total (Millions)	9.1	9.8	7.7	7.5	16.8	17.3
%	54.4	56.7	45.6	43.3	100.0	100.0

Source: JNTO (2009).

destinations and the size of particular groups of travellers have varied in the forty years since then (Cha et al. 1995; Yamamoto and Gill 1999; March 2000; Reisinger and Turner 2003; Agrusa et al. 2005; Kim et al. 2005; Takai-Tokunaga 2007), the importance of Japanese outbound tourism has remained high. More males than females travel overseas (Table 5.4), but on average they tend to be older, except in the 60 and over age group, where the proportions of male and female travellers are the same. The largest single group of female travellers is that of the so-called 'office ladies' or the 20 to 29 age group, although this has been declining in recent years. Under their influence, often in search of sites associated with TV and music stars, South Korea was the top destination for Japanese outbound travellers for many years until China became more important in 2002 (Table 5.5). These two leading destinations are followed by the mainland USA, Hong Kong, Thailand, Taiwan and Hawaii. From the end of 2007 until very recently there was a decline in Japanese visitors to China, largely due to concerns over food safety and security (Table 5.5). Food poisoning in Japan from *gyoza* dumplings made in China, immediately followed by issues over Tibet, temporarily discouraged Japanese visitors to China. Nevertheless, there has been a shift over the last decade in Japanese international travel from traditional long-haul to short-haul destinations, mostly in Asia. The background to this shift in destinations is the increasing business traffic within Asia and an increase in capacity to China and South Korea, coupled with the downsizing of aircraft for trans-Pacific and European routes. As a result of airline policies of allocating more space to profitable business class passengers, the supply of economy-class seats for the leisure market has been reduced (MLIT 2008b).

Table 5.5: Number of Japanese overseas travellers by destination, 2002 to 2011.

Year	Korea	China	Taiwan	Hong Kong	Macao	Malaysia	Singapore
2002	2,320,820	2,925,500	991,224	1,395,020	142,588	354,563	723,420
2003	1,802,163	2,251,266	659,972	867,160	85,613	213,527	434,064
2004	2,443,070	3,334,251	890,444	1,126,250	122,184	301,429	598,821
2005	2,439,809	3,389,976	1,127,184	1,210,848	169,115	340,027	588,535
2006	2,338,921	3,748,882	1,163,835	1,311,111	220,190	354,213	594,404
2007	2,235,963	3,977,479	1,170,582	1,324,336	299,406	367,567	594,511
2008	2,378,102	3,446,117	1,090,225	1,324,797	370,409	433,462	571,020
2009	3,053,311	3,317,400	1,007,621	1,204,490	379,241	395,746	489,940
2010	3,023,009	3,731,100	1,102,054	1,316,618	413,507	415,881	528,817
2011	3,289,051	3,658,300	1,300,022	1,283,687	396,023	386,974	656,406

Year	Thailand	Philippines	Indonesia	Vietnam	Canada	USA	Hawaii
2002	1,239,421	341,867	326,862	279,769	436,492	3,627,264	1,483,121
2003	1,042,349	322,896	181,635	209,730	262,182	3,169,682	1,340,033
2004	1,212,213	382,307	316,448	267,210	413,997	3,747,620	1,482,085
2005	1,196,654	415,456	301,989	320,606	423,881	3,883,906	1,517,439
2006	1,311,987	421,808	253,003	383,896	386,485	3,672,584	1,362,710
2007	1,277,638	395,012	354,138	410,515	332,934	3,531,489	1,296,423
2008	1,153,868	359,306	345,923	392,999	276,077	3,249,521	1,160,732
2009	1,004,438	324,980	319,473	358,691	197,741	2,918,268	1,168,080
2010	993,674	358,744	246,350	442,089	235,508	3,386,076	1,239,438
2011	1,139,439	375,496	182,908	481,506	211,060	3,249,659	1,176,546

Year	Guam	N. Marianas	Australia	New Zealand	France	Germany	Spain
2002	786,957	786,957	715,457	173,567	N/A	240,146	596,997
2003	659,593	659,593	627,735	150,851	1,253,753	645,300	546,379
2004	906,104	906,104	710,351	165,023	1,398,020	715,300	575,868
2005	955,245	955,245	685,466	154,925	1,459,097	730,200	604,175
2006	952,687	952,687	651,070	136,401	1,353,623	759,834	706,503
2007	932,175	932,175	573,045	121,652	1,295,253	661,169	599,462
2008	846,599	846,599	457,236	102,482	1,139,756	597,314	574,218
2009	825,129	191,111	355,456	78,426	1,112,588	538,751	511,772
2010	893,865	185,032	398,200	87,735	1,128,967	604,778	611,531
2011	824,005	142,946	332,653	68,963	1,106,754	639,772	615,079

Year	UK	Switzerland	Italy	Netherlands	Czech R	Austria	Croatia
2002	314,000	416,329	N/A	185,100	100,567	240,146	N/A
2003	348,000	321,685	N/A	136,700	93,110	227,675	N/A
2004	332,000	N/A	1,656,213	163,700	122,613	256,541	22,932
2005	324,000	335,199	1,657,688	156,900	153,980	278,686	32,748
2006	314,000	347,299	1,648,220	141,600	145,804	267,909	64,751
2007	366,000	324,463	1,474,014	128,900	136,587	229,343	86,404
2008	239,000	278,448	1,307,729	114,300	123,408	221,577	143,704
2009	236,000	275,505	1,298,068	99,200	114,777	198,865	163,173
2010	220,000	297,562	1,363,444	119,000	133,052	213,581	147,119
2011	237,000	275,411	N/A	110,600	121,858	228,559	131,630

Source: Compiled from JNTO reports, various years.

Another recent trend is 'bipolarization' (JNTO 2008a). Japan has long been considered to be an equal society, a society where there is no big gap between the rich and the poor. However, an analysis of Japanese overseas travel reveals an increase in low-cost travellers (or at least trips to closer and therefore usually cheaper destinations) but also of big spenders at destinations. On the other hand there are consumers who seek luxury travel, including a sharp increase in business-class purchases by Japanese holiday travellers. Table 5.5 details the main destination markets and flows in Japanese outbound tourism from 2001.

Provisional figures are also available for 2011, the latest at the time of writing, and these show an increase in Japanese visitors to South Korea of 8.8 per cent compared with 2010 (MLIT 2012). The same is true for Taiwan (18.0 per cent), Thailand (14.7 per cent), Singapore (24.0 per cent), Germany (5.8 per cent) and the Philippines (5.0 per cent). In other markets there has been a decline in Japanese visitors: to the North Marianas (down 22.7 per cent), Guam (7.8 per cent), Indonesia (25.8 per cent), Canada (10.4 per cent), USA (4.0 per cent, Hawaii 5.1 per cent), Australia (16.5 per cent), New Zealand (21.4 per cent), China (2.0 per cent), France (3.3 per cent) and the UK (6.8 per cent). Overall though, the pattern is one of a revival in absolute numbers, with minor changes in actual destinations. The majority of outbound travellers continue to undertake travel for sightseeing, with business trips the second most important reason, and visiting friends and relations the third (Table 5.6). These patterns will be elaborated on in Chapter 6.

Regional and Local Economic Impacts

Effects of Tourism on other Sectors of the Japanese Economy

As well as having direct economic effects on tourism-related industries, Japan's tourism industry also has an effect on a broad spectrum of domestic industries through its stimulation of household consumption by employees in tourism-related industries. The direct economic effects of the value of tourism consumption on related industries included ¥6.36 trillion in the transportation industry and ¥4.26 trillion in the accommodation industry in 2005 (MLIT 2007). A study carried out by MLIT in 2005 estimated the economic effects of tourism consumption on other industries besides those mentioned above (Table 5.7). For example, the impact on agriculture, forestry and fisheries was estimated to be ¥1.28 trillion, that on the food industry overall as ¥3.88 trillion (from a direct expenditure of ¥1.49 trillion), and that on the restaurant industry as ¥3.7 trillion. If these impacts are traced further to employment, their effect was estimated to be the creation of 540,000 jobs in agriculture, forestry and fisheries and 720,000 in the retail industry, revealing significant downstream effects, not only on the accommodation

Table 5.6: Breakdown of reasons for overseas travel by Japanese travellers, 2006.

Purpose of Travel	Percentage of Travellers
Sightseeing	67.6
Honeymoon	2.3
VFR	6.2
Business	12.2
Attending conferences	1.7
Studying abroad/School trip	1.3
Other/No response	6.2

Source: JNTO (2009; yearly a).

Table 5.7: Estimated economic impact of tourism, 2005.

Sector	Travel Consumption (¥ trillion)	Production Diffusion Effect (¥ trillion)	Employment Generation Effect (number of jobs)
Agriculture, Forestry & Fisheries	0.28	1.28	538,000
Food	1.49	3.88	168,000
Retailing	1.52	2.91	718,000
Transport	6.39	8.32	485,000
Travel Services	1.42	1.76	167,000
Restaurants	2.56	3.07	439,000
Accommodation	4.26	4.45	468,000
Others	6.14	29.63	1,709,000
Total	24.4	55.30	4,692,000

Source: MLIT (2006; 2007).

and transportation industries, but also on agriculture, forestry and fisheries, food, retail and other industries.

Economic Effects of Tourism in 2010

In 2006, the then Ministry of Land, Industry and Transport estimated the likely economic effects of tourism in the year 2010, based on the accumulated results of several national policies (notably 'Yōkoso! Japan'), trends in demand and in population change (JCO 2007). Specifically, it was assumed that the number of foreign travellers to Japan would reach ten million by 2010, that there would be an increased tourism demand by the postwar baby-boomer generation after retirement, and there would be an improved ratio of paid holidays for those still in employment. The results of this study showed that, if the number of foreign travellers to Japan should reach ten million in 2010, an increase of ¥840 billion in the value of domestic tourism consumption could be expected. Under this scenario the total value of tourism consumption by foreign travellers to Japan would be ¥2.48 trillion. However, as a result of the financial crisis beginning in 2008, the number of visitors actually fell 17.1 per cent from its peak in 2008 of 9.15 million to 7.6 million in 2009, rising to 8.6 million in 2010, only to fall again after 11 March 2011. The projected economic benefit from this source thus did not reach the projected level. However, it should be noted that the number of Japanese who travelled abroad also declined at the same time, only reaching a total of 16.64 million in 2010 (MLIT 2012: 3), so total tourism economic activity also declined.

On the positive side, the impact on domestic tourism consumption due to increased leisure activity following retirement by the baby-boomer generation (assumed to be persons aged 55 to 59 in 2005; that is, 5.08 million males and 5.18 million females) was expected to be higher than that of previous generations, and reach about ¥1.1 trillion by 2010. While no follow up research has been done on this factor there is reason to be optimistic according to the MLIT White Paper of 2012 (MLIT 2012) that this level of impact has been reached.

The impact on domestic tourism consumption due to an increased in workers' paid holidays was also factored into likely patterns of domestic travel demand. The total of paid holidays in Japan as a whole due to an increased ratio of paid holidays reached 72.62 million days in 2010. Based on the fact that day trips represent 33.3 per cent of these days and 41.0 per cent of them are used for overnight trips, and also that family travel accounts for 45.2 per cent of all travel, the increase in the value of tourism consumption from this source was projected to be ¥2.16 trillion by 2010. It should be noted here that this factor was included in the analysis as a result of a decision by the Council on Measures for the Society with a Declining Birth Rate in December 2004 to seek longer holiday entitlement for Japanese workers (MLIT 2007). However, caution was advised concerning this result, as so far, all attempts to introduce longer, consecutive holidays have proven unsuccessful in Japan.

The overall impact in 2010 of all these factors was projected by this study to be in the order of ¥30 trillion. As a result the actual value in 2010 of ¥23.8 trillion represented a shortfall of about ¥6 trillion on the cumulative effect of the above scenarios (MLIT 2012: 35). Nevertheless, MLIT's projection that the overall value of tourism consumption in 2010 would be more than 20 per cent greater than that in the fiscal year of 2005, as well as their projection of economic effects based on this, should not be seen as having been overly optimistic, since even in the very difficult times that actually occurred the value of tourism production did not decline from the level of the mid 2000s. For tourism to contribute to the further growth of the Japanese economy, however, the key will be for regions, residents and the tourism industry to take positive steps to enhance the attraction of regional resources to both domestic and inbound tourists and make more effective use of them, rather than passively waiting for leisure activity by baby boomers to increase (MLIT 2007: 7).

Finally, assessing the current contribution of the tourism industry by using data from the 'establishment and enterprise' census conducted every two or three years offers some additional insights into the sector's contribution to the economy. These data show that, in 2006, the accommodation sector accounted for 1.1 per cent of all establishments, and 1 per cent of male and 1.7 per cent of female employees in the country. If we add travel agencies, golf courses, amusement parks, museums and zoos, the tourism industry contributed 1.4 per cent of all establishments, and 1.4 per cent of male and 2.5 per cent of female employees (MIAC 2006b). This clearly shows the strong emphasis on a female workforce in the tourism industry. With eleven employees per establishment, accommodation establishments are also slightly bigger than the average small and medium enterprise in the service sector. The structure of the accommodation sector, forming the most important part of the tourism industry, is examined further below.

The Structure of the Accommodation Sector

In the Edo period and earlier, a variety of accommodation facilities catered to different social classes and offered several levels of service. After the opening of the country to Western influence, the first European-style hotel was opened in 1888, starting the dualism of Western and Japanese styles in the country's accommodation sector. Even now, operating permits for accommodation are given to three categories of establishment: *ryokan*, hotels and so-called *kani shisetsu* or 'simple facilities'. *Ryokan* and hotels are defined as predominately Japanese-style or Western-style respectively. In the 1950s, most facilities were Japanese style with tatami floors, futons and communal baths and toilets. During that period, Government initiatives to improve accommodation were aimed in two directions.

First, to make travel more affordable for domestic tourists, 'people lodges' (*kokuminshukusha*) and other public facilities were developed throughout the country, often in scenic locations in national parks. As has been seen in similar developmental sequences in other countries (for example, in Vietnam; Cooper 2000), each ministry had its own type of accommodation facility, and prefectural and municipal lodges added further variety. These attempts at social tourism were abandoned in the late 1990s, when public finances became tight and the ageing facilities, with their large rooms for group travel and low -level service, no longer met consumer needs. In the 1990s such lodges were shifted from national to municipal responsibility or sold off to investors. Municipal facilities too have been increasingly handed over to the private sector for operation. However, these facilities can still play a major role as core facilities for the development of small-scale tourism in rural areas, as affordable accommodation for students, and as venues for other group activities.

The other initiative was directed towards inbound tourism. The Act on Development of Hotels for Inbound Tourists (1949) created new quality standards in accommodation. *Ryokan* and hotels registered under this law had to provide a certain standard of facilities: a minimum room size and size of common facilities, safety requirements and private baths and toilets for at least ten, and in the case of hotels, fifteen rooms. However, as these standards required substantial investment, this type of accommodation made up only 3 per cent of all accommodation facilities registered in 1992 (Asamizu 2007). The law was therefore changed in 1993 loosening regulations on size, but introducing requirements for staff capable of catering to foreign tourists. By 2008, the number of registered establishments of this quality had reached around 3,000. This is important, as Japan does not have a hotel quality ranking system, so in the absence of such a system for accommodation facilities, registration as an international *ryokan* or hotel is the only measure of quality available. Nevertheless, general standards in the accommodation sector have benefited from the 1993 act, and from the increasing attention to tourism accommodation standards.

The 1960s saw the development of domestic mass tourism and an increased interest in outdoor activities. To serve the needs of urban families spending a weekend in the mountains or by the sea, *minshuku* sprang up between 50 and 200 kilometres around metropolitan areas (Ishii 1980). Farmers offered this type of accommodation as a side business. Rooms are simple, furnished with a low table and a TV, sometimes separated only by sliding doors from adjacent rooms. Futons are spread out in the evening and folded by the guests themselves in the morning; baths and toilets are communal. Meals are included in the price and often feature local products. Also, the number of persons staying in one room can be handled flexibly, allowing for families to stay together in one room and for student groups to negotiate cheaper prices for higher numbers per room. *Minshuku* tend to concentrate in certain locations near ski slopes, hot springs or beaches where they are organized in a cooperative that handles bookings and often sets a common price. *Minshuku* centres include Niigata and Nagano prefectures for skiing and hiking, and the coastal prefectures of Chiba, Shizuoka, Kyoto and Hyôgo.

As Western influences increasingly affected daily life, tourists expected more comfort even in rural locations. *Penshons*, defined as small Western-style lodgings (NKK 1995) and probably named after the German word *pension* or lodging, were created to answer these needs in the 1970s. In contrast to *minshuku*, which are run by their owners part-time, *penshon* owners came from urban areas, bought a plot of land offered by developers and built their dream house in sometimes a rather fancy Western style. Developers buy large pieces of land which they then connect to the road network and water supply, later selling it off in small plots, so that often several *penshons* can be found clustered together in a kind of village.

The personality and hobbies of the owner form a major sales point, as they can variously offer facilities, courses or information for bikers, sky gliders, surfers and other types of outdoor sports. Their number increased from 100 in 1975 to about 2,000 in 1985. However, as they are not registered as a special category of accommodation, more recent detailed numbers are unobtainable. Locations are similar to those of *minshuku*, but mainly in mountain areas, as large plots of undeveloped land are rarely available on the coast.

Two other segments of tourism accommodation popular in Europe play a rather minor role in Japan: second homes and camping. Second-home development is closely connected to economic upturns as a form of capital investment and development, and locations are restricted to the surroundings of metropolitan areas and to Okinawa. A first postwar wave in the late 1960s saw some second-home development projects, but many were cancelled after the oil shock of 1973 or later incorporated into the relentlessly expanding urban sprawl. The second boom in the late 1980s concentrated on the construction of apartment buildings in famous *onsen* and coastal and mountain resorts around the Tokyo metropolitan area. However, time budgets severely restrict the possible usage of second homes in Japan. Expectations are nevertheless high that some retired baby boomers will divide their time between an urban base and a second house in the countryside.

Camping has changed in character from no-frills accommodation for hikers to a comfortable option for family outings where tents and equipment can be rented on the spot or brought by car. 'Auto-camping' became popular with the boom in SUV (sports utility vehicle) ownership during the 1980s. However, as space in homes to store camping gear used only once or twice a year is scarce, most camp sites are equipped with blockhouses, fixed tents and rental services for everything needed.

In the postwar years, the accommodation sector changed from one where *ryokan* were predominant to a mixed structure where the hotel sector expanded quickly, especially in urban areas. Figures 5.2 and 5.3 illustrate the change in balance between these two types of facilities. In general, while the number of facilities is decreasing, capacity is not, so that both categories show a move to larger units. An examination of the regional distribution of accommodation gives a picture of the economic importance of tourism in different regions across the country (Figure 5.4). The number of accommodation establishments is highest in Tokyo itself and the neighbouring prefectures of Chiba and Kanagawa, with famous tourist attractions like the Disneyland Resorts, the historic city of Kamakura and a coastline popular for its marine leisure life. Around this core, a belt of prefectures in the Chûbu, Hokuriku and southern Tohoku regions have large numbers of accommodation facilities, forming a pleasure periphery for the capital metropolitan area. In the second biggest metropolitan area of Japan, the Kansai region (around Osaka and Kyoto), Hyôgo Prefecture houses the most establishments due to a combination of urban areas, hot springs, and mountain

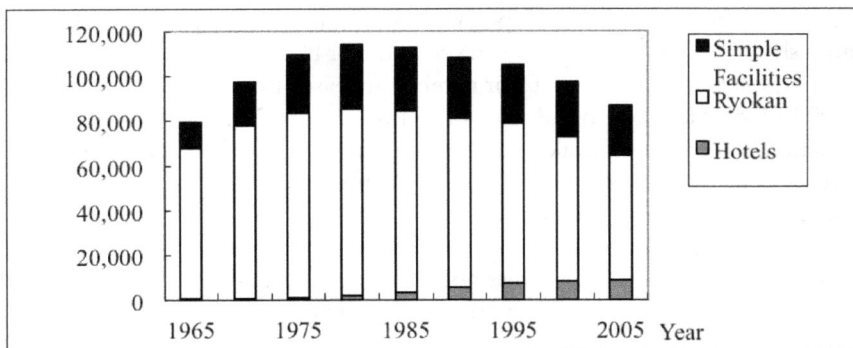

Figure 5.2: Breakdown of accommodation sector types and numbers of facilities, 1965 to 2005.

Note: *Minshuku* are registered as *ryokan* or simple facilities, *penshons* mainly as hotels.

Source: MHLW (yearly c).

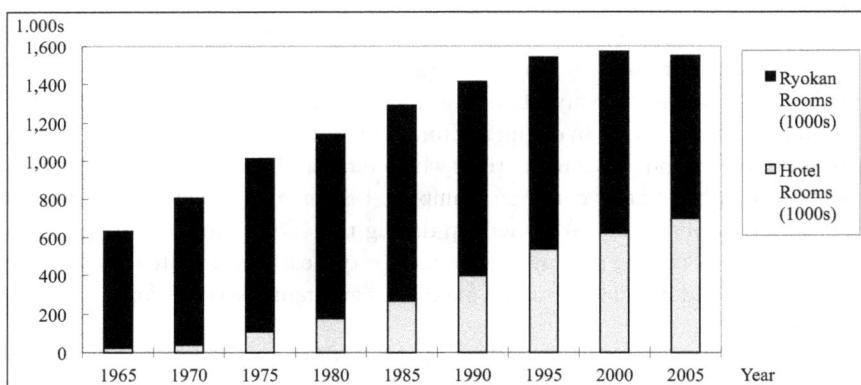

Figure 5.3: Changes in numbers of rooms in *ryokan* and hotels, 1965 to 2005.

Source: MHLW (yearly c).

and coastal resorts. In Hokkaidô, the accommodation industry is also well established for both foreign and domestic visitors.

Figures 5.5 and 5.6 show a slightly different regional pattern to the absolute numbers of establishments. The percentage of the workforce in the accommodation sector is highest in prefectures that are home to famous *onsen* resorts like Ôita (Beppu), Wakayama (Shirahama) and Ishikawa (Figure 5.5). Famous domestic and international tourist destinations like Matsue City in Shimane Prefecture on the Sea of Japan coast and Nagasaki in Kyûshû) also draw a sufficiently large number of visitors to support a strong accommodation sector, and therefore employment, as does the national pleasure periphery based on Hokkaidô and

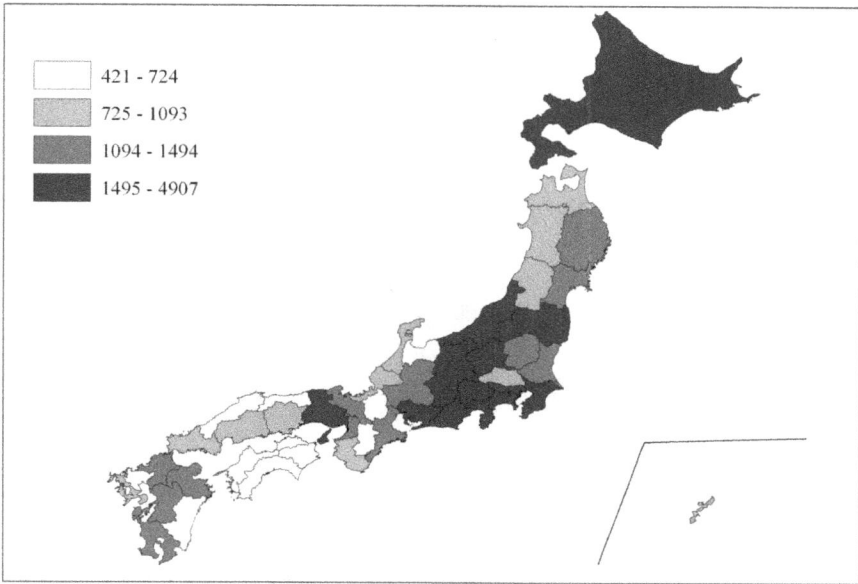

Figure 5.4: Number of accommodation facilities by prefecture, 2006.
Source: MIAC (2006b).

Okinawa. Other than these concentrations, the data is as might be expected in a country with large domestic tourist flows, showing a broadly linear relationship between population size and numbers of rooms (Figure 5.6), except for Saitama and Kanagawa on the one hand, which have fewer rooms than their size would suggest, and Shizuoka, Nagano and Niigata on the other, which have more.

Within these categories there is a differentiation in the provision of tourist accommodation facilities between urban tourism and new resort development areas on the one hand, and established tourist destinations with predominately Japanese-style accommodation on the other. Western-style hotels play an important role in the urban conurbations of Kantô and Kansai and large urban centres like Sendai, Hiroshima or Fukuoka. They also feature in resort areas like Miyazaki Prefecture, as explained in Chapter 4, and in Okinawa. Japanese-style accommodation predominates elsewhere. However, it should be noted that even facilities registered as *ryokan* often offer Western-style rooms. Thus, although *ryokan* still account for the largest number of establishments in many areas, they have undergone a number of changes. Their concept of service still, however, represents the Japanese style of travelling and it is therefore worthwhile examining the changes they have undergone. In the 1950s, *ryokan* were the main form of accommodation in urban areas as well as in tourist destinations like hot springs. However, urban *ryokan* have been almost completely replaced by hotels. The few

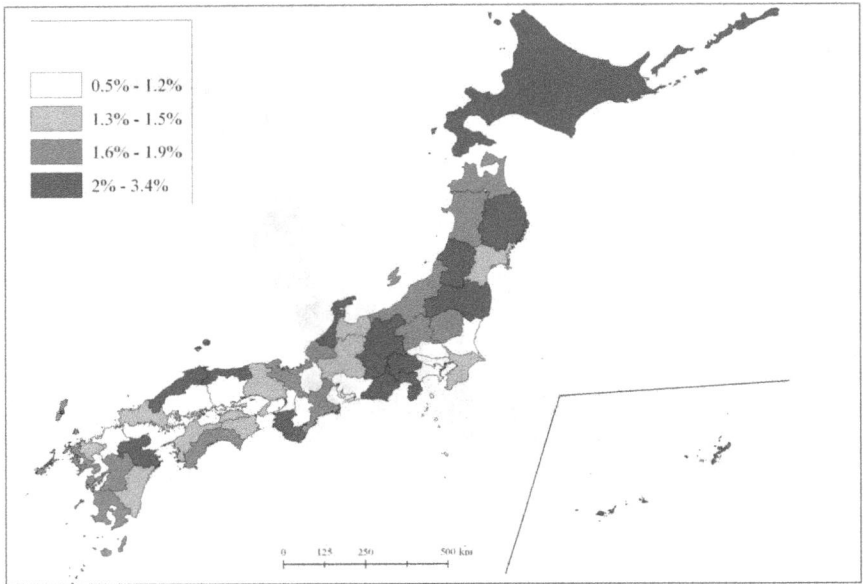

Figure 5.5: Percentage of the workforce in the accommodation sector, 2006.
Source: MIAC (2006b).

that are left are small facilities that cater to foreign travellers looking for cheap and authentic accommodation.

Today, *ryokan* can be found mainly in tourist destinations and this accommodation type is almost synonymous with *onsen* bathing and fine dining. Typical features of a *ryokan* include large tatami rooms that can be occupied by a flexible number of persons, tea-making facilities and a TV. Meals are served in the room and futon bedding is spread out after the meal. Rooms are equipped with a small bath and toilet. A large common bathing area, often with outdoor baths (*rotemburo*), is the main attraction, but bars, karaoke facilities, souvenir shops and rooms for large groups to dine together, sometimes with a stage for performances, are provided in larger facilities. Prices include breakfast and dinner. This structure has been gradually changing to adapt to the needs of smaller groups and families on the one hand and the necessity to cut down on expensive labour on the other. Buffet-style breakfasts are now offered, as has long been common in hotels, and parts of the bathing area have been separated into smaller units that can be reserved for private use. Some have even added Western-style rooms.

The process of diversification has also occurred in the hotel sector. Two varieties of hotels developed: so-called 'city hotels', with restaurants, wedding facilities, conference rooms and a higher price; and 'business hotels', providing cheaper accommodation. The *kapuseru hoteru* is a special Japanese variety for busy

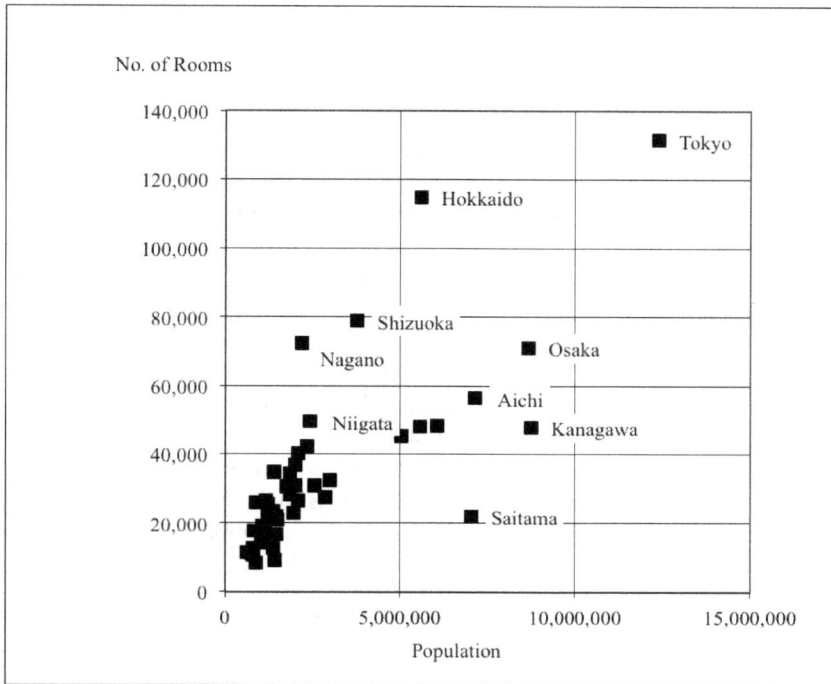

Figure 5.6: Tourism intensity index: number of rooms per 1,000 inhabitants, 2007.

Source: MHLW (yearly c); Report on Public Health Administration and Services; Ministry of Internal Affairs and Communication Statistics Bureau. *Population Census of Japan* 2000.

company employees who have missed the last train home and can pass the night in a box-type room just the size of one bed. Another very visible feature of the Japanese hotel landscape are the so-called *rabu hoteru* ('love hotels'). Although they are sometimes used by travellers as cheap accommodation because they charge per room and not per person, their main function is to offer couples a place to escape from the eyes of society or from crowded living conditions in order to meet or have sex. They can be easily distinguished by their flashy design, neon lights and prices by the hour indicated on large signs. All these varieties of hotel are mainly located in urban areas, although 'love hotels' can also be found near highways to give their customers privacy.

The late-nineteenth-century tradition of offering Western-style accommodation to wealthy travellers in famous scenic destinations was revived by developers in the 1980s. Resort hotels sprang up all around the country in connection with ski slopes, golf courses and marinas. In contrast to the *ryokan* sector, large chains predominate in hotel development. Domestic chains have been recently joined by international ones both in the high-price and business sectors.

The accommodation sector has thus adapted itself to the changing needs of domestic tourists and now faces the challenge of adapting to international visitors and their standards. Generally, in addition to the large segment of reliable and well-appointed mid-price hotels, there are an increasing number of high-end international hotel chains and individual *ryokan* offering a comfortable modern version of the 'traditional' Japanese experience. It is possible to say that the ability of *ryokan* to re-invent tradition and create a unique modernity has helped them to keep and even increase their popularity (Guichard-Anguis 2009). At the low end, self-service and backpacker hotels and cheap run-down *ryokan* are concentrated in urban areas.

Finally, it is necessary to look at the contribution the accommodation sector makes to local and regional employment. As is common in this sector, employees are divided into a small group of qualified personnel in permanent positions and a larger group of part-time or seasonally hired staff with few qualification requirements. This is especially true of Japan, where concentration of demand on national holidays, weekends and special seasons is high. As Funck (1999a: 168) has pointed out, at the beginning of the 1990s, the accommodation industry was characterized by a higher percentage of women and elderly employees than tertiary industries in general, as one third were older than 55 years. Wages per person only reached 83 per cent of the average in other service industries. More recent interviews in several destinations have revealed that these employment patterns have not changed. A reliance on elderly women working part-time in *onsen* locations or students in seasonal employment in skiing destinations still exists and is supplemented by an increase in mainly female workers recruited through temporary staff agencies. Employees in accommodation and catering enjoy the lowest rate of holidays taken of any industry, 29.4 per cent compared to 74.4 per cent in the electricity, gas and water industries (MHLW yearly a). Providing accommodation therefore offers few permanent, attractive jobs that could lure young people back to depopulating areas. It does however contribute to mixed sources of income, which is typical for rural areas, and also offers lifestyle choices for those who prefer the countryside and want to start their own small-scale business.

The Structure of the Travel Agency Sector

Travel agencies form an important part of the tourism industry. The travel agency sector in Japan is divided into Type 1 agencies that can produce and handle international and domestic trips, Type 2 agencies that are restricted to domestic trips, and Type 3 agencies that specialize in retail trade. The number of Type 1 agencies has fluctuated since 1996, when these new categories were introduced, while Type 2 and Type 3 agencies have been declining since 2003. While Type 1 agencies only account for 7.7 per cent of all agencies by number, their sales made up 84.2 per cent of the whole sector. Concentration becomes even more evident when we

Table 5.8: Number of registered travel agents in Japan, 2003 to 2007.

Year	Type 1 Travel Agency	Type 2 Travel Agency	Type 3 Travel Agency	Travel Agency Total	Travel Agency Business	Total
2003	841	2,782	6,314	9,937	1,129	11,066
2004	783	2,765	6,259	9,807	1,061	10868
2005	781	2,727	6,179	9,687	1,015	10,702
2006	817	2,757	6,088	9,662	959	10,621
2007	808	2,793	6,153	9,754	930	10,684

Source: Mimura (2008).

look at the fifty most important agencies, all Type 1, which control 74.5 per cent of all sales (Horie 2006: 123). In 2007, JTB Group sales accounted for more than one third of the sales of the sixty most important agencies (JATA 2008).

The travel industry is often referred to as an example of a labour-intensive service industry. The industry's low productivity in comparison to other industries has long been a subject of debate (Witt and Moutinho 1995; Weaver and Lawton 2002). In Japan it is possible to illustrate this situation and its effects through an analysis of travel agent sub-sector data (Table 5.8). According to the 2006 profit and loss statements of the registered Type 1 travel firms in Japan (such as HIS and JTB), their average yearly sales were ¥12.9 billion, of which 89 per cent was paid to transportation and accommodation providers. After deducting operating expenses from their revenue of ¥1.4 billion, the operating profit was a mere ¥71.4 million. Their operating profit margin was therefore only 0.5 per cent, which is extremely low compared to the average for non-manufacturing industries (2.5 per cent) or that of all industries (3.1 per cent).

As noted above, part of the problem is that the travel industry is quite labour-intensive (Witt and Moutinho 1995; Weaver and Lawton 2002); in Japan the proportion of labour cost to total operating expenses was as high as 48 per cent in 2006, which is generally higher than other labour-intensive sectors such as wholesaling, retailing and the transport industry (Mimura 2008). Increasing productivity and reducing labour use will be indispensable for the travel industry in Japan in order to ensure survival in the face of a continuing squeeze on cost margins, as will the impact on travel agents of travellers using IT-based solutions such as information searches and bookings using the internet.

The Youth Travel Market

In order to understand what is happening in economic terms in the current Japanese tourism market, it is important to know on what factors different groups of travellers base their consumption decisions. A survey by the economic analysis firm Japan Tourism Marketing Company (JTM), carried out in 2007, looked at the youth and young-adult market to determine under what conditions they consider travelling and what types of travel they actually undertake (Kono 2008). The results are interesting in that they show that young people (in their 20s and 30s) rank day-to-day consumption activities as their highest priority, much the same as youth everywhere in developed countries. For males this may or may not include some forms of local recreation and short-term tourism, but certainly includes dining out, other forms of socializing with colleagues, and/or hobbies. Female respondents, however, primarily spend money on fashion items, with socializing very much in second place, and quite often only with other females.

Looking at survey respondents according to their income levels, the higher the annual income the more is spent on dining out (although this pattern may also mean that they are too busy working to cook at home). Of respondents with annual incomes of less than ¥3.5 million, more than 40 per cent of males answered that they would spend discretionary money on hobbies, including movies, concerts, games and books. A high percentage of females belonging to this income group also spend money on movies, concerts, games and books. Young consumers with lower incomes may think they can save money enjoying such things by themselves rather than dining out with friends (Kono 2008). But when all were asked what they would spend a sum of say ¥300,000 on (a half-yearly average bonus level amount for many people), male respondents' top three choices were saving (40 per cent), audio-visual appliances (35 per cent) and domestic travel (30 per cent). Female respondents identified their top priorities as saving (40 per cent) and overseas travel (40 per cent), closely followed by domestic travel (39 per cent). These results show that travelling, both domestic and overseas, which was considered low in priority in responses to the previous question on spending, is in fact highly prioritized by both males and females, but only if they think that they will have the disposable income (Kono 2008, Part 2). Female respondents are particularly eager to travel overseas. Men seem to prefer domestic travel regardless of their income level.

The JTM report includes further analyses of travel trends among young Japanese in their twenties, including what types of travel experiences young consumers have had, and what styles of travel they prefer. The results show that approximately 80 per cent of females and 78 per cent of male respondents in their twenties have taken a domestic trip at least once a year in the last three years. Around half of them travel more than twice a year. Domestic travel thus appears to be a common activity for Japanese youths in their twenties. There are several reasons for this pattern: First, Japan has abundant tourism resources such as hot springs and local food. Second, domestic travel is comparatively easy to schedule or re-schedule in accordance with budgets and holidays or in response to friends' wishes. Third, in contrast to overseas travel, domestic travel raises fewer concerns about language, safety and security, and sanitary conditions. These factors make all Japanese age groups feel that domestic travel is easier to participate in than overseas travel (Kono 2008).

Looking at travel trends according to respondents' household annual income levels, there is a visible contrast between males and females (JTM 2008). For males, the higher their income, the more frequent is domestic travel. In contrast, more than 40 per cent of female respondents with low incomes (less than ¥2 million per year) travel domestically two or three times a year, which is more frequent than for males in the same income group. Among those whose annual household income is between ¥2 million and ¥7 million, there is little difference in travel frequency. The number of young Japanese, both male and female, who have no overseas travel experience tends to be lower among higher income groups (JTM 2008), as with other age groups and societies. However, male respondents with higher incomes (over ¥7 million) appear to travel less frequently than those with incomes between ¥5 million and ¥7 million (possibly because they are too busy earning extra income through massive amounts of overtime). For females, travel frequency is lower in the ¥5 million to ¥7 million income group compared to those earning ¥5 million or less, but frequency of travel is much higher among female respondents earning over ¥7 million, unlike the pattern found with males.

For Japanese youths in their twenties, travel companions are also an important factor in deciding on overseas trips (JTM 2008). To the question 'How do you like to travel?', nearly half (45 per cent) of the JTM respondents chose 'with spouse or boyfriend/girlfriend', followed by 'with a few friends' (21 per cent), 'with family' (18 per cent) and 'by oneself' (14 per cent). The survey results also show that Japanese youths in their twenties adapt their style of travelling to suit their travel companions. Overall, this important survey disclosed characteristics of young travellers that show that they select rationally what to spend money on and where to travel, and within this they attach as much importance to human relations during the trip as to what a destination has to offer (An 2012).

The Structure of the Tourism Industry in Regional Economies

Many communities in Japan are already turning their landscapes into quasi if not actual theme parks in order to attract tourists, capital and more residents (see Chapter 4). Over the next fifty years, this process of conversion could become a Darwinian struggle for survival as the population outside major cities across the country diminishes in line with the predicted decline in the Japanese population overall (Cooper and Eades 2007). A large percentage of the more than seventy million Japanese of the future will be accounted for by the megacities of the heartland – the Tokyo and Osaka regions – and the other regional hubs of over a million inhabitants along the high-speed railway line from Tokyo to Fukuoka.

That will mean few people in the rest of the country, so we have to ask the question: As demographic shrinking gathers speed, what are people going to do with the surplus rural space?

Speculation about these matters is not of course new. It is a commonplace that an ageing population needs more expensive care and medical facilities, and that as society ages the number of people actually working and paying taxes to support them is gradually reduced, creating a crisis for both the pension and welfare systems. It is also well-known that after the Second World War, Japan urbanized quickly in one of the most dramatic periods of economic growth of any country in history (Johnson 1989). The European countries sourced their labour for reconstruction from their colonies and refugees. Refugees figured in the reconstruction of Japan as well, but after that the labour for reconstruction came increasingly from rural communities, freed of debt to landlords because of the Occupation land reforms (Dower 1979: 329–32). Farming became increasingly mechanized, with a reduced demand for labour, and farmers themselves dwindled in number and aged, forming now perhaps the most geriatric agricultural labour force in history. In the process, rural men ran out of potential wives and had to import them from overseas (Hisada 1992, cited in Yamashita 2003: 155; see also Knight 2003a, Faier 2009) or stay bachelors, and members of many rural communities simply voted with their feet. Is this the picture of life in the peripheral community of the future, even with tourism?

Tourism and Economic Life in Provincial and Rural Japan

This section reviews some of the studies that have been carried out in what we might call peripheral Japan – that is to say in the *mura* (villages), *machi* or *cho* (towns) and smaller *shi* (cities) – over the last few years on the economic and social pressures facing these types of settlements in modern times. As in many other countries, the classic response to these kinds of pressure has been the amalgamation of communities to pool their resources and services, together with attempts to, first, raise the profiles of local communities through various types of *machizukuri* (literally 'making the town', see Knight 1994; Traphagen 1998), and second, bring back jobs and people through the aegis of tourism. As is often the case in Japan, many of these attempts have not been generated locally but have reflected national policies. The most extreme case is the rearrangement of communities around 2005, called the *heisei daigappei* (Great Heisei Amalgamation Initiative). Based on a law of 1999, communities were encouraged to merge, with the result that their number shrank from 3,232 in 1999 to 1,820 in 2006 (Thompson 2008: 368). Other attempts to combine tourism and regional development include the *furusato sosei undo* or 'home town campaign' of the late 1980s, and the finance provided under the Resort Law of 1987 (Funabiki 1992: 61; Rimmer 1992; Funck 1999b; Thompson 2003: 92; Cooper and Flehr. 2006). The latter were in the main bubble-economy extravaganzas, in which communities were given large sums of money to shore up their local identities and attract visitors. Despite the excesses of some communities in the ways in which they invested the money – one mayor bought a lump of gold and put it on display as a tourist attraction, while another invited two American artists to construct a dune out of 29,700 tons of sand, which was, alas, soon blown away (Funabiki 1992: 61–62) – two broad themes emerged from these policies: the encouragement of specialized niche agriculture, and the promotion of local tourism as an economic saviour of peripheral regions.

In reporting on research carried out in a town formed through the amalgamation of five villages after the Second World War, Knight (2003a) noted that many Japanese writers see the depopulation of the countryside and its return to nature as a national disaster, or at the very least as the loss of a vital national resource. In the five villages of the 1950s, the population stood at over 10,000, but by the 1990s it was under 5,000, with 20 per cent of the population leaving during the period 1965 to 1970 alone. Most of the emigrants were of course younger people, resulting in a drastic fall in births and marriages, and bachelors who found it increasingly difficult to find wives. Some migrants return every year at the time of the August *Bon* festival, but then return to the cities immediately after the festivities. This rural depopulation, however, is in a perverse way in line with government policy, particularly with attempts to reduce the acreage of land under rice cultivation. Some villagers have even planted their fields with trees, effectively helping extend the boundaries of the forest. As a result, the community self-image is not surprisingly one of terminal decline, to which the town hall has attempted to respond: they have tried to stimulate return migration, promoted *furusato* ties with migrants so that they want to do this regularly, and tried to attract new settlers and/or tourists.

As with other communities, these are recurring themes. Interestingly, one initiative has been to try and attract the elderly to return, through the still available concentration of care and medical services. Clearly, with growing numbers of elderly, this is not a bad revitalization strategy for the Japan of the next generation or so. They have also tried to stimulate more marriage and reproduction locally and lure migrants back from Tokyo by providing lists of empty houses which could provide accommodation for young couples and returnees. *Furusato* ties have also been encouraged by developing a mail-order service of local products and sending details to migrants throughout the country (Knight 1998). In addition to the elderly, some of those who have been attracted back are counter-cultural types with an interest in the arts, rebuilding traditional industries and culture through tourism, or organic agriculture. Needless to say, not all of them manage to put down roots, and they become serial settlers as they move on to the next community in their quest for rural authenticity. But Knight's gloomy conclusion is that none of these initiatives has reversed the trend, and his alternative scenario is for wild animals such as macaques, bears and boars moving in, making life seemingly even more insecure, and thus hastening the rural-to-urban exodus (Knight 2003b).

Traphagen's (1998, 2000, 2003) discussion of the impact of population change on the town of Kanagasaki is of interest regarding the management of the economic impact of tourism on rural areas. In the 1980s and 1990s the town still relied on agriculture, though there was some local industry in the form of semiconductor and pharmaceuticals manufacture. Farming was in fact part-time, however, and agricultural cooperatives were a significant development for pooling resources. By the mid 1990s, the town had been trying for fifteen years to revitalize itself through a *machizukuri* campaign. The local people organized lectures, meetings and campaigns to create a 'living environment' and they had reinvented tradition in the form of festivals and celebrations of public holidays (Respect the Elderly Day on 15 September being an important day in the local calendar). Generally the discourse was one of lifelong education, a healthy environment and good social relations, everything that an elderly population could in fact want. Other initiatives included improved home help, a centre for life-long education, meeting rooms, classrooms, computer training facilities, kitchens and fitness facilities, improved sports facilities, better sewage systems, the promotion of local eco-tourism, and a town hall.

Another city on a similar scale is Tôno, famous from the collection of folklore stories collected there by Yanagita Kunio in the Meiji period, *Tôno Monogatari* (Yanagita 2008; see also Yamashita 2003). Tôno now projects itself as a rural museum (tourist) city, the city of myth, and the *furusato* of folklore. The original manuscript of Yanagita's book is prominently displayed in the museum, while his study has been brought from Tokyo and reconstructed in Tôno. At the centre of the town's regeneration is the Tonopia theme-park project, with a complex of facilities including a city museum, a folklore village and a heritage park. While there is something of an irony in the fact that Yanagita himself was a Tokyo bureaucrat, given that regions of Japan often see their own decline as the corollary of the growth of the capital, his contribution has been localized through the appropriation of his study and his manuscript, to create a mythic landscape that probably never was, using a combination of local *machizukuri* and the tourist gaze (Urry 1990) backed up by the domestic tourist yen. How far these factors will be sufficient to sustain the tourism industry in future if the population of the region as a whole suffers a meltdown is anyone's guess, but certainly Tôno is making a concerted effort. It may be that in the long run the only way to sustain this kind of tourism is to develop it into the full theme-park experience, as has happened in the examples of national and literary tourism described in Hendry and Raveri (2002).

National Players, Local Players: The Private and Public Sectors in Tourism Development

The development of tourist facilities typically begins with an investment concept based on preliminary analyses of demand (Cooper and Flehr 2006). Normally, the developer then obtains capital from lending institutions, secures land, hires architects and engineers to formulate physical plans, employs consultants to conduct various surveys regarding the characteristics of the land and of the projected demand, and begins to seek development approval from the relevant authorities. For major projects a developer may incur substantial debts in this early development phase, often spending significant amounts of money before any actual or implied development approval can be gained. In most countries this type of situation produces a climate of uncertainty for investors, as local authorities might enact zoning or other ordinances that render the development financially impossible. Alternatively, administrators responsible for environmental protection and building codes, for example, might react negatively to a politically desirable local development by hedging it with conditions that again make it impossible for the developer to carry through on the project. In both of these situations the developer is subject to a local approving authority's discretion and may be left stranded once initial work and financing has been arranged but before the right to develop land has been secured, if planning approval is refused or unduly delayed.

In addition, the extent to which such problems conflict, or are perceived to conflict, with the resource management and development policies of higher levels of government can constitute a political difficulty. This is why in Japan and other countries the power of the state may sometimes be invoked to ensure desired outcomes for public sector policy making, especially where regional development is perceived to be at stake (for more discussion on this point, see Chapter 3). Economically, major tourism developments resulting from state intervention have been made possible in Japan through the ability of prefectural governors under the Japanese land-management system to designate urban or peri-urban land as an 'urban promotion' area, and in national laws which bind local communities to act in a certain manner (Sorensen 2002; Cooper and Flehr 2006). This power, which can remove particular development proposals from the purview of local government and thus of local communities and force development in particular directions, may be used by higher levels of government to reduce the inherent uncertainty of tourism development at the local level, thereby producing the desired effect of enabling developers to protect their investment in many cases (Shapira 1994: 1–11; Hall 2000). This process then provides the developer with vested rights, often by invalidating the local zoning regulations applicable to a property because the higher public benefit of the development, economically and/ or socially, is said to over-ride such local considerations.

Gilman (2001) analyses two examples of theme-park development in the context of deindustrialization in Japan and the United States. In the Japanese example, it was the local government in cooperation with the company closing a coal mine that secured public funds to create a theme park – only to have it closed after two years due to lack of visitors. The fact that expected visitor figures calculated by the consultants often mysteriously fit with the predicted running costs perhaps gives additional proof that these projects are regional development strategies rather than promising investments. Therefore, as returns on investment are not the absolute priority, luring investors with offers of deregulation and political support, including reorganizing festivals into a regular calendar of events which are then used to promote tourism to the destination throughout the year, forms a vital part of these strategies (Graburn 1983; March 2000).

The Law on the Development of Comprehensive Resort Areas, 1987

To further examine the connection between public and private development in the economics of tourism in Japan, we now look at the Law on the Development of Comprehensive Resort Areas, or as it is commonly known, the Resort Law, of 1987 as a prime example of higher-level government involvement in local tourism development. Japan's strong dependency on the construction sector for economic development is famous (Wolferen 1989; Kerr 2001), especially in peripheral areas with a weak economic structure that rely on public works projects for jobs and investment. The shift during the 1980s and 1990s to the active government promotion of private investment saw the commencement of so called 'third sector' developments or public–private joint ventures all over the country. The tourism sector, requiring large initial investment and at the same time cooperation from regional and local government for deregulation and planning security, saw a particularly strong boom in third-sector companies promoted by national policies for resort development.

Japan has a strong tradition of promoting economic growth through national development initiatives. Growth pole development through large-scale industrialization in selected localities in the 1960s and the spread of high-tech industries through technopolis projects in the 1980s are the most famous examples. The Resort Law was the first attempt to extend this concept to the service sector. It took resort development outside the Japanese local land-use planning and control system and led to massive investment in local tourism projects designed to influence the pattern of regional and local economic development. This was seen at the time as a way of reducing uncertainty for developers of resorts and golf courses, which were considered at the national level to be ideal bases for rural regeneration and regional economic development, and a way to promote the effective use of leisure time and stimulate domestic tourism demand (Klamann 1990; Hebbert 1994). As part of the bubble economy, it created an investment boom across the country that would have affected about 3 per cent of all national land if the original plans had been completed. While this strategy was evaluated positively in general and scientific publications in the 1980s, voices critical of environmental destruction and a one-sided emphasis on 'hardware' development were raised in the early 1990s (Sato 1990; Suzuki and Kobuchi 1991). Since then, silence has covered many shelved development plans and bankruptcies after the bursting of the bubble economy.

The Resort Law has however to be seen in the context of the emphasis on private-sector development by the then Nakasone government, as exemplified by the privatization of Japan National Railways and Nippon Telegraph and Telephone, and in connection with the Fourth National Development Plan. As a national response to international pressure to increase domestic consumption and an invitation to companies to invest their surplus capital in regional economies, the law aimed to provide an enrichment of lifestyle through the development of recreation facilities and better balanced regional development. Low-interest loans, public infrastructure development, tax exemptions and, most important of all, deregulation of land-use restrictions were used to lure private enterprises to the countryside; the overall planning framework was left to prefectures. When the law came before parliament in May 1987 it took less than a day of discussion to be passed. By the end of 1991, 35 prefectures had a resort development plan approved; by 1994, their number had risen to 41 out of 47. Plans focused on areas with weak economic structures rather than on those with rich tourism resources or easy access, in an attempt to create new, artificial destinations on the drawing board. Golf courses, ski slopes, marinas, holiday apartments and hotels were the core projects included in all plans, as sales of golf course and club hotel membership and apartments promised a quick return on investment. Investors looked for public cooperation in the form of third-sector companies to qualify for low-interest loans and to achieve faster planning permission through the deregulation of restrictions on the use of forest, agricultural land and national parks. The Seagaia ocean resort in Miyazaki Prefecture, theme parks like the Spain Village in Mie Prefecture or Huis Ten Bosch in Sasebo (Nagasaki Prefecture), and many ski slopes in the northern parts of Japan are examples of developments which followed this logic.

However, many developments soon ran into difficulties. Environmental groups opposed golf course construction as they feared negative effects of pesticides on water resources; and tourists preferred to fly to cheap destinations abroad rather than stay in new, overpriced domestic hotels. Legislation to promote consecutive holidays was suggested but never enacted. Finally, the bubble economy burst and those prefectures and municipalities who had not yet started construction turned out to be the lucky ones, as they didn't have to take over oversized tourist facilities after investors withdrew or went bankrupt. The resort development boom left theme parks, golf courses, ski slopes, marinas, museums and hotels scattered around the country that since then have faced closure, takeover by domestic or foreign investment firms, and scaled-down operation. Now, fifteen to twenty years after construction, they are in need of additional investment to keep them attractive for tourists.

The Resort Law thus turned out to be an extreme example of private investment promotion with little regard being paid to environmental costs, responsible use of public funds and planning regulations, but also without any attention to market needs. The following case studies further illustrate the cooperation and combination of the public and private sectors in regional and local tourism development in Japan.

Case Study 1: Spa Resort Hawaiians

The Spa Resort Hawaiians in Iwaki City, Fukushima Prefecture, north-east of the national capital metropolitan area, is probably the first example of a theme park and resort in Japan constructed by an industrial company to make up for the decline of their main business (Aburakawa et al. 2009). The operation in question was the Jôban coal mine, which started operating at the end of the nineteenth century. Until the 1950s, the towns that in 1966 merged to form Iwaki City flourished as mining towns based on the company's investments, with an adjacent important *onsen*. When demand for coal became sluggish, the mining company developed plans for a spa resort using hot water from coal mining operations and themed on Hawaii, at that time still the distant dream resort for many Japanese. About 600 former mine workers were employed. Japan's first technical school for flamenco and Polynesian dance was established to educate dancers dedicated to the stage, and in 1966 Jôban Hawaiian Centre opened its doors. Since its first year of operation, more than one million people have visited the resort each year, and in the forty years that that have elapsed since then fifty million visitors have enjoyed the spas, hotels, water-themed attractions and the Polynesian dance show at this site.

Continued renewal and new attractions have created a solid base for business, and in 1990 the name was changed to the current one of Spa Resort Hawaiians. Even during and since the 1990s, when many similar theme parks declared bankruptcy, the company has continued to invest in new attractions and expand its water- and spa-based facilities for all ages in both the European/American and Japanese styles. The *onsen* town nearby has also profited, while accommodation facilities have doubled and capacity has increased more than tenfold. In 2007, a new Hawaiian-themed shopping area and a movie based on the story of the girls who learned Hawaiian dance in the 1960s to work in the new resort boosted visitor numbers to 1,546,000 during that year. The resort's continued success, however, owes much to its location relatively close to the Tokyo metropolitan area and the fact that many attractions are covered by a dome, making them all-weather attractions. Marketing efforts – like package offers including the trip by bus from the capital area, promotion on the internet, and moderate prices have paid off too. The sheer number of facilities, grouped in five themed areas, calls for at least one overnight stay, but repeat day-trip visitors from nearby areas are also frequent. The attractions have also always been adapted to the changing tastes of the time; whereas banana trees fascinated tourists in the 1960s, a historic spa facility in the Japanese style attracts the tourists of the twenty-first century. Spa Resort Hawaiian is thus a rare example of a successful local shift from industrial production to the tourism industry, made possible by the consequent investment and the involvement of a single company with strong links to local government.

Postscript: the resort had to close in 2011/12 due to the impact of the March 2011 earthquake and associated nuclear accident, when the groundwater supply dried up and the spa proved to be too close to the troubled Fukushima nuclear plant. The resort reopened in February 2012.

Case Study 2: Space World

As noted by Cooper and Flehr (2006), while the Japanese system of local land-use controls through zoning has much in common with other developed planning systems, actual development planning is top-down and based on regional rather than local economic considerations (Callies 1994: 60–66). The growth of the tourism industry is no exception to this pattern. The Japanese system tends to target particular areas for development, by means of such special laws as the Resort Law, and this is perhaps both a cause and effect of the activities of a coalition of property developers, landowners, and central and prefectural government authorities, which for many years has dominated local government development policy and practice (Sorensen 2002: 290–95). As elsewhere, the end result is that local government in Japan seeks to control development pressures, but under existing regulations there is generally no local objection to, and there can even be considerable involvement in, development projects that have central government backing. Indeed, if necessary, the land in question will automatically be rezoned to facilitate approval of a central-government-backed development (Cooper and Flehr 2006). When this is coupled with the considerable investment incentives available through special laws or the land readjustment grants (*kukaku seiri*) available at prefectural and city level from the MLIT, investors in major tourism developments are favourably placed to obtain approval for their projects.

Kitakyûshû City, on the northern coast of the island of Kyûshû, has long been a centre of heavy industry and, like the industrial heartlands of North America, Western Europe and Australia, has undergone massive economic restructuring over the past three decades. Steel, shipbuilding and coal mining have been particularly affected, and the result has been a considerable downsizing of the local workforce, many directly employed by Nippon Steel, the largest local company, and its subcontractors, in favour of the development of high-technology industries in the adjacent city and prefecture of Fukuoka. As a result, the city has had to define a new economic future and rationale, and has used several of the regional and economic measures created under the legislative programmes outlined above, especially the finance available under the Resort Law and the Comprehensive National Development Plans of the past twenty years.

The city entered into a number of third-sector (public–private) projects involving city and prefectural agencies, central government and private investors. One of these was the Space World complex, occupying 20 hectares of the former Nippon Steel Yawata plant and the biggest single project in Nippon Steel's diversification program. Modelled on a similar development in Huntsville, Alabama, USA, and opened in 1990, Space World contains a large-scale amusement park with a space theme and an overnight-stay space camp for children (Klamann 1990). Nippon Steel was the primary sponsor of the ¥30,000 million (US$214 million) project, with minority participation by Kitakyûshû City, Fukuoka Prefecture and MITI's facilitation fund for industrial structural adjustment (implemented under the Law Concerning the Promotion of Local Economic Development and the Resort Law, both of 1987; see Shapira 1994: 171). In this respect, Kitakyûshû's economic development strategies are similar to those adopted elsewhere in Japan – and in comparable cities in the USA, Australia and Europe. The main thrust is to achieve economic diversification through a combination of image building, organizational development, technology, infrastructure improvement, small business and tourism. Many of the city's hopes for tourism, image improvement and the regeneration of the old Yawata works therefore hinged on Space World, as it was expected to attract two million visitors a year after opening, and progressively more thereafter. However, attendance did not reach the planned levels. In the year after it opened (1990), there were 1.85 million visitors, but numbers then declined to 1.65 million in 1992, climbed slowly to 2.1 million in 2002, before falling back to 1.64 million in 2004, the last date for which reliable figures are available.

When it opened, Space World employed approximately 250 full time and 500 part-time workers; in 2004 there were approximately 200 full-time and 300 part-time. About a half the full-time workers are regular or permanent employees, with the other half on one-year temporary contracts. However, although some 7,000 Nippon Steel workers lost their jobs between 1985 and 1990, only about 80 found work at Space World, largely in park maintenance programs (Shapira 1994: 159). And when the park opened, average wages for all part-time employees were set just below the level paid by the local Japanese McDonalds (Shapira 1994). In short, Space World generated few well-paid regular jobs to replace those formerly available in the steel industry and its part-time salaries were lower than the norm locally – not a recipe for confidence in the tourism industry as a replacement for the steel industry.

How, then, was Space World created as a planned local tourism development? As noted above, it is one of the numerous theme parks and leisure resorts developed by private developers with support from MITI and local government, but generally without local planning approval under such ordinances as the City

Planning Law of 1968 (Sorensen 2002: 214–16, 316). MITI provided financial incentives for leisure developments in areas of industrial depression and encouraged industrial cities to become partners in these third-sector projects, but it did not conduct any planning background studies or require comprehensive evaluation of any of the proposed projects (Sorensen 2002: 316–17). This lack of critical evaluation of large development projects under the Resort Law and other regional investment vehicles also extended to the planning policy framework of local government. Although Kitakyûshû City was a financial contributor to Space World, the city government did not carry out any independent evaluation of the project either. It was simply notified by Nippon Steel and asked to participate. It carried out no cost–benefit analyses and explored no alternative uses for the site, even though there was a shortage of land in the city and the authorities knew that Space World was likely to create few new jobs (Shapira 1994: 177).

However, in following Nippon Steel's lead, while the city authorities seem to have abrogated (or at the very least disregarded) their responsibilities under the City Planning Law of 1968, they had little choice because of the way the major projects system actually runs in Japan (Shapira 1994: 177). Officials took the view that if the private company was willing to risk its own money, so was the city. In making this investment, however, they failed to alert planners to the fact that the project, to be located in an old industrial area, had no adjacent tourism-related facilities, that there were few other visitor attractions in the local area to enable the city to build an integrated and viable tourism industry, and that transport connections to the chosen site were extremely limited. Such considerations might have made the city question the extent to which the project would enhance its tourism image. Instead, with no attempt to demand a review of the investment proposal under local planning ordinances, redevelopment of the industrial site was left to Nippon Steel and was not part of an overall land-management process under the control of Kitakyûshû City (Cooper and Flehr 2006).

Case Study 3: The Reconstruction of Beppu City

As a final case study of recent economic impacts and trends in Japanese tourism, this section briefly discusses tourism to the city of Beppu, on the southern island of Kyûshû, and scenarios for its tourism future. Beppu is a city of some 120,000 located on the east coast of Kyûshû in Ôita Prefecture and attracts annually more than eleven million tourists, mainly from domestic sources (Table 5.9). The core reason for their visit is the more than 2,600 natural hot springs in and around the city, delivering a volume of hot mineral water second only to Yellowstone National Park in the USA (Figure 5.7; Lund 2002). Traditional bathhouses such as Takegawara *onsen* are a definite tourist attraction both from the architectural and the healing perspective. At the other end of the scale are natural *onsen* like Hebinoyu *onsen* hidden in the forested hills around the city. There is also a beach sand bath (hot, wet sand is used to cover the body as a wellness treatment) which has been used by locals and visitors for centuries (Cooper and Erfurt-Cooper 2009).

Unlike the Spa Resort Hawaiians complex in northern Japan, however, the majority of Beppu's hot springs are solely utilized for small-scale *onsen* facilities within the hotel industry, or within local community or private baths. As a result, while the city offers special view-points where the steam rising from many vents can be observed (Figure 5.8), it has little attraction for a number of the market segments we have identified within Japanese tourism, and its facilities are not oriented to inbound tourists unless they desire the traditional Japanese bathing experience.

There is another side to the use of hot springs for tourism in the city, a special tourist attraction – the *Jigoku Meguri* (Erfurt-Cooper and Cooper 2009). *Jigoku* is the Japanese word for hell and *meguri* refers to a tour or pilgrimage to certain specific locations. This 'pilgrimage', however, is not strictly religious, although each of these 'hells' have several sacred shrines on site. The several *jigoku* of Beppu are a group of ten small geothermal parks with different themes (see Figure 5.7), utilizing a range of hot-spring manifestations like boiling ponds, bubbling mud pools and steaming geysers to their full potential, attracting vast numbers of visitors on a daily basis. Several *jigoku* offer pleasantly warm foot and hand spas for their visitors, and hot-spring-cooked food as well as the more dramatic geothermal attractions. The tour of the 'hells' is one of the most popular tourist attractions of the

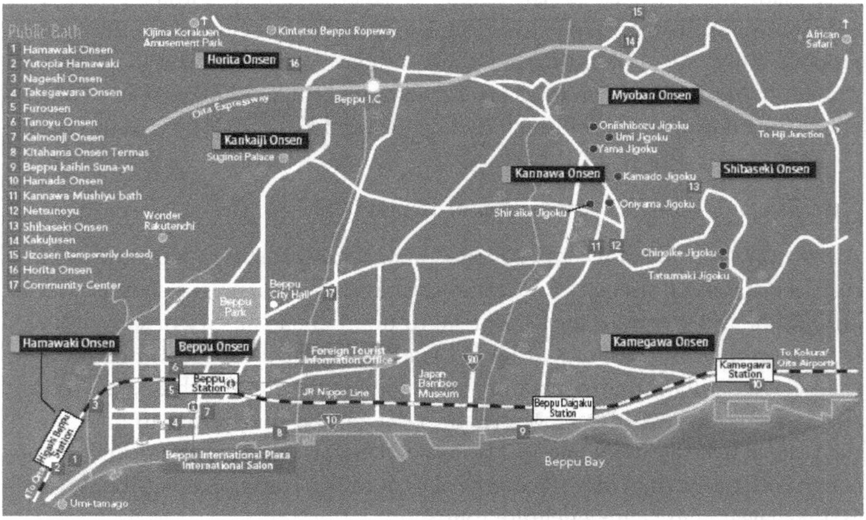

Figure 5.7: City of Beppu *onsen* resources and locations.

Source: Cooper and Erfurt-Cooper (2009).

Figure 5.8: Beppu's active steam vents identify the thousands of individual thermal springs which supply the town with an abundance of *onsen* facilities (photo courtesy of Malcolm Cooper).

city and, as with many locations throughout Japan, repeat visits during different seasons are encouraged.

Even though the overnight-stay market has largely collapsed due to the decline in domestic school excursions in favour of overseas trips in recent years, *onsen* tourism is still the basis of the local economy, with demand still fairly buoyant (Table 5.9). However, the local population is ageing and the nature of the tourism market (heavily weighted to *onsen* and to *ryokan*) tends to attract mainly older people by definition; with the smaller 'green tourism' resort of Yufuin 24 kilometres away competing for a wider range of customers, there are concerns for the future of the area, not just for Beppu City but for Ôita Prefecture as a whole.

Not enumerated but still important is the tourism based on Beppu's 'soapland'. This has been a feature of the *onsen* city for many years, and is where foreign 'entertainers' were often employed to service the traditional sex industry and/or provide a source of brides for Japanese men. This proved a source of contention in the city as in the rest of Japan when the quota of visitors was reduced at the end of 2004 (Garcia Dizon 2006).

The Failures of the Tourism Industry in Beppu

Today, there are two major problems discussed in Beppu's local tourism forums. One is the failure of the larger hotels and facilities in the city, and other is the decline of the local economy in the downtown area. Both of these are regarded as

Table 5.9: Shifts in patterns of population and tourism in Beppu since 1965.

Year	Population of Beppu (April)	Number of Tourists	Number of Day Visitors	Number of Overnight Stays	Number of School Excursions	Number of Jigoku Meguri visitors	Number of Foreign Visitors
1965	118,938	7,528,890	5,582,105	1,946,785	1,423,233	N/A	N/A
1970	123,786	9,585,621	4,650,068	4,935,553	1,117,189	1,300,074	N/A
1975	130,554	12,035,418	6,540,991	5,494,427	722,240	1,128,664	N/A
1980	134,403	12,174,342	7,015,284	5,159,058	678,168	715,956	N/A
1985	133,164	11,774,438	7,236,385	4,538,053	534,095	620,535	N/A
1990	130,071	12,156,993	7,915,539	4,241,454	508,393	617,994	N/A
1995	127,982	11,197,243	7,098,509	4,107,734	283,945	N/A	56,947
2000	125,649	11,850,681	7,854,052	4,006,061	77,030	N/A	125,844
2005	123,275	11,735,741	7,810,551	3,925,190	45,165	N/A	176,641
2006	123,015	11,765,789	7,828,823	3,936,966	28,333	N/A	226,013
2007	122,621	11,676,910	7,842,305	3,834,605	30,583	N/A	265,187
2008	122,074	11,518,360	7,779,620	3,738,740	28,514	N/A	251,684
2009	121,398	11,999,003	8,346,658	3,652,345	26,608	N/A	162,122
2010	120,818	N/A	N/A	N/A	N/A	N/A	N/A

Note: total population figures did not include residents of foreign origin until July 2010; this change increased the total population by approximately 3,800 in 2012, to 123,000.

Source: Beppu City Council (2012).

failures of Beppu tourism. In the case of the hotel industry, the number of hotel beds has been decreasing consistently because of severe competition for declining numbers of patrons. Since the modernized, large hotels and expensive *ryokan* attract most overnight tourists, the medium and small hotels have tended to lose business, and some of them have closed. The major reason for the decline in the hotel industry is that although the total number of tourists per year to the city has been stable in the range eleven to twelve million per year for more than thirty years, the number of visitors staying overnight in Beppu is decreasing (Table 5.9).

After the bursting of the bubble economy in the 1990s the situation worsened for the big hotels as well. There were fears of bankruptcy concerning the Suginoi Hotel, the biggest hotel in Beppu, and the Company Resuscitation Law has been applied to the Suginoi since 2001. In addition, the 'modern' hotels and attractions which invested heavily during the period of rapid economic growth have become 'old' today. The style of tourism which Beppu developed during this period has stagnated, and its tourism has been left behind by the latest trends in short-break tourism since the end of the bubble economy.

The situation for local tourism attractions and the downtown area is even worse than that of the hotel industry, but it is the large facilities which contributed to the golden age of Beppu tourism which have lost the most visitors. They are the African Safari Theme Park, Rakutenchi Amusement Park, Takasakiyama (Mount Takasaki) with its resident monkeys, Kijima Amusement Park and the Jigoku Meguri; for example, the Jigoku Meguri has typified local tourism for a long time, but very few individual *jigoku* have updated their facilities. Visitor numbers have been dropping rapidly, and it is obvious that the Jigoku Meguri needs to refresh its image. The decline in the local economy in downtown Beppu from these trends is also being discussed seriously. In spite of the still large number of tourists, the impact of visitors downtown has declined. A number of businesses have closed and there are few visitors in the shopping arcades because day trips to *onsen* and other attractions do not include shopping, as that is usually much better where the domestic visitors come from.

Responses from the City

Government still has an important role in the development of Beppu tourism today. Tourism infrastructure including municipal hot springs is being managed and improved by the city administration. Redevelopment of the seaside in the city over a then to fifteen year period is being planned as the largest public enterprise supporting tourism today. Also, while the development of public infrastructure has continued, there have been new trends in tourism developing to replace overnight group tourism. These new trends are a response to the recession in the local economy and the declining tourism industry. Beppu tourism has relied on large-scale tourism facilities for a long time, but a greater range of tourism facilities and attractions are required to transform its decline. In this situation, the concepts of *Beppu Hatto* (visiting the eight hot springs of Beppu and their urban environments with guides) and *machiaruki* (walking around the town) have emerged as key words for the regeneration of local tourism.

Given the density of hotels and the ageing population, another obvious way forward might be to establish the city as a 'silver service' centre, which will attract both ageing (hence 'silver') tourists and retirement capital. There are similar models elsewhere: some European spas, starting with Baden Baden and Monte Carlo in the nineteenth century, managed to establish themselves on the tourist map with a combination of facilities for ageing aristocrats and gambling (Turner and Ash 1975), where the richer members of society could deposit some of their wealth for the benefit of urban development. It also needs to be recognized that a revitalized health and wellness campaign based on hot springs is currently a successful strategy in many parts of Europe, and would probably appeal to the kinds of clientele that Japanese cities like Beppu already attract or could attract. It is obvious that medical and hot-springs tourist facilities designed to attract a much younger and/or much more international clientele are needed in Beppu. This would, however, require a complete change of mind-set from that found in present debates (Erfurt-Cooper and Cooper 2009), and this is discussed in Chapter 6.

Tourism as an Economic Strategy in the Context of Deindustrialization, Ageing and Depopulation

We have noted in previous sections that the central question – What will the predicted changes in population structure mean for Japan? – is becoming more and more important for the country, and this question must be asked of the economics of tourism as well. Despite the Japan Tourism Agency's recent moves to redefine Japan internationally (MLIT 2009), we believe that we must for the moment discount the idea that it will ever attract large numbers of overseas tourists: it is still seen as too expensive and insular for that. Therefore the market for tourists will have to rely on a declining pool of domestic clients who also have the option of spending their time and money overseas. While the growth of a low-cost airline network in East Asia and Japan could deliver the same kind of boost to traditional Japanese holiday destinations that cheap trips in Europe have had on travel patterns and destinations, an increasing number of Japanese pensioners might well decide at some point to spend most of their lives in warmer places outside Japan (Yamashita 2003: 87–101).

So what will the effects of these changes be on the economics of tourism in the smaller cities and towns, and the rural areas of Japan? Listed below are some broad hypotheses first put forward in Cooper and Eades (2007), and it will be interesting to see how far they are supported by the experiences of different parts of Japan over the next few years.

In the new slim-line geriatric Japan, communications will be vital. Many rural communities will survive – but they will only do so if they are easily accessed and have local attractions. So increasingly those that can compete will be located along the main motorway or railway lines – particularly the *shinkansen* in the case of the latter – or near airports. Perhaps the enthusiasm for local airports that are not justified by market demand will, in the fullness of time, appear to have been a rational strategy should an East Asian low-cost air network eventually take off.

First, settlements which are on the periphery of the major cities could do quite well, following the British 'new town' or American 'edge city' model (Garreau 1991). These towns are often attractive to live in, are within easy commuting distance of major city centres by rail, and even provide attractive locations for new businesses wanting to provide good living environments for their employees. As one example, the towns on the eastern side of Biwako from Otsu to Nagahama are thriving as dormitory suburbs of Kyoto, Osaka and Nagoya, thanks to good rail and motorway links with all three.

Second, settlements away from these main transport arteries will have a much more difficult time. The rural settlements described by Knight, Thompson and Traphagen appear to be pretty much doomed. On the other hand, places like Tôno, with a plausible basis for a tourist industry and an integrated concept for tourism development, will continue to appeal to tourists and even attract inbound tourism for their 'Japanese-ness'. Success through new man-made attractions, on the other hand, seems unlikely. The most successful theme parks in Japan are those near the major urban hubs. Others, like Huis Ten Bosch (Hendry 2000), which are more peripheral, are already in trouble. So a Tonopia Disneyland, however appealing a project, is probably not going to happen. Even for traditional attractions, access remains a key issue. The Gifu villages of Shirakawago and Gokayama with their surviving thatched houses as described by Carle (2003) are clearly on the tourist routes and highly visible due to their listing as world cultural heritage – but mainly because they lie close to the major population centres of Kansai, Aichi and Hokuriku. If they were in Aomori, probably they too would have long since disappeared. New forms of tourism based on media-induced content (see Chapter 8) or other fashions will mainly lead to short-term impulses for development.

Third, some existing urban tourism destinations like Beppu may be able to compete, but only if they take full advantage of their competitive advantages and pour all of their resources into those. Beppu actually has the communications infrastructure, accommodation facilities and the geothermal resources to become the Baden Baden of Japan – but it will need the cultural and recreational facilities to go with them. The disjointed set of local and regional development policies of the last twenty years in its environs, focusing as they did on distractions such as 'silicon valleys' and high-cost sports facilities and resorts should not continue to detract from the central aim of repositioning Beppu and Ôita in the national and international tourist market. A major arts festival, casino complex, marine tourism facilities, spa resort or a good quality symphony orchestra able to make more effective use of the venues which already exist in the area might be projects which could be considered. What is needed is something which will not only bring the tourists but keep them around to spend money over a longer period, and keep them coming back.

As for the rest of Japan, if the population declines at the rate of over a million people per year further rural areas will become deserted and the problem will remain of what to do with them. Luxury hotels serving the eco-tourism industry, massive expansion of the national parks system, and good feeder roads into them so that visitors of the future can enjoy them are one possible solution. Redevelopment of rural areas through *satoyama* (a rural agricultural and social heritage protection and enhancement concept in Japan) tourism is another (see Chapter 8). This will happen if the economic stimulus from tourism is enough to attract people to *satoyama* lifestyles; however, the biggest challenge to *satoyama* revitalization through tourism is first to keep newly introduced tourism enterprises sustainable, and second to attract new populations to move into an area by creating enough job opportunities. Management of the negative environmental impacts of rural tourism is not a priority in such considerations as yet, as tourism development is in an early stage and natural resources are still underused, but it will also need to be considered later as an inseparable part of sustainable rural tourism development.

Summary and Conclusions

The purpose of this chapter has been to document the role of tourism in Japanese local, regional and national economic development. The discussion shows that a positive economic impact from major tourism developments is virtually always assumed, and that once government at all levels has been persuaded of the value of a development, it will do almost anything to ensure that it is approved, even if the actual economics are less than clear. This type of outcome is achieved through direct investment by national government institutions, a process which often requires local land use regulations to be suspended. For example, by using the financial resources established under such programmes as the Resort Law of 1987, developers were able to obtain land cheaply, and local and prefectural governments were able to issue bonds to finance tourism infrastructure without reference to their constituent communities (McCormack 1996: 105). Like the earlier programmes that created a number of prefectural industrial cities in the 1960s throughout the country, resort development in the 1990s was intended to be a heavily subsidized magnet for capital and employment in specific areas, and it was anticipated that the Resort Law would attract some ¥830 billion from public and private sources to be invested in tourism-related developments.

It is this last point that indicates most forcefully how development under the Japanese land-management system is facilitated and made financially possible. In fact, since the 1960s all national planning and economic development programmes in Japan seem to have assumed that local planning ordinances are essentially irrelevant wherever a government-endorsed tourism development plan applies. While this clearly reduces inherent uncertainty in the development process and enables developers to protect their investment, it has also given rise to the slogan *fukoku hinmin*, 'enrich the country, impoverish the people' (McCormack 1996: 106), as well as considerable local opposition to many development decisions (Sorensen and Funck 2007). Under this system, a (usually) small group of developers receives an almost unfettered right to develop land, and zoning regulations are frozen, allegedly in exchange for public benefits. As shown in this discussion, payment for the site, at least in part, comes from the public purse, while developers reduce their risks and gain cheap land and finance.

In this system, then, the net effect of state involvement in tourism development planning is a form of boosterism rather than the fostering of a community-oriented approach to such development. A higher level of government can promote the idea that a particular development will provide social and economic benefits to a local community, with negligible disadvantages, and should therefore be supported by state policy even if such policy effectively results in public loss for private gain; and the mechanisms discussed in this chapter allow for this to happen. From the perspective of the state, however, continued capital accumulation is necessary, and in the twenty-first century this depends largely on private investment. The government therefore needs to encourage private investment in tourism, while private investors need to find a home for their money, and such mutual interdependence has meant that the planning agenda for major tourism investment has been dominated by state and business concerns rather than local community objectives (this is by no means confined to Japan – see Cooper and Flehr 2006). Unfortunately, when tourism-based major development projects fail, which they often do due to unpredictable market changes and the difficult structure of a domestic tourism market relying completely on short trips, it is usually the local communities that are left with the unfinished projects and debts.

In conclusion it can be seen that the relationship between tourism investment and economic development policies and management practices in Japan is no different from that involving any other industry able to influence the state's policy-making processes. Major tourism facility development has just been the most recent beneficiary of the *dokken kokka*, the Japanese 'construction state' ideology (McCormack 1996: 32; Kerr 2001). In this system, decisions on many major tourism projects are made centrally by the state, for the benefit of political and business interests that operate at that level. It remains to be seen whether recent changes in local government structures through large-scale community mergers, new legal systems to allow for stronger land and building regulations, initiatives like *satoyama*, and the so-called regionalization of responsibilities will offer better chances for sustainable economic development through tourism at the local level for the benefit of the country as a whole.

6

THE JAPANESE GAZE ON THE WORLD

This chapter documents the development and strength of Japanese outbound travel, long a mainstay of several tourism destinations around the world and one still eagerly competed for (ABTR 1990; Bolkus 1991; Mak and White 1992; Kobayashi 2003; Kômoto 2004). It pays attention to the changing patterns of Japanese and North Asian international tourism as a result of the transformation of consumption patterns in the region, and notes the influence of position in the life cycle on international trips and particular destinations. Another important factor has been the influence of terrorism and potential disease epidemics on the consumption of international travel by Japanese travellers. However, noticeable in this area is the propensity of the Japanese traveller to modify but not abandon their travel when faced with such issues (Cooper 2005). As a result, the chapter spends some time analysing the psychology of Japanese tourist travel.

In recent years there has been a diversification in the travel patterns of Japanese outbound tourists, from packaged sightseeing group tours to honeymoon vacations (and, indeed marriages offshore), golf tours, sex tours, shopping tours, visits to South Korea to see Korean music and TV show actors, and a general expansion of destinations to places like Central Asia, the Arctic and Antarctic, and many others. The average Japanese traveller remains a wealthy high-spender but has specific requirements in terms of safety and security when they travel. Nevertheless, their preferences regarding destinations and desired experiences have changed (Johnson 1989; ABTR 1990; Mouer and Sugimoto 1995; Asamizu 1998; Sakai et al. 2000; Slattery 2000; Sakakibara 2003; Mak et al. 2005; Maksay 2007). The chapter examines these changes and adds specific material through case studies of the impact of SARS and other crises on the travel patterns of Japanese tourists, of battlefield tourism on both the senior- and the youth-traveller markets and that of the changing preferences of all travellers for destinations like Hawaii.

As part of this discussion, the chapter also examines the process whereby Japanese outbound tourism has become inextricably associated with national and international social, economic and political issues. The emphasis here is on the way in which the political and economic spheres of social life are intimately bound up with tourism, in keeping with the argument of the book overall. The basic features of twenty-first-century Japanese social life at all levels are thrown into sharp relief through observing and making sense of the patterns of twenty-first-century tourism through case studies of the impact of disasters, and issues of post-colonization (diving in former Japanese islands), as well as of the changing consumption patterns of youth on Japanese outbound tourism.

Japanese Outbound Travel

Immediately after the Second World War, Japanese citizens were not allowed to travel for pleasure overseas (until 1964) as this was thought likely to remove much needed liquidity from the national economy (Carlile 1996; Mak 2004). With the end of postwar hardships and the hosting of the Tokyo Olympic Games in 1964, the government signalled the end of restrictions on overseas travel by Japanese who could afford it (Figure 6.1). Much of the travel during the initial phase of liberalization was for pleasure, comprising group and package tours and often supported and controlled by people's place of employment. However, the rapid increase from 1964 in outbound travel can also be seen as a policy aimed at changing the image of Japan abroad in order to aid and support the equally rapid globalization of Japanese industry (Carlile 1996; Asamizu 2005). In any event, the increase in the number of outbound travellers cemented the place of Japan in the world tourism

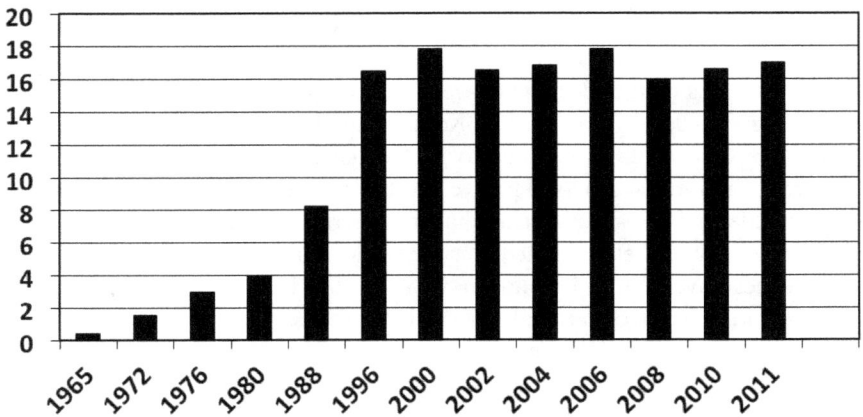

Figure 6.1: Outbound tourism, 1965 to 2011 (millions).

Source: JNTO (2012).

consciousness as a wealthy and important market because with these numbers came their higher than average spending on luxury goods, food and entertainment, tours, gifts for those back home (*omiyage*), and other goods and services. In other words, they were the ideal tourist from the point of view of the host country or region (Mak et al. 2004; Schumann 2006) despite the realization that their group tour style of travel reduced opportunities for interaction with local communities.

The number of Japanese overseas travellers grew from 266,000 in 1965 to nearly eighteen million by the year 2000 (Figure 6.1), stabilized at a level of about seventeen million until 2009, when numbers dropped to just over fifteen million as a result of the global financial crisis, and since then has again stabilized at about sixteen million. Despite the bursting of Japan's bubble economy in the late 1980s (Wood 2005), the Asian financial crisis of the late 1990s, and the terrorism, health epidemics and the occasional political manipulation of traveller sentiment through the so-called 'travel advisories' system (the information is generally on where *not* to travel), the number of Japanese travelling overseas has not varied greatly in recent years. Nevertheless, what has to be understood is that despite this constant there have been considerable shifts in Japanese domestic and international spending and in attitudes to overseas travel, as well as those changes to be expected in the adjustment of a mature travel market to its ageing and other internal traveller-based developments. In turn, these changes have had a profound effect on particular destinations – such as Hawaii, the Australian Gold Coast, the Pacific islands, parts of Europe – that have relied for some time on Japanese tourism for their economic survival. Shono et al. (2005) note that there needs to be more research if destinations reliant on Japanese travellers are to fully understand the implications of these changes in Japanese society for their success or failure to attract such travellers in the future.

The 1950s to the 1970s

After the Second World War, Japan was not in a position to allow its citizens to travel the world in an unrestricted manner, even if it had desired to return to the prewar situation. The exigencies of modern nation building during the postwar period imposed the same restrictions as had been in place under the late Shogunate until 1964. Kelly (1992: 79) describes the impact of government policy making through a content analysis of consumer advertising during these decades: what were considered affordable goals for the Japanese citizen in the 1950s were goods such as *senpûki* (electric fans), *sentakuki* (washing machines) and *suihanki* (rice cookers); by the 1960s these had become *kâ* (cars), *kûrâ* (air conditioners) and *karâ terebi* (colour televisions); and by the 1970s, *juerî* (jewellery), *jetto* (air tickets) and *jûtaku* (home ownership).

By the time of Tokyo Olympic Games in 1964, government policies and the Japanese worker had spurred the national economy to unsurpassed levels of growth, and this in turn allowed a shift from discouragement to the active encouragement of overseas travel. International travel was to become incorporated into the lifestyle of the modern Japanese individual with the simultaneous creation of systems to handle the mass marketing of overseas travel and the mass transportation of travellers through package tours organized by air carriers and sold by major travel agencies and wholesalers. One of the many restrictions removed was the foreign currency quota. On 1 April 1964 the amount of foreign currency allowed out of the country as spending money in addition to the prepaid cost of transportation was set at US$500 per person per year; this was raised to US$700 in 1969. A restriction on the number of trips per year was also lifted by the government in 1966 as new international air routes were opened and more airlines began serving Japan. Bulk fares, with as much as 60 per cent off the regular economy class fare, were introduced in 1968, and Boeing 747s came into service in 1970 (JTBB 1986; Schumann 2006).

The period from 1965 to 1973 saw large increases in the numbers of Japanese visiting foreign countries, only interrupted by the first global oil crisis in 1973. The amount of foreign currency allowed out of the country was increased to US$1,000 in 1970, and later to US$1,500 (plus ¥30,000) in 1975. In 1976, this was raised again to US$3,000 (and ¥100,000), and finally in 1978 all currency limits were abolished. These changes are important to our understanding of Japanese outbound travel patterns and their impact due to the traditional Japanese system of *senbetsu* and *omiyage*, parting gifts and souvenirs (see Chapter 2), which obligates travellers to repay any farewell gift or money presented by friends and relatives on their departure with a gift brought back from overseas. Repayment cannot be made with just any souvenir, however; the repayment is expected to conform with several rules: it has to be worth half the yen value of the original gift; it has be a specialty of the locale visited on the trip (a *meibutsu*), and it has to have a legitimizing mark (*kinen*), for instance the tag or wrapper, proving that it was purchased on-site (Brannen 1992: 223). Hence, the more currency allowed out of the country, the more obligated travellers were to shop for and bring back the appropriate souvenir, which of course proved to be a great and much sought after boost to destination economies. The first oil crisis ended very quickly, but the second period of growth in outbound travel (1974 to 1979) also came to an end with an oil crisis and an economic recession in Japan (JTBB 1986: 102), and in retrospect it can be seen from the data in Figure 6.1 that one of the highlights of world tourism since the 1970s has been the emergence of Japan as a leading tourist-generating country (Schumann 2006: 132).

The 1980s to 2012

By 1981 the number of Japanese travelling overseas for pleasure and business had risen to over four million a year, with the bulk of them visiting US destinations like Hawaii and the Pacific west coast. From 1981 to 1990, the number rose very quickly to nearly eleven million at the end of the decade. This period included an effort by the Japanese government to encourage outbound tourism in an effort to contribute to international society and to improve the quality of Japanese people's lives, including the promotion of internationalization at home, and to announce to the rest of the world that Japan had become a normal advanced industrialized country (Leheny 2003). Encouraging Japanese overseas travel was also seen as preferable to opening up Japan's domestic markets, widely seen as closed, to foreign competition.

The 'Ten Million' programme was introduced to double the annual number of Japanese tourists going abroad from 5.5 million in 1986 to over 10 million people in the next five years, or to 10 per cent or so of the population (MLIT 1987). The goals of this plan were in fact achieved one year earlier than expected, in 1990, when the number of Japanese travelling overseas reached 10.1 million (MLIT 1991). By 1995 this had further grown to over 15 million, but thereafter climbed more slowly to the highest ever figure, recorded in 2000, of 17.8 million. Within this pattern there have been several fluctuations, all reflecting the fact that at these levels the total outbound flows are susceptible to both economic and social pressures (the impact of SARS and the Asian financial crisis are discussed below).

One further factor should be mentioned here, that of the relative value of the yen against other currencies. At the beginning of the liberalization of foreign travel in 1964/65 the yen stood at 360 to the US dollar, effectively providing a ready-made means of soaking up excess funds held by the richer members of society if they could be persuaded to go overseas and spend it. Table 6.1 shows how the value of the yen has fluctuated, from a low of 360 yen in 1965 to as high as 75 yen to the dollar in 2011. During the implementation of the 'Ten Million' programme from 1987 to 1991 for example, the value of the yen strengthened from

Table 6.1: Average value of the yen against the US dollar, 1965 to 2012.

Year	Value	Year	Value
1965	360	2005	115
1970	360	2006	120
1975	297	2007	125
1980	227	2008	88–110
1985	239	2009	93–96
1990	145	2010	90–93
1995	78	2011	75–92
2000	108	2012	77–91

Source: Lloyds TSB online currency calculator historical data as at December 2012.

145 yen to the dollar in 1987 to peak at 128 yen in 1988, and closed at 135 yen in 1991. The rising value of the yen encouraged Japanese citizens to travel overseas to take advantage of their purchasing power to buy items that cost much more in the domestic market, as well as travel services.

After the shocks of the SARS non-epidemic and the American invasion of Iraq in 2003 had worn off, the number of Japanese travelling abroad rose again by 2006 to the second highest ever figure of 17,534,565. However, 2007 showed a slight decline to 17,295,000, a 1.3 per cent fall from the previous year, and 2008 another decline, to 15,987,250 (down 7.6 per cent on 2007). The reasons for the latest declines can be found in continuing structural problems in the Japanese economy and society: an growing unemployment rate among the younger generation, increases in crude oil prices, and an ageing population. The result up to September 2008 was a rise in airfares including fuel surcharges, and consequently higher package-tour prices, while a weak yen against several currencies such as the euro and the Australian dollar put extra pressure on travel to these destinations. In September 2008, though, everything changed: the USA's own bubble economy burst, resulting in worldwide financial chaos and an immediate downturn in international travel. The yen also appreciated rapidly against local regional currencies like the Korean won and others further afield, like the British pound, the euro and the Australian dollar.

Recent Trends in the Japan Outbound Travel Market

In 2007 the number of Japanese international travellers declined for the first time in history without the impetus of major changes in the travel environment. Certainly there were pressures on travel prices through fuel surcharges and terrorism threats but, as we will see later, the Japanese normally do not take these things particularly seriously and keep travelling regardless, albeit perhaps to proven safe and/or closer destinations. The decline had in fact begun prior to September 2008 and the global financial meltdown, and may have continued at a slow pace if this event had not taken place. So, while it was overtaken by the impact of the global financial crisis, the other possible causes for the recent decline are in fact more serious for outbound tourism from Japan. These include: an absolute decline in the number of younger people in Japan; a relatively slow growth in the seniors market; a rise in international airfares and overseas tour prices as a result of a sharp rise in fuel and other travel surcharges (though these had begun to decrease by September 2008); a shortfall in the supply of air seats to major holiday destinations; and increasing competition for the relatively short Japanese holiday periods from domestic destinations and recreational activities other than travel.

Discussing these in turn, the number of male travellers has been stable since 2004, but the number of female travellers has fluctuated. It was highest in 2000 with 8.3 million, and has not exceeded this since. Some female travellers have obviously left the overseas travel market after such system shocks as terrorism and health epidemics raised concerns over the safety and security of travelling, but another factor that should be kept in mind is a continuous decline of the number of women in their 20s. In the 1990s, this age group was the largest and the most influential segment in the Japanese outbound travel market. In 1994, 17.5 per cent of international travellers were women in their 20s, but now the figure is down to just above 10 per cent. Factors contributing to this decline are the decrease in the population of younger people, decreases in the average disposable income of young workers, and their lack of interest in overseas travel. Unlike the pattern of earlier years, when they were active in travelling internationally, many young Japanese today try to avoid the trouble related to overseas travel and prefer staying at home.

In recent years, the reluctance of young people, including university students, to travel overseas has become the subject of attention (Nihon Kôtsû Kôsha 2007) and has been highlighted as a symbol of an inward-looking, passive generation. Tourism statistics show a clear difference between Korean and Japanese young people. Although this population group is shrinking in both countries, Japan witnessed a decrease in outbound travellers in their 20s of one third between 1995 and 2010, whereas the number of Koreans in their 20s travelling abroad more than doubled in the same period. On the other hand, there is a steady increase of senior travellers and of women travellers in their 30s from Japan.

Despite the changing numbers, Japanese travellers as a whole are becoming more independent as a result of changes in the country's culture. In earlier years when travellers ventured overseas for the first time, packaged group tours were the most popular way to travel. As noted above, the early growth of Japanese overseas tourism was in large part supported by package tours (Yamamoto and Gill 1999). This form of travel eliminated the need to speak a foreign language and lessened the need to plan an itinerary in a foreign land. The tendency was also to follow a pattern, staying with a familiar itinerary and visiting well-known sites as directed by a guide. However, a study conducted as early as 1989 found three distinct clusters distinguished by age and education among Japanese travelling overseas, showing that variety was developing (Cha et al. 1995). Young, highly educated white-collar workers were dominant among the 'sports seekers', as were enterprise owners, clerical sales staff and students with lower educational levels among the 'novelty seekers', and slightly older travellers with higher incomes among the 'family/relaxation seekers'. The study identified 'relaxation', 'knowledge' and 'adventure' as the dominant motifs for Japanese tourists.

Since the time of this study, outbound travel has diversified further. Certainly, the old stereotype of a Japanese tourist with a camera blindly following a flag-bearing guide no longer applies to this market. Japanese tourists today have access to massive amounts of information for just about every overseas destination, and many of them do not hesitate to explore new territory. Similarly, the lack of foreign language-speaking skills, which was a limiting factor in the past, is becoming less of an issue given that more and more Japanese students are studying foreign languages in schools and may even have first-hand overseas experience by the time they become independent overseas travellers.

The evidence relating to travel preferences now shows that while many Japanese overseas travellers still travel with tour groups, increasing numbers are designing their own itineraries and making their own inexpensive air travel and accommodation arrangements online or through a travel agent (Milne et al. 2002). Internet bookings in Japan are becoming ever more popular (in Japan – which still makes little use of credit cards – you can book air tickets online, obtain a digital barcode, and then pay in cash down at a local convenience store), and special interest groups are also increasing in numbers to enjoy all types of activities, including hobbies or educational opportunities in an overseas environment, and sex tourism to China and other destinations (Jeffreys 2004). One trend that is apparent with all mature markets including Japan is that individuals with special interests now pursue these interests on holiday. And the result for traditional destination markets is that special-interest tourists want to spend the major part of their holiday involved in a specific activity. It is apparent that many Japanese travellers are no longer content with just going to an overseas destination, taking photos, shopping at the duty free store, and coming home.

The Influence of the Media

Schumann (2006) makes the point that television and movies can, even inadvertently, provide marketing for tourism destinations, especially if the programme or film proves to be popular in the source market. This is because most tourism organizations lack the financial backing to finance an advertising campaign that could even begin to approach their desired markets. And this is what has happened in the context of Japanese outbound travel on at least two celebrated occasions when television has had a major impact on destination choices. In this regard, Iwashita (2003: 332) has commented on 'movie-induced tourism' and 'media-related tourism' that involves visits to places renowned for being associated with books, television programmes, films and authors. The first example of this can be seen in contemporary tourist flows out of Japan that have been strongly influenced by travel shows that feature long-stay or home-stay opportunities in other countries (Asamizu 2005: 34). The second type of phenomenon influencing travel recently in Japan has been the combination of sporting events and local culture (Schumann 2006: 134). When Korea and Japan co-hosted the 2002 football World Cup, this created an interest in Korean culture in Japan, resulting in a 'Korea boom' or *hanryu*. With this came a number of Korean television programmes that were broadcast in Japan. One of these, a drama called *Fuyu no Sonata* ('Winter sonata') became a huge hit (Asamizu 2005: 34–35; Schumann 2006: 134–35), and the interest in it resulted in large numbers of mainly middle-aged women and 'office ladies' visiting the Korean sites shown in the programme.

Major Destinations Today

Apart from the USA, South Korea was the top national destination for Japanese outbound travellers for many years until China overtook it in 2002 (Figure 6.2). Europe as a whole remained the top destination in 2010, followed by China and the US. These leading destinations are followed by South Korea, Hong Kong, Guam, Hawaii, Taiwan and Thailand. However, even the China market has had its share of problems since 2007. Since 2008 there has been a decline in outbound travel to China, largely due to concerns over safety and security when travelling in that country. The food-poisoning scares relating to imported dumplings (*gyoza*) did not encourage Japanese travel to China, nor did the flare-up in the Tibetan issue in 2007/8, or the Senkaku Islands incident in 2011/12. Underlying these trends has been a shift of Japanese international travellers from traditional long-haul destinations (noticeably a very large proportionate decline in travel to the US) to short-haul destinations in Asia over the last decade (China, Vietnam, Thailand, Taiwan). The background to this shift in destinations is found in

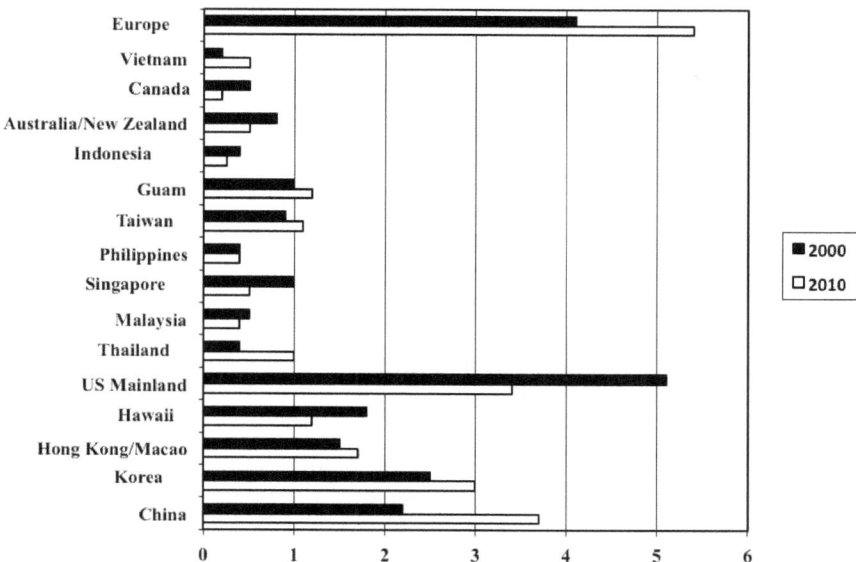

Figure 6.2: Major destinations for Japanese tourists, 2000 and 2010 (millions).
Source: JNTO (2012).

increasing business traffic within Asia (in other words a re-orientation of economic activity towards intra-regional trade from trade with other regions), and an increase in seating capacity on the China and Korea routes, coupled with a downsizing in numbers of aircraft on trans-Pacific and European routes. As a result of airline policies to further concentrate their seat allocation to profitable business class passengers, the supply of economy class seats for leisure markets outside Asia has been reduced.

Just as Japanese overseas travellers have been influenced by a combination of television dramas and film and the economic recession to visit new short-haul destinations, they are beginning to become more selective in pursuing what they personally want to do as well as where they want to go. A shift has taken place in consumer preferences (see Chon et al. 2000), and this in part can be attributed to the natural outcome of an expanding 'repeater' market, which means that the need for all-inclusive tours has in many cases diminished in favour of basing travel on personal experience. There is also the increasingly adventurous nature of many young Japanese, the explosion in the amount of reliable travel information available throughout Japan, and a rise in discount air and charter travel.

The Impact of Technology

The efficiency and convenience of information technology is also having a great influence on some of the latest travel trends. The Internet is growing in importance for Japanese tourists (Milne et al. 2002), in line with increasing computer use in the country as a whole (101 million users, 80 per cent penetration in 2011). While the IATA target of 100 per cent e-ticketing for travel by the end of 2007 (Bisignani 2005) did not materialize, e-ticketing has become a cheap and convenient way to book travel reservations. The growing opportunity presented by the internet is also felt inside the country. In 2004, online reservations accounted for just over 11 per cent of total hotel sales domestically, and travel retail via the internet reached more than ¥1,700 billion in value during the same year (Euromonitor 2005). While there appear to be no up-to-date figures for internet use for overseas travel, in the comparable case of the USA nearly forty million households booked travel online in 2007, spending US$86 billion. Web travellers now make up 79 per cent of the US travel population, and 55 per cent of them buy leisure travel online, and there is no reason to expect Japanese consumers will use the web any less. Just as consumers have found in other countries, online booking in Japan serves as the most convenient way for consumers to seek out the best deals in the travel and tourism industry. Reservations and payments via the internet and mobile phone in Japan also began in 2004, and mobile phone technology now allows for online booking, electronic ticketing, payment and replacement of boarding passes for those that make use of it.

Traveller Responses to the Above Issues

The various segments that make up the Japanese outbound tourism market react to these issues and opportunities in different ways. In this section we will look primarily at the seniors and middle aged, with youth and 'office ladies' discussed as required, within a general discussion of the influence of changes in the demography of Japan. Substantial change has also occurred within Japanese society and culture during the period following travel liberalization in 1964. As Japanese society continues to change, we are seeing a reflection of these changes in the profiles, activity preferences and consumption patterns of Japanese overseas tourists.

It is a general assumption that tourism provides a form of escape from the familiar home environment, based on the contrast between ordinary, everyday life (the familiar) and the faraway and extraordinary (Urry 1990). Tourism allows for a break from the everyday monotony of modern living, including a break from obligations and responsibilities. But the pattern of responses to this opportunity varies. Some tourists are in search of new or different experiences from those they encounter in their daily routines, while others may seek to include aspects of their everyday life in their holiday experiences, and still others seek freedom from social mores in a different culture. Tourism thus allows people to remove themselves physically and socially from their native social system, and the cultural difference or contrast that they encounter provides a sense of pleasure and curiosity. Iwashita (2003: 334–35) links the social construction of tourism practices to tourism motivations and notes that consumption in the form of purchasing products and services, including those related to sex tourism, is another everyday life activity influenced by societal norms and structures. One of the interesting aspects of modern Japanese society in this respect is the acceptance among observers that it is a culture that values conformity in the sense of membership in an in-group. In creating these in-groups, consumption appears to play a major role in the way individual Japanese create their own identities within them. Although self-cultivation in the form of traditional modes of character formation is still occurring, self-cultivation is pursued increasingly through practices of individual consumption: fashion, commercialized sports, diet and hobbies (Clammer 2000: 215). Choices that are made in relation to travel destination, tour activities, lodging and so on can be heavily influenced by the ways in which wider society identifies with those products, activities or services (Kotler and Gertner 2004).

This can be seen in the rise in popularity of the young female Japanese tourist since the late 1980s as a market segment with a high disposable income (Iverson 1997). With young Japanese females, materialism and a longing for a higher social class have had an effect on not only their souvenir shopping patterns but also on their perception of sexuality and human relationships. These perceptions are the result of how young females are viewed in contemporary society. As a response to these perceptions, young female Japanese are becoming more and more selective about tourism products and prefer to personalize their travel purchases.

An examination of these changes is important for destinations that want to remain competitive in attracting the Japanese overseas traveller. It is not possible to predict with certainty what will happen with Japanese overseas tourism in the future but it is expected that Japanese tourists will prefer to stay longer in particular destinations and to focus on experiential travel as opposed to simple observation. Tourists from mature markets like Japan will pursue more individual interactions with local residents (Yoo and Sohn 2003). In addition, it is important to note that the Japanese economy will probably remain relatively strong in the coming decades, despite the current problems. A strong Japanese economy will continue to allow for the growth and maintenance of leisure time for its citizens (Hall 1997).

The Changing Demographics of Japan and Outbound Tourism

As already noted, Japan is experiencing major demographic changes which will affect the pattern of outbound tourism growth. This situation, of course, leads to serious questioning of how the country will cope with the social implications of such a demographic change, but our discussion here is limited to its impacts on outbound tourism. By 2012 the bulge in the Japanese population made up the baby boomers, born from 1946 to 1949, had almost all reached the retirement age of 65. Sakai et al. (2000) note that the generation that carried Japan's economic boom has the potential to create a new type of age-based wealth given their privileged position in society. They give the following as characteristics of this age group: they have known neither war nor material shortage; they have never questioned economic growth; they have lived within a system of lifetime employment and seniority-based promotion; and they can adapt to any environment. These baby boomers will set trends and create new demands, transforming the impression the Japanese hold of people over 60 as being elderly, and contributing to outbound tourism and second-home purchase overseas in a massive way for at least another ten years of their lives (Schumann 2006).

So what do these patterns mean for outbound tourism? Japan's changing demographics did raise early concerns that overseas travel from the country may slow dramatically in the future, despite the maturation of the Japanese travel market (You and Leary 2000), the main fear being that fewer younger people would naturally equate to a fewer outbound travellers, along with a shrinking work force and slower economic growth. While slower economic growth will not stop Japanese citizens from travelling overseas, it will certainly not be a condition that will encourage greater demand. This means that capturing travel by tourists from Japan may become even more difficult for overseas destinations relying on this market. Although there has been an overall increase in the number of overseas trips that Japanese take in a year, this trend will have to be monitored more closely as Japan's population ages.

Mak et al. (2004) have studied the impact of population ageing on travel propensity and note that it tends to decline with age. They also note that in Japan's case the highest travel propensity is seen among the population in the 25 to 29 age group. Thereafter, the propensity to travel declines with age and, among adults, those in the 65-and-over age group have the lowest propensity to travel abroad (Mak et al. 2004: 6). They also point out that Japan's overall overseas travel propensity reached a historic peak in 2000 at 14.04 per cent of the total population compared to 0.64 per cent in 1970, 3.34 per cent in 1980 and 8.90 per cent in 1990 (Mak et al. 2004: 198–99). So the ageing population in Japan may have a significant effect in slowing down the overall rate of growth in the propensity to travel in coming years.

Senior Citizens: The Silver Market

This situation has been anticipated. In the 1970s, when Japan achieved an initial degree of affluence, the Ministry of Foreign Affairs began a programme encouraging the resettlement of elderly people overseas. The rationale behind this push was that, especially in Third World countries, retired Japanese should be able to live there comfortably with their pensions due to differences in the cost of living. This programme was criticized from its inception on the grounds that the Japanese government was trying to rid itself of its welfare burden by exporting economically useless and medically costly elder citizens (Befu 2000: 27).

However, overseas travel is one form of leisure activity that many elderly Japanese are enjoying in greater numbers. This age group typically represents senior Japanese citizens who are pursuing their leisure activities after fulfilling their duties at work or in the home during the high-paced expansion of the Japanese economy in the postwar decades. These citizens were unable to freely enjoy time for travel during their younger years and are now making up for it. The number of senior travellers is expected to increase sharply in the coming years. By 2025 Japanese over the age of 60 will likely account for 26 per cent of all Japanese overseas travel (compared to less than 15 per cent in 2000). This group of senior citizens will account for 60 per cent of the predicted 5.6 million increase in outbound trips. By 2025, the seniors will have displaced travellers in their 20s as the largest group of overseas travellers (Mak et al. 2004: 17).

The older senior citizens or 'silver market' travellers have a number of advantages over younger groups: they are not limited to certain holidays such as Golden Week, the summer vacation, *Bon* (the August holiday in honour of deceased family members), or New Year. The silver market can travel at any time, and can fill empty hotel rooms during non-peak and shoulder seasons. Another advantage for the silver market is their economic strength. They have a variety of interests related to their daily hobbies, and they have the funds to pursue these hobbies on overseas travel. The elderly Japanese are therefore an excellent market to target for overseas travel destinations that are prepared to welcome these visitors.

Other Markets

The future of Japanese overseas travel is not only about the silver market, although it is an important market segment to keep in mind for all destinations welcoming Japanese visitors. Table 6.2 (after Mak et al. 2004) suggests that different age groups will experience different frequencies of overseas travel at different times up to 2025: the 35 to 39 age group to 2010, the 40 to 49 age group to 2020, and the 50 to 64 age groups between 2015 and 2025. The cohort groups made up of baby boomers will peak with over four million outbound travellers over the age of 65 in 2025. These projections are now probably on the high side given that Japanese outbound travel has dropped significantly since 2008/9 (to about sixteen million) due to the on-going world financial crisis.

Some markets continue to do well though, such as South Korea; Macau also showed increases because of the popularity of new resorts and casinos and World Heritage sites with 23.7 per cent more visitors, while Malaysia received 17.9 per cent more visitors, and was one of the few Asian destinations to show higher traffic compared to 2007. Business and technical visits and incentive travel (company rewards for exemplary performance) all continued to fall, but the student segment saw a significant increase with the arrival of the student holiday season in February/March 2008 (JATA 2008). Other customer segments have also shown a slight improvement in recent months. Further increases are predicted over the next three months in all segments, with the exception of the student one.

In addition to these data on the inherent flexibility of the Japanese outbound tourism market even under extreme conditions (in this case financial), while Japan has been struggling with a lagging economy it still ranked in the top four in travel expenditure by country until 2004 and among the top ten since then. The 2010 ranking had Germany as the leader (US$78.5 billion), followed by the USA (US$75.5 billion), China (US$54.9 billion), the UK (US$48.6 billion), France (US$39.4 billion) and Canada (US$29.5 billion); next was Japan at US$27.9 billion, followed by Italy (US$27.1 billion), the Russian Federation (US$26.5 billion) and Australia (US$22.5 billion) (UNWTO 2009). Within this pattern of high expenditure, the Japanese travel market can be divided into segments: younger travellers under 60 who prefer activities such as shopping and gourmet sampling; and elderly travellers who prefer visiting historic and cultural attractions, art galleries and museums, and going to natural and scenic attractions. An earlier survey by JTB (2001: 30) showed that tour content is important to women and elderly travellers, and reliability is a prime concern for middle-aged women and the

Table 6.2: Observed and forecast Japanese overseas trips, 1970 to 2025.

Year	Age Group						
	15-19	20-29	30-39	40-49	50-59	60-64	65+
1970	10	178	183	136	76	32	33
1975	39	729	640	552	274	104	106
1980	71	1002	1031	824	547	203	207
1985	115	1358	1149	943	730	251	262
1990	374	3062	2134	2763	1612	541	531
1995	535	4242	2890	2886	2353	848	906
2000	632	4179	3589	2785	3268	1124	1373
2005	730	3616	4055	3045	3060	1093	1553
2010	686	3427	4189	3608	3069	1617	1880
2015	834	3274	3792	4380	3566	1483	2395
2020	804	3291	3588	4495	3958	1721	2465
2025	891	3421	3476	4064	4765	1903	4017

Source: Mak et al. (2004), National Institute for Population Security Research (2008).

elderly: 80 per cent of the elderly use full package tours, a percentage high above the average Japanese utilization rate of 53.5 per cent (JTB 2001: 47).

Free Independent Travellers

There is a growing number of free independent travellers (FITs) in the Japanese outbound market (Schumann 2006). Unlike the 1960s to 1980s, when Japanese travellers relied on guided tours, many are now making arrangements to travel on their own via the internet, telephone or through convenience-store kiosks. Such travellers are more sophisticated in the sense that they have more confidence in their ability to communicate, and even if they do not have fluency they are more confident to attempt communicating in a foreign language. In the early stages of Japanese outbound tourism, travel provided increased status for the traveller, even though many Japanese had little knowledge about travelling overseas, and did not know whether they had to be able to speak foreign languages. This uncertainty has been minimized to an extent by the proliferation of guidebooks written in the Japanese language.

Research also reveals that Japanese overseas travellers are returning to destinations that they found to their liking due to convenience, cost and other factors. An analysis of Japanese travel experiences by JTB in the early 2000s showed that

5.3 percent of travellers were taking their first trip in 2002, while 14.4 per cent reported that it was their second or third trip, 13.6 per cent said it was their fourth or fifth trip, 18.2 per cent noted that it was their sixth to ninth trip, and 46.3 per cent indicated that it was their tenth or greater trip (JTB 2003: 41). Repeat visits are a critical factor in measuring the success of any destination, and with the tendency of Japanese overseas travellers to still spend more than most other travellers, repeat business by Japanese visitors will weigh heavily on a destination's revenue stream.

Changes in Japanese Outbound Tourism: Three Case Studies

The SARS 'Epidemic'

We have seen how Japanese outbound tourism has developed since the lifting of restrictions on overseas travel in 1964, and how one of the most important world source markets for international tourists has reacted in general to the various shocks and constraints it has faced over the past forty-five years. We have also seen that during the first Gulf war of 1991, the Asian financial crisis of 1997/8 and the 9/11 terrorist attacks of 2001, anything that might affect traveller safety consistently results in short-term avoidance of affected areas or particular modes of travel (Faulkner 2001; Cooper 2005). However, while 9/11 contributed to a reduction of only 9 per cent in Japanese outbound travel from the previous year of 2000, in response to the SARS 'epidemic' of 2003 the total number of outbound travellers fell by 24.3 per cent in the three months of the so-called 'crisis'; overall it fell to 13.3 million for the year, a 19.5 per cent decline (Cooper 2005). Nevertheless, despite this sequence of demand-dampening impacts, Japan remains a very important generator of overseas travellers even in times of such crises, with several external markets very heavily reliant on what Japanese tourists might do in each case. In the case of SARS, the decline probably reflected Japan's proximity to the worst affected areas, even though it had no cases itself. However, the decline in numbers of travellers was even more short-lived than normal, indicating that once reliable information about the likelihood of contracting SARS while travelling to, from or in Japan was available in Japan's major tourist markets, the 'crisis' quickly evaporated in the minds of Japanese travellers.

Richardson's (1994) analysis of crisis management in organizations provides another perspective on the adjustment capabilities of Japanese outbound tourists by distinguishing between 'single' and 'double loop' learning approaches. In the former, the response to disasters involves a linear reorientation 'more' or less in keeping with traditional objectives and traditional responses (Richardson 1994). In the Japanese case this has the central feature of avoidance of potential risk in a specific market, but not usually complete avoidance of overseas travel (Cooper

2005). Alternatively, the double-loop learning approach challenges traditional beliefs about what society and management is and should do. This approach recognizes that management systems in fact can themselves engender the ingredients of chaos and catastrophe, and that managers must also be more aware and proactively concerned about organizations as the creators of crises. If we accept this distinction, it is possible to see the disquiet that emerged in Japan and other countries over the role of the media and the World Health Organization in the SARS saga at the time as reflecting concern over these organizations' role as 'creators' of the crisis. Similar concerns were voiced over the 'swine flu' crisis and led to an almost complete disregard of the implications for overseas travel of this later 'epidemic'.

Outbound to Hawaii

Although destinations for Japanese overseas travel have diversified over the years, Hawaii remains one of the favourites. The dream of travelling to Hawaii was actually apparent even before travel restrictions were lifted in 1964 and has a strong connection with worker emigration from Japan to Hawaii in the nineteenth century. Between 1885 and 1924, more than 200,000 Japanese emigrated to earn their living on the sugarcane plantations of Hawaii, mainly from the poor rural regions of western Japan. Many of the former immigrants and their offspring took American citizenship in 1949 and became involved in the developing economy. In the 1950s, cinemas in the Japanese quarter of Honolulu showed Japanese movies and their owners and agents invited actors and also sports athletes to Hawaii. The image of famous actors enjoying life on Waikiki beach soon replaced the grim picture of sugarcane plantations. The same agents also promoted Hawaii as a film set. The story of a Japanese man visiting Hawaii and falling in love with a 'native' girl of Japanese ancestry, played out in the tourist spots of Hawaii, soon became a popular movie theme, imitating the Hollywood story of a white American falling for a pure, exotic native beauty. Hawaii became the island paradise of the Japanese, like the South Pacific was for Europeans in the eighteenth century (Sudô 2009).

When travel abroad became unrestricted in 1964, the Hawaiian dream could be finally fulfilled, although it would cost the ordinary office worker six months of his salary for a one-week trip. Visitors focused on Waikiki beach, enjoying an American paradise while speaking Japanese. Companies run by people of Japanese ancestry that had been involved in receiving Japanese immigrants decades ago now took care of Japanese tourists. JTB and JAL began to offer package tours to Hawaii in the late 1960s. In the 1970s, travel became cheaper and trips shorter, and shopping centres next to the hotels on Waikiki Beach catered to the new affluence of Japanese tourists. The number of Japanese tourists increased tenfold, from 130,000 in 1970 to 1.3 million in 1989. Japanese companies started to invest in the Hawaiian tourism industry, especially in the early 1970s and during the period of Japan's bubble economy of the late 1980s. As a result, much of the money spent by Japanese visitors flowed back to Japan. In 1997, travel to Hawaii reached its peak with 2.2 million visitors from Japan. However, as Japanese tourists started to discover nearby Asia and to look for more individual travel experiences, numbers began to decline. In 2008 they had almost halved, but Japanese tourists still form an important part of the Hawaiian tourist industry (Sudô 2009).

Battlefield Tourism

The third case study is that of the Japanese tourist's increasing involvement in battlefield tourism in the Pacific theatre of the Second World War (Cooper 2006). Several important sites in the tourist geography of war and peace are in this region, most notably the Pearl Harbor, Hiroshima and Nagasaki memorials, battlefield detritus throughout the Pacific and Asia, and battlefield sites on Okinawa, Sakhalin, the Solomon Islands and the North Marianas. As the war progressed, land, sea and air battles left a trail of discarded equipment, war graves and fortifications in the jungles and lagoons of South-east Asia, China, Micronesia and Melanesia. These are now tourist attractions with visitors ranging from very old ex-combatants to young scuba divers, and are on one level outstanding examples of the disaster of war turned to peace-time profit. On another, they are memorials to battlefield action and human suffering. As many authors have noted (Seaton and Bennett 1996; Lennon and Foley 2000; Douglas et al. 2001; Weaver and Lawton 2002; Ryan 2007), nostalgia has long been a potent factor in tourism; the incorporation of the Second World War's legacy into Asia Pacific tourism and travel not only rekindled interest in some destinations; it was largely responsible for creating interest in others, while at the same time laying down the infrastructure in the form of ports and airfields to support it, as in the Solomon Islands (Cooper 2006).

The Pacific War is known by Japanese as *daitôa sensô*, the Greater East Asian War, a war ostensibly entered into to liberate Asia and the Pacific from bolshevism and white colonialism (Biao 2005; Kibata 2005), but in fact it was more about trying to break America's stranglehold on essential resources (Buruma 1994). Too brief to consolidate the resources of the Asia Pacific region in Japanese hands effectively, it nevertheless contributed to breaking the European colonial hold in Asia and helped pave the way for Japan's postwar economic success, at the same time as it resulted in a humiliating national defeat for the Japanese and immense suffering for both Japan and the peoples of its former empire and Pacific War conquests. This paradox is important, as it goes some way towards explaining both the Japanese national and individual attitudes to battlefield tourism and the reluctance on the part of former colonies and conquests to welcome Japanese veterans at battlefield sites (Kibata 2005).

In the postwar period, former Western enemies clamoured for involvement in the new Japanese economic miracle, as astute Japanese private investment in America and Europe (as well as in former conquered territories) created dynamic transnationals out of Japan-based conglomerates. However, at the same time, references to the activities of Japanese forces of occupation in China, Korea and other parts of the Asia Pacific region during and before the Second World War in Japanese school textbooks were censored (Buruma 1994; see Kibata 2005: 104–7 for a description of how this was done). In fact, the former ruling LDP coalition in Japan systematically promoted selective historical amnesia during the fifty years following the American occupation while at the same time focusing the minds of the Japanese people on such programmes as 'double your income' (in the 1960s) rather than on the sort of soul-searching about past actions that occurred, for example, in Germany (Buruma 1994: 65; Biao 2005).

For the Japanese, symbols of the war abound in the Asia Pacific region: the Saipan cliffs; the Soviet and Mongolian gulags for Japanese army prisoners; and the battles of Midway, the Coral Sea, Savo Sound and Okinawa are particularly important. For the few remaining armed-forces veterans, the Malayan campaign, Singapore and Burma, as well as the much longer Sino–Japanese War and the Kwantung Army's experiences at the hands of the Soviet Union are just as important. However, their experiences of these theatres as soldiers are to a great extent overshadowed by external views of the Nanjing massacre, the Sandakan death march, the human cost of building the Burma railway, and the Nagasaki and Hiroshima atomic bombs. The images of Japanese behaviour that are conjured up for an outside observer in certain parts of Asia and the Pacific evoke a corresponding embarrassment for would-be Japanese battlefield tourists to these areas, and often hostility on the part of potential hosts to their desire to visit them, thus limiting the potential of tourism to heal the wounds of war between former combatants (D'Amore 1989; Butler and Mao 1996; Glosserman 2004). Nevertheless, Japanese tourism to overseas battlefields does exist and may be growing, as younger generations make the events of the past a concern. However, official statistics do not allow any reliable count to be made of these flows at the time of writing.

Veterans on both sides of the Pacific War now mingle mainly in private, as on Iwo Jima, where a yearly meeting takes place between former adversaries on this largely uninhabited island, amicably bringing together veterans and relatives of the war dead on both sides in the conflict (Talmadge 2004). Close to Pengkalan Chepa airport on Kelantan, Malaysia, is a Japanese war cemetery typical of those across South-east Asia. A local firm, Sampugita Holidays Sdn Bhd, is one of the battlefield holiday tour operators in this part of Malaysia, and one of its specialties is covering the actions of 8 December 1941 to 15 February 1942, the fall of Singapore. The company reports that Japanese war veterans are among Kelantan's regular visitors, along with British and Australian veterans (Ahmad 2004). And at Kuching in Malaysia (Batu Lintang) there is another cemetery, also host to many Japanese war-veteran visitors, generally in groups of ten to twelve people, throughout the year (Sakai Kazue, personal communication, January 2004).

On the other hand, while 15 June 2004 marked sixty years since the United States invaded the Japanese League of Nations-mandated islands of Saipan and Tinian in the North Marianas, Japanese veterans were not invited to commemorate the events, However, tour operators such as Battlefield Expeditions to Saipan make no such distinction between their clients, although it is unclear exactly how many Japanese veterans they attract on their tours (http://www.battlefield-expeditions.com/). It is more likely that Japanese veteran associations run parallel tours to Saipan and other islands, although the extent of these is also unknown. Such firms, however, specialize in offering an on-going series of in-depth historical explorations of the battlefields of Saipan, Tinian the North Marianas and other Pacific islands. Each expedition provides a detailed examination of the battles from both the Japanese and American perspectives, and includes optional hiking and walking tours of these remote battlefields along the ridgelines, hillsides, mountains and jungles of the islands. Their clients include as many young people as veterans.

Finally, touring sites related to the battle of Okinawa is an activity which attracts many US military personnel (the US maintains control over a significant proportion of Okinawa to this day), but also some Okinawans, Japanese and other foreign tourists (Siddle and Hook 2003). One of the most popular tours is that organized by the US Marine Corps Community Services every second week, which attracts tourists because it includes the battlefield perspectives of all participants. Again, though any discussion of Japanese battlefield tourism in the Okinawan context needs to take into account the tensions still evident concerning the Japanese military's treatment of native Okinawans during the battle, the fact that Okinawa (though officially part of Japan from 1972) is still occupied by American forces, who control some of the best land, must be understood, as well as the desire of the Okinawans, Americans and the Japanese to commemorate their war dead as best they can (Figal 2012).

Summary and Conclusions

We have seen in this chapter how Japanese outbound travel rapidly developed in the decades following 1964, when overseas travel was finally liberalized. By the 1980s the Japanese traveller had become one of the major source markets for international tourism, and this remains true today for many countries. Nevertheless, the nature of Japanese outbound tourism has changed over the years, with an expansion and then contraction in the 'office lady' singles group, the rise of the 'silvers', and the even sharper rise in the FIT group. The latter has taken over from the group tour as the main way of travelling (couples and individuals travelling with their own agenda), although the travel agencies and the airline and accommodation sectors continue to provide their services on a group basis to many individuals. This change is more related to the financial and operational requirements of the service providers rather than the desire of the Japanese traveller to travel in a close-knit group to an overseas destination.

A major factor in the growth of outbound tourism has been the Japanese government's policy of encouraging it in an effort to contribute to international society and to improve the quality of Japanese people's lives, including the promotion of internationalization at home, and to announce to the rest of the world that Japan is a normal, advanced industrialized country (Leheny 2003). Encouraging Japanese overseas travel has also been helped by a strong yen during much of this period, and the fact that it was seen as politically preferable to the opening up of Japan's domestic markets, widely seen as closed by outsiders, to foreign competition. Such major efforts as the 'Ten Million' programme were introduced from time to time to increase the annual number of Japanese tourists going abroad, from 5.5 million in 1986 to over 17 million in the 2000s. Within this pattern there have been several fluctuations, all reflecting the fact that at these levels the total outbound flows are susceptible to both economic and social pressures.

Major impacts in this respect have been felt from terrorist activities, and war and health scares in other parts of the world, but as we have shown these have in the main only served to redirect Japanese outbound travel to alternative destinations, not reduce it permanently. We have also shown that, given understanding of the past has been systematically affected by the censorship actions of the establishment in postwar Japan, it is not surprising that information on Japanese battlefield tourism in the Pacific theatre of the Second World War is hard to come by, or only surfaces as a by-product of the broader debate on how to overcome such censorship. While the idea that silence on such matters as the actions of the Imperial Army and colonial bureaucracy during the 1930s and 1940s may be preferable to the embarrassing controversies that periodically erupt in the newspapers or that strain Japan's relations with regional countries, it has served to obfuscate and promote ignorance about the propensity of the Japanese to undertake battlefield tourism. Nevertheless, there is a strong tradition of battlefield tourism in Japan in relation to the Pacific War, promoted by many of the same type of organizations that do so for other former combatant countries, the returned services leagues and families of the war dead. These organizations are supplemented by battlefield tourism-oriented travel companies whose tours cater for all sides in the conflict, and who attract at least some Japanese veterans and/or their families. But perhaps the most positive aspect is that younger generations of Japanese travellers and some of the remaining veterans are no longer willing to put up with official silence on past actions, and are prepared to visit battlefields (including those in Japan itself) or enter into media debate to try to aid understanding of how the dehumanizing processes of war come about (Cooper 2006; Figal 2012).

7

WELCOME TO JAPAN

In contrast to the rapid development of outbound tourism since the 1980s, inbound tourism has played a minor role in the development of tourism in Japan, especially since the Second World War. An exception was the Meiji period, when foreigners from Western countries became involved in the rapid modernization process of the country and brought with them Western forms of leisure. Starting in late 2002, the Japanese government embarked once again on a policy of actively enticing foreign tourists. However, this stands in contrast with continuing restrictive policies on labour migration and immigration issues, which has created a conundrum for tourism policy makers and the industry. The aim of reviving regional economies through inbound tourism, though, will also affect social structures and daily life across the country, even in areas that so far have experienced only limited contact with foreign visitors, and will ultimately put pressure on the immigration authorities. This chapter therefore pays attention to the range of policy questions that arise from the promotion of inbound tourism. Will it be possible to separate 'good' foreign tourists and 'bad' labour immigrants, as the government is attempting to do? What other socially relevant, and perhaps unexpected, issues will emerge during the course of the next few years as Japan opens up its domestic tourism industry to inbound tourism? Will inbound tourism become a source of innovation in Japanese tourist destinations?

In 2002, the Japanese government under then Prime Minister Koizumi embarked on the 'Inbound Tourism Initiative of Japan' and proclaimed its aim to increase the number of foreign tourists from about five million in 2002 to ten million by 2010. On the official English website of MLIT the significance of tourism promotion is explained as follows: 'Tourism is said to be the biggest industry in the world. Tourism has a ripple effect on many industries and contributes to regional development. International exchange through tourism will contribute to world peace. Visits by tourists will lead to a renewed interest and pride in regional communities' (MLIT 2009a). This chapter will look at the background to this recent change of policy and examine the consequences from the national to the local level.

Immigration Policies and Foreigners in Japan

Japan has been long known for restrictive immigration policies (Befu 2000; Vafadari and Cooper 2007). As in Germany, nationality is defined on the basis of the blood principle rather than place of birth, and the somewhat antiquated system of family registers further limits access to Japanese society and citizenship. Even during the bubble economy, when the country suffered from a severe labour shortage, importing workers from abroad was not an easy option. The problems of multicultural societies in Europe, where Germany, Britain and France built their postwar economies with the cooperation of 'guest workers' and migrants from former colonies, often serve as a negative image of the future to policy makers should Japan ever allow foreigners to come to work in the country in large numbers. However, in true Japanese fashion, loopholes had to be created to deal with the real demand for personnel to work in low-paid, dangerous jobs or in the entertainment and sex industry. South American workers with Japanese ancestors and Filipino entertainers and trainees on a three-year visa were allowed to fill these gaps; foreign brides mainly from Asian countries for farmers have also been welcomed.

The general public attitude, however, nurtured by restrictive government policies for decades and fed by shock-horror media reports of crimes committed by foreigners, remains cautious. As a result, in a questionnaire conducted by the government in 2003, 32.4 per cent of respondents voted against an increase in the number of foreign tourists, mainly due to a fear of increasing crime (NDKSK 2003). But under the influence of the 'Yôkoso! Japan' campaign this percentage had declined to 9.6 per cent by 2005. Apparently, the campaign not only attracted more foreign tourists but also convinced many Japanese of the benefits of inbound tourism.

The Evolution of Policy

It is important now to take a short historical look at the evolution of immigration policy, as past experiences influence present-day attitudes towards foreigners – whether migrants or tourists. Migrants from nearby Asian countries have for centuries brought new technical and cultural practices to Japan. In the nineteenth century, Western specialists were actively encouraged to help modernizing Japanese society and the economy. With their country under Japanese colonial rule from 1910, Korean workers were recruited and later forced to come to Japan to fill the factories, so that 2.1 million Koreans resided in Japan by 1945. This group still forms the largest segment of permanent foreign residents in Japan, after Korean and Taiwanese residents had the Japanese nationality they had held during colonial rule revoked. While after the Second World War, unlike European countries, Japan still had sufficient surplus rural population to call to the cities for low-wage jobs during the postwar period of high growth, the economic upturn of the 1980s made it necessary to find a cheap workforce outside the country. Illegal migrants from nearby Asian countries had been increasing, with women working in the entertainment and sex industries since the 1970s and men filling the '3K' dirty, dangerous and difficult jobs (*kitanai, kitsui, kiken*). Illegally working foreigners normally enter the country on tourist, cultural or student visas and then work without permission and/or overstay their visa. From 1989 onwards a number of changes were introduced that basically confirmed the government's intention to close the door on unskilled labour immigration, but at the same time responded to the lobbying efforts of the business world to provide a continuing cheap workforce.

A new visa category for 'trainees' was established that allows a person to work for up to three years in Japan. In theory a trainee enters a training programme for up to one year to learn industrial techniques or skills under curricula which satisfy the standards set by the Ministry of Justice (MoJ) and they can then work as a trainee-in-practice under contract with the same organization or company for two more years. However, this system has been heavily criticized for its low wages and poor working conditions under the guise of 'technical transfer'. Trainees often work long hours at hard jobs in small factories, but also in agriculture and fisheries, thus supporting industries that have been given up by young Japanese.

Despite repeated calls for reform to the system, from 2003 to 2008 the number of trainees doubled to about 88,000. In 2007, the MoJ revised the guidelines for participating organizations by clarifying acts that fall under 'unfair conduct' such as requiring trainees and interns to hand over their passports and alien registration cards or prohibiting them from leaving their dormitories (MoJ 2008: 74). In 2009, the immigration law was changed and a new 'Technical Intern Training Programme' became the main way to employ low-qualified foreign workers for up to three years. Under this programme, participants are covered by Japanese labour laws from the first year. On the other hand, trainee programmes were restricted to specific organizations and purposes (Kremers 2011).

The employment category 'entertainer' was introduced at the same time as the trainee system. Until 2004, when severe restrictions were introduced in the light of international criticism of Japan for not acting sufficiently against human trafficking, visas of this type provided the entertainment and sex industries with sufficient workers (Eades 2007; Roberts 2008). More than 130,000 persons entered Japan under this category in 2004; their number has since declined to about 38,000 per year. However, 'entertainers' still account for the largest number of foreigners newly arriving with employment visas. Entertainment visas are a good example of the high degree of segmentation according to nationality and gender in migration to Japan, as this category used to consist mainly of Filipinas. In 1996, three-quarters of the migrants from the Philippines were female, most in their twenties, and about 90 per cent of them were estimated to work in the entertainment or sex industries (Douglass 2000: 115). In 2004, the Japanese government started an enquiry in the Philippines and decided that criteria were not applied strictly enough by the Philippine side. The ensuing enforcement of rules led to a decline in the number of entertainment visas issued from 2004 to 2007, with a decrease in Filipina migrants entering Japan under this category from over 80,000 to 5,533. However, critics pointed out that this move would push workers in the entertainment industry towards prostitution, which is officially illegal in Japan, while also restricting the opportunities for Japanese men to meet urban hostesses and marry them (Faier 2009). In 2007, the percentage of women amongst arrivals from the Philippines was still 73 per cent, by far the highest of any country of origin.

In another attempt to find substitutes for Asian migrants, people of Japanese ethnic decent (*nikkeijin*), mostly from South America, were permitted to work in Japan for up to three years under the status of long-term resident. However, as they are legal residents, they do not fill real low-paid jobs but rather work in large companies and have a tendency to stay for longer periods. Since many of them live close to the companies employing them and don't speak much Japanese, they form their own communities. In a report by the Ministry of Justice in 2006 on the 'basic stance on admittance of foreigners in the future' it is suggested revising the *nikkeijin* policy and the trainee system and requiring Japanese language skills as a condition for continuation of work (MoJ 2006).

There are also workforce shortages regarding nurses and caregivers. After the establishment of the nursing insurance scheme in 2000 to address the problem of caring for the ageing population, some *nikkeijin* women filled low-qualified jobs in the care sector. Recent trade agreements with the Philippines and Indonesia allow for a limited number of qualified nurses and welfare care givers to enter Japan for three or four years, after which they have to pass the Japanese qualification exam for their profession. If they pass, they can continue to work on three-year visas; however, this forms a very high hurdle as pass rates are low in general and the exam has to be taken in Japanese.

Other important aspects of immigration by different groups and nationalities to Japan have increasingly been the subjects of research (Faier 2009; Liu-Farrer 2009; Ryang and Lie 2009) but have not been discussed here in detail as our emphasis is on tourism rather than migration, although the line between both is becoming increasingly blurred in the context of globalization.

After having lived in Japan for several years, it is possible to apply for permanent residence. An applicant has to be of good conduct, have sufficient assets or an ability to make an independent living, and the person's permanent residence has to be regarded as in accord with the interests of Japan. In principle, ten years of residence are required, but a person that has been recognized to have made a contribution to Japan in diplomatic, social, educational, economic, cultural or other fields, and has been in Japan for more than five years, can also be eligible. To clarify this rather obscure rule, the MoJ's Immigration Bureau has listed some examples of successful and unsuccessful applications on its homepage. A look at the list shows that professors, researchers and others active in science or technology have a good chance of success, whereas artists or foreigners running their own business or working for language schools will find it hard to be accepted (MoJ 2009).

It should be noted that up to July 2012 all categories of foreigners residing in Japan, even permanent residents, wishing to travel abroad during the validity period of their visa had to obtain a re-entry permit before leaving Japan. Also, all foreigners on anything other than short-term visas had to register as residents, like Japanese, with their local administration. They were then issued with a foreigner's registration card, which they had to carry with them all the time – unlike Japanese citizens, who need no identification. In July 2012 a new system of residence management was implemented. Re-entry permits were abolished for most cases and the registration of foreigners integrated into the general residence registration system. Visa extensions and other procedures will subsequently be simplified. However, registration cards will still be required for foreigners only. The new regulations will also improve the exchange of information between immigration and local authorities as the existing dual system was seen as causing problems in ensuring immigration control (MoJ 2010: 77).

As a result of this rather restrictive handling of immigration, 2,134,151 foreigners were registered in Japan as of December 2010 accounting for only 1.7 per cent of the overall population (this proportion has been stable since 2007). Figure 7.1 shows the change in numbers and identities of foreigners registered in Japan from 1997 to 2007. While Chinese have replaced Koreans as the biggest group of foreigners, other nations – such as Vietnam, Thailand, Indonesia and India – show an increase of more than 10,000 persons over this ten-year period, proof of increased diversification in countries of origin.

Through the changes of immigration categories in the 1990s, in combination with a stricter persecution of persons overstaying their visas and tighter controls at points of entry, the number of foreigners overstaying their visa is estimated to have been reduced from 298,646 in 1993 to 91,778 in 2010; the number of illegal entries has also decreased since 2006 (MoJ 2010). In a fashion similar to Germany but on a much smaller scale, Japan can be characterized as a de facto country of immigration, where immigration policies are designed to control in-coming workers as a flexible labour supply rather than as potential citizens, keeping them under the dual pressures of legal insecurity and exclusion from social life (Douglass and

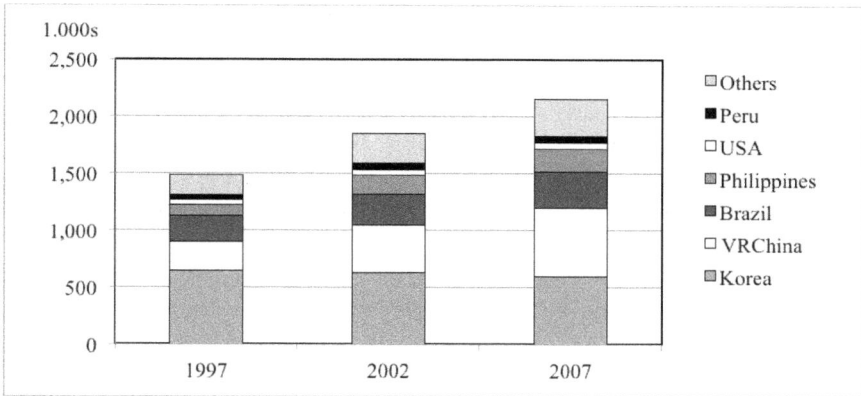

Figure 7.1: Foreigners registered in Japan, 1997 to 2007.
Source: MoJ (2008).

Roberts 2000: 13). With respect to the subject matter of this book, while such strong control may well inhibit the new policies of increasing inbound tourism overall, it certainly has helped to cement an informal hierarchy among foreigners. While workers from Asian, South American and other Third World countries, no matter how well-educated, are perceived as low-class individuals, and beneath the largely middle-class strata of Japanese, 'old foreigners' from Europe and North America form a separate group, providing images that inform the Japanese upper-class life (Lie 2000: 75). This classification of foreigners is mirrored in attitudes towards tourists, but is slowly being overturned by realities in the tourism market.

Tourists and the Visa System

For short-term visitors to Japan, a tourist visa of three months is available. However, this possibility of easy access is restricted to certain nations. Repeated entrance on this type of visa is also handled in an increasingly restrictive way. On the other hand, visas have been granted to a wider range of nations and with fewer conditions from time to time, especially in connection with events like the World Expo held in Aichi in 2005. Recent changes also include the lifting of visa requirements for South Koreans and high-school students from China, permitting tour groups from more areas in China, and finally opening the country to individual tourists from China under certain conditions since summer 2008 (Yu and Shimoyama 2010: 95). An explosive growth of visitors from Asian countries has been seen whenever visa restrictions have been lifted; for example, in 1989 South Korean visitors to Japan sharply increased by 78.7 per cent due to the complete liberalization of overseas pleasure travel from that country. As visitors from Asia clearly form the biggest market for Japanese inbound tourism, lifting restrictions for Chinese tourists is the subject of an argument between the MoJ and agencies and interests connected to tourism. It is also a bilateral problem, as Japanese can usually enter China as tourists without visas. As a result of debates like this, the current policy of promoting inbound tourism, while at the same time restricting access for most neighbouring countries, leaves the impression of a driver pushing down on the accelerator and the brake at the same time.

Following the lead of the USA, Japan introduced fingerprinting and photographs for all foreigners entering the country in 2007, even permanent residents, on the assumption of the increased risk of terrorism. This caused protests from foreigners in Japan, because the practice of fingerprinting all foreigners upon resident registration had been abolished several years ago for being discriminatory. Many observers also pointed out that all terrorist acts in Japan, like the sarin gas attack in Tokyo in 1995, have so far been committed by Japanese. This policy therefore aims at the restriction of migration rather than terrorism (Cooper et al. 2007). Having said that, the process itself is conducted with typical technical proficiency, costing the tourist no more than a few minutes on arrival. As a further control, once inside the country, foreign tourists since 2005 have been required to leave a copy of their passport at each place of accommodation they stay at. While this is not required of foreigners residing in Japan, poor front office training and/or undifferentiated procedures often mean that some hotels make no such distinction in practice until the almost inevitable protest comes from the client.

The Promotion of Inbound Tourism

Japan's pattern of international inbound tourism is quite peculiar. Other large tourist generating economies like the USA, Germany, France and Britain have a thriving inbound tourism market. Japan, on the other hand, ranks among the top ten countries for tourist departures and spending but sits somewhere around thirtieth for the number of incoming visitors. However, the number of inbound tourists has been growing almost constantly in recent years, and the deficit from tourism expenses has been almost halved from its peak in 1995. In 2000 the ratio of outbound to inbound tourists stood at 3.74; by 2007 this had improved to 2.07, though it has since dropped back as a result of the March 2011 earthquake and nuclear power plant accident.

Soshiroda (2005) divides Japan's inbound tourism policy into five phases. During the two phases before the Second World War, the government aimed to use inbound tourism policies to raise the international status of Japan and to generate foreign currency (see Chapters 3 and 5). For this purpose, tourist routes along the railways to Japan's major attractions were recommended and hotel construction was sponsored by the government and the railway companies. After the Second World War, phases of inbound promotion (1945 to 1964 and 1997 until the present) alternated with a period emphasizing outbound travel (1964 to 1996). Directly after the war, inbound tourism was promoted to bring foreign currency into the country but also to establish a new image for Japan as a peaceful nation. In 1949, laws to introduce a qualification for tour guides in foreign languages and to set standards for hotels and *ryokan* aimed to provide a better travel environment for foreign tourists. The Tokyo Olympic Games in 1964 were an excellent opportunity to spread the image of Japan around the world, so the Japan National Tourism Organization (JNTO) was established for this purpose.

However, when overseas travel was liberalized in the same year, outbound trips began to increase. The rise of the yen since 1985 and the ensuing years of economic upturn lead to a rapid growth in travel abroad, whereas the image – and its reality in Tokyo – of Japan as an expensive country helped to suffocate inbound tourism. Generally, during this phase, outbound tourism dominated realities and policies. The introduction of the designations International Tourism Model District in 1986 and International Convention City in 1988 were exceptions. These can be seen as attempts aimed at bringing foreigners, foreign goods and the possibility of overseas travel to every village within the framework of internationalization, a central concept of that period. Forty-two districts were designated to create an environment where foreign tourists could explore sites by themselves, even places off the traditional international tourist routes. However, the introduction of the Japan Rail Pass in 1981 probably had a much stronger and longer-lasting effect, as it is popular with individual travellers and allows them to visit every corner of the country that can be reached by train. These efforts notwithstanding, the gap between inbound and outbound tourism widened considerably during the 1980s. The resulting unbalance was actually welcome at the time, as the deficit in tourism helped to adjust Japan's trade surplus. It only became to be perceived as a problem in the late 1990s.

In the 1990s the continuous economic growth in neighbouring Asian countries and the deflation that plagued Japan during its 'lost decade' made the country a more affordable destination. In 1996, when economic depression had firmly set in, a panel of experts established by the Ministry of Transport suggested the 'Welcome Plan 21' to increase the number of inbound tourists, especially visits to more regions across the country. For the first time, the aim of doubling the number of visitors to Japan was introduced. It was hoped that this would have positive effects on the image of Japan abroad and on regional economies. To implement this plan, in 1997 a law on attracting foreign tourists introduced three sets of measures: the establishment of theme districts for international tourism that would be promoted specially by JNTO; regionally restricted Welcome Cards that would offer foreign tourists price reductions; and new qualifications for tour guides on a regional basis that would not require passing the national tour-guide exam. These ideas finally led to the new inbound tourism policy of the early 2000s.

It was an extremely rare move for Prime Minister Koizumi (2002–2006) in his yearly outline of policies to take up the subject of tourism, especially inbound tourism. In his speech of 2002, he mentioned that the football World Cup, hosted jointly by Japan and South Korea, was a chance to increase interest in and understanding for Japan, and that tourism would play an important role in improving ties with China and South Korea. In 2003, he set the goal of ten million visitors by 2010. In 2004, he promoted the slogan 'a country good to live in is good to visit'; and in 2005, he delivered on concrete measures like the abolition of visa requirements for Chinese high-school students and the placing of international signs in underground stations (JNTO 2005b: 428–29).

Under the Koizumi administration, inbound tourism for the first time was emphasized as an important policy, which found its expression in the 'Yôkoso! Japan' campaign and later in the establishment of the Tourism Agency within the MLIT (see Chapter 3). In the economic strategy established by the cabinet for 2002, tourism, especially inbound, was part of the action programme to revitalize the economy, and MLIT developed and published 'The Inbound Tourism Initiative of Japan' in December 2002 (MLIT 2002b). The aim of promoting inbound tourism was to contribute to international understanding, trigger economic revitalization and enhance confidence and pride in local communities and their culture. Three basic strategies were outlined: promotion, increasing the sophistication of the tourism industry, and improving visitor reception structures concerning information, transportation and destinations. On the basis of this paper, a 'Visit Japan' campaign was started in 2003, aiming at ten million overseas visitors by 2010. Promotion concentrated in the first years on the five biggest markets of origin: South Korea, Taiwan, the USA, China and Hong Kong. Britain, Germany and France were added in 2004, and Australia, Canada, Thailand and Singapore followed in 2005. A 'Visit Japan' campaign bureau was established to coordinate efforts between the public and private sector. Sub-groups within the bureau for each target market and projects organized for regions like Kyûshû and Hokkaidô helped to diversify and adjust the strategy.

The 'Visit Japan' campaign was integrated in a larger political frame with the implementation of the Tourism Nation Promotion Basic Law of 2007 and the subsequent Tourism Nation Promotion Basic Plan, which have been explained in detail in Chapter 3. Of the five numerical targets set by the plan, two were connected to inbound tourism: the already fixed goal of ten million international visitors, and a fivefold increase in international conferences held in Japan, both initially to be achieved by 2010. Considering arrival numbers, the inbound campaign was quite effective as long as it coincided with economic growth in China and other nearby Asian countries, a soaring euro and a generally weak yen. However, growth came to a halt in autumn 2008 as a result of the global financial crisis and the free-fall of most currencies against the yen. The triple disaster of the earthquake, tsunami and nuclear accident in March 2011 dealt a further, much deeper blow to inbound tourism as it destroyed Japan's image as a safe destination. More difficult questions about the plan's ultimate success arise when not only arrivals but also lengths of stay are included in the calculation. The period of constant promotion and success since at least 2003 in inbound tourism has been replaced by one of turbulence. The following section will look in more detail at travel flows to Japan.

Travel Flows into Japan

In contrast to domestic tourism, inbound tourists can be easily traced from immigration statistics. The Ministry of Justice's Immigration Bureau each year releases the number of foreign nationals entering Japan (MoJ 2008). However, most public or official reference to data about inbound tourism is usually based on the number of visitor arrivals published by JNTO (yearly a). This is calculated on the basis of the number of foreigners entering Japan as given by the Immigration Bureau, excluding those foreigners living permanently in Japan, then adding short-term visitors who only use the country as a transfer point. Visitors are divided into tourists, business people and others. The category of 'others' also includes researchers, students, trainees, diplomats, entertainers, family members and those on other types of visa. Some of these would not be covered by the international definition of tourists as set by the UNWTO. Similarly, 'business' includes visas for investors, managers and intra-company transferees that might also contradict this definition. However, since 90 per cent of foreigners enter Japan on a temporary visa, the inclusion of these types of visitors will not overly inflate arrival numbers given for inbound tourism. Figures 7.2 and 7.3 show changes in number and composition of visitor arrivals, based on data from JNTO.

Data collected on the origin of tourists show a large increase in visitors from Asia (China especially) over recent years. By 2007, the top five countries or regions – South Korea, Taiwan, China, USA and Hong Kong – accounted for 74 per cent of all arrivals. While the top five countries or regions have not changed in ten years, China has moved from fifth to third place and Australia replaced the UK in sixth position at the end of the first decade of the twenty-first century. In terms of the gender of these visitors, about half of all visitors are female. However, this proportion is slightly higher for arrivals from Asia and much lower for arrivals from Europe and North America, where males account for two thirds. As for the age of visitors, men in their 30s (13.5 per cent of all visitors) and 40s (12.2 per cent) and women in their 20s (11.5 per cent) and 30s (10.9 per cent) are the most common (MoJ 2008).

Points of entry to Japan vary between different nationalities. In general, Narita airport accounts for more than half of all arrivals, but some small regional airports

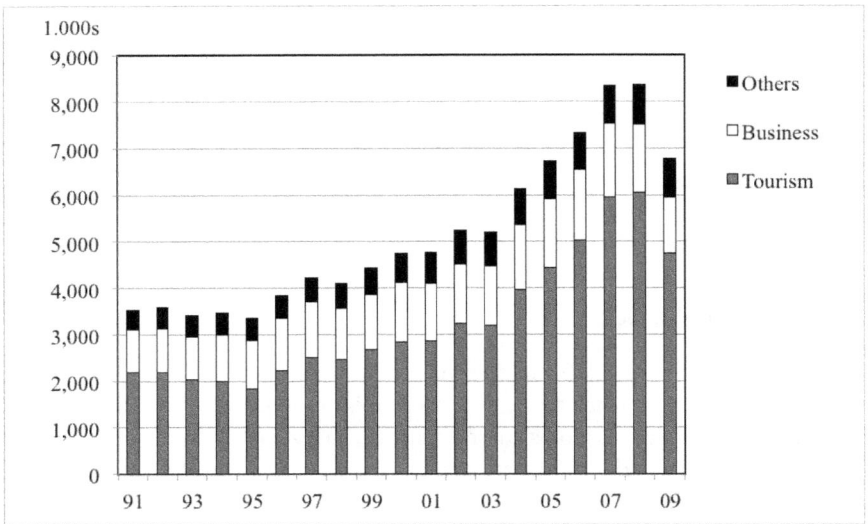

Figure 7.2: Changes in the number and purpose of visits, 1991 to 2009.

Source: JNTO (yearly a).

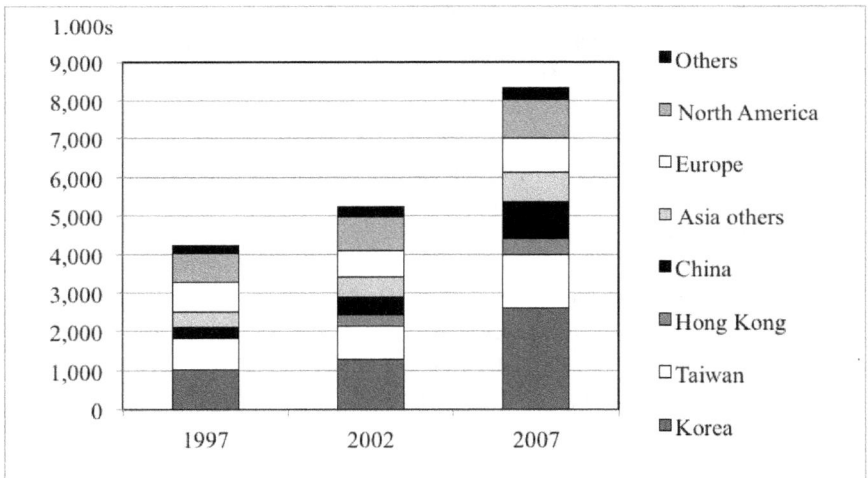

Figure 7.3: Changes in origin of overseas visitors to Japan, 1997 to 2007.

Source: JNTO (yearly a).

with charter connections and some ports are used almost exclusively by foreigners. Taiwanese and South Koreans arrive in Japan through a large variety of entry points, whereas Chinese and Western travellers concentrate in the hub airports of Kansai, Nagoya and Narita. Charter tours play an important role in tourism to

Hokkaidô and a lesser extent to the Sea of Japan coast from Taiwan, Hong Kong and South Korea, as will be explained later. For Koreans, flight and sea connections to Kyûshû and the western end of Honshû are a cheap and fast way to enter Japan (JNTO 2008a).

Travel Flows inside Japan

Once inside the country, foreign visitors are more difficult to track because many destinations do not keep separate records of them. In 2004, only 21 prefectures collected data on foreign tourists (MLIT 2004). The yearly surveys of travellers by JNTO (JNTO yearly a,b) and the 'Overnight Trip Statistics Survey' conducted by the government since 2007 (MLIT 2008a) therefore form the main sources of information used in this section. The JNTO surveys ask visitors at the point of departure from Japan to name the destinations they have visited. However, given the fact that the survey is carried out only at six major airports, problems of recall (many visitors make trips of several weeks), lack of familiarity with place names, and restricted space on the questionnaire all suggest that only a small proportion of destinations will be picked up. Figure 7.4 illustrates clearly that the well-known urban conurbations receive the most visitors according to this survey, with Tokyo a distant leader with 58.9 per cent.

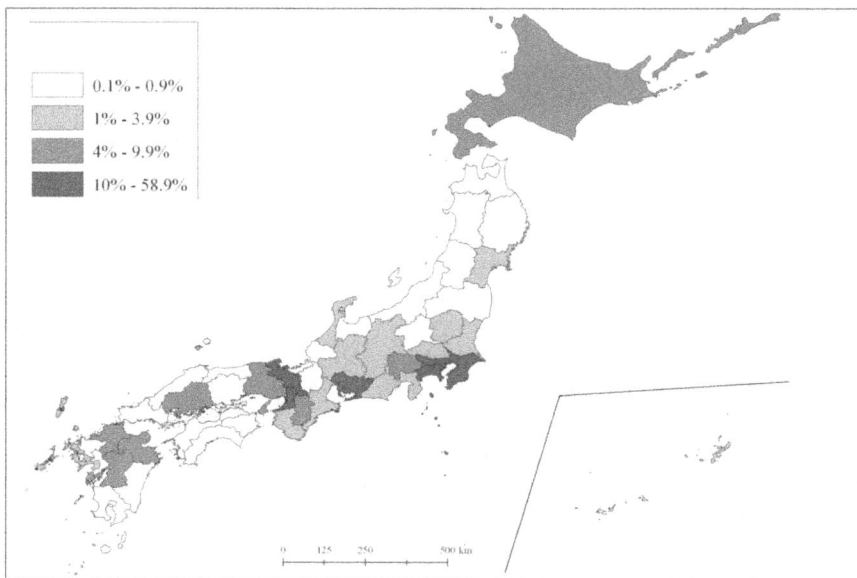

Figure 7.4: Percentage of foreigners visiting each prefecture, 2007.
Source: JNTO (2009).

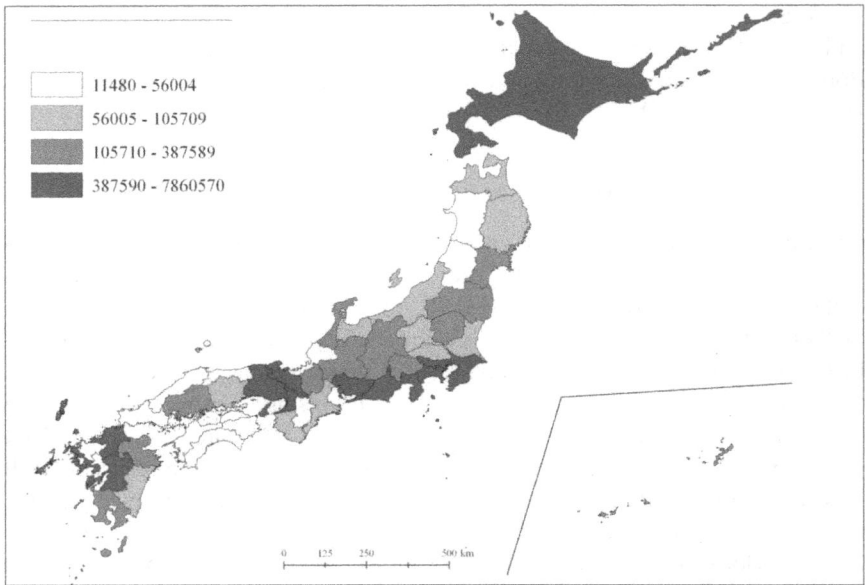

Figure 7.5: Number of nights stayed in accommodation facilities by foreigners in each prefecture, 2007.
Source: MLIT (2008).

Osaka, Kyoto, Kanagawa, Chiba (Disney resorts) and Nagoya all attract more than 10 per cent of visitors; Fukuoka with 9.7 per cent also belongs to this group. Prefectures with famous natural attractions, sites or hot springs like Hokkaidô, Yamanashi with Mount Fuji, Nara with its historical attractions, Ôita with the Beppu hot springs, Kumamoto with the Aso mountain range and Hiroshima and Nagasaki are visited by between 4 and 9 per cent of visitors. The rest are almost untouched by inbound tourism (JNTO 2009). For a more precise picture, Figure 7.5 shows the number of nights spent by foreigners in each prefecture. The pattern varies from Japanese tourists as illustrated in Chapter 4. Foreign visitors spend most nights in the coastal area between Chiba and Nagoya, in the Kansai conurbation including Kyoto, in Hokkaidô and the northern part of Kyûshû.

The largest differences between foreign and Japanese tourists occur in Hokkaidô, in Yamanashi prefecture where Mount Fuji is located and in almost all of Kyûshû, where foreigners spend more nights. On the other hand, around the capital metropolitan area stretches a belt that is mainly visited by Japanese, as it is convenient to reach for a one-night trip. As for individual locations, seventeen of the thirty most frequently visited locations are situated inside Tokyo, showing once again the dominance of the capital city in inbound tourism (JNTO 2009). The regional distribution of foreign tourists differs for each nationality and is influenced by a range of factors that will be examined in the following sections.

In the mass-tourism sector, package tour development by tourist agencies in the countries of origin plays an important role and is closely connected to regular flight routes and, increasingly, charter flights. For individual tourists, although reliable information on the internet has increased considerably, guidebooks still strongly influence trip itineraries. Local actors like accommodation owners actively lure international visitors and resident foreigners active in tourism and the media help to create local hotspots for inbound tourism. Finally, some municipalities and prefectures have also been successful with focused inbound strategies. Through a combination of these factors, some regionally restricted inbound clusters have evolved that have gained a status as symbols of successful inbound tourism policies reviving local economies. Australian skiers in Niseko (Hokkaidô), Taiwanese tourists driving the Tateyama Kurobe Alpine route (Toyama) by bus, Koreans soaking in Beppu's (Ôita) hot springs after playing golf, Western tourists enjoying Miyajima after a visit to the Peace Memorial Museum in Hiroshima, and Chinese shopping for electronic goods in Akihabara (Tokyo) are some famous examples.

Charter and Cruise Tourism

The development of mass tourism in Europe, especially in the Mediterranean area, would have been unthinkable without charter flights and packages. Although these have in recent years been partly replaced by low-cost carriers (LCC), all-inclusive charter tours still play an important role in some destinations. On the other hand, as tourism to and from nearby destinations in Asia is a newer phenomenon and Asian open-sky policies lag behind their American, Australian and European counterparts, charter tourism in Japan has developed rather hesitantly, and it received a heavy blow from the SARS panic in 2003. However, since Japan actively developed regional airports in the 1980s to overcome the transport obstacles of its mountainous landscape and promote regional economies, ninety-two regional and local airports are now scattered around the country, many of them without or with hardly any regular domestic flights. These airports have been encouraging charter tourism from Taiwan, Korea, Hong Kong and China, sometimes even offering financial benefits. Regional airports in Hokkaidô, Tôhoku, along the Sea of Japan coast and in Kyûshû have successfully attracted Taiwanese charters since restrictions on the number of charter flights between Taiwan and Japan were lifted in 2003. In 2005, thirty-nine regional airports were used by international charter tours, with the number of flights ranging from four in Iôjima (Ogasawara Islands) to 927 in Hakodate (Hokkaidô) (KKS 2007: 345). Fourteen airports had more than 100 flights; of these, six were located in Hokkaidô, three in the Tôhoku area and two in Kyûshû, thus showing the important role charter tourism can play in peripheral regions.

Whereas visitors on regular flights to small regional airports face the problem of inconvenient transportation from the airport and outside the metropolitan areas, charter tourists don't have to worry about that. The all-inclusive tours only last a few days and stay within the region, often not even visiting major tourist areas like Tokyo and Kyoto. They are therefore popular among repeat visitors to Japan, as well as for their cheaper prices as they avoid high-cost destinations. Ski and snow tours to Hokkaidô and Tôhoku, spring trips across the Tateyama Alpine route that used to be popular among Japanese in the 1960s, and autumn foliage and rural *onsen* along the Sea of Japan coast and in the Tôhoku region are especially enjoyed by charter tourists. Among visitors from Taiwan and Hong Kong, the numbers of tourists and rates of repeaters are higher than from other regions (JNTO 2008b: 62), a phenomenon closely connected to this type of charter tour, based on minor regional airports. Charter flight demand is, however, also highly volatile in the face of international crises, exchange-rate fluctuations, demand factors and the structure of travel agencies in the country of origin. The forthcoming introduction of scheduled flights by low-cost airlines within Japan may serve to integrate regional airports into the national transport system as has been done in Europe and Australia. For example, the Australian low-cost airline Jetstar began domestic flights in Japan in late 2012.

Cruises, although on a much smaller scale, have also contributed to inbound tourism. Terminals able to accommodate large cruise ships have been developed in several port towns like Kobe, Nagasaki and Hiroshima. Cruises have been organized from Taiwan to Okinawa, from China combining South Korea with Okinawa or Kyûshû, and from the USA to several ports along the East Asian coast. In 2007, ten American cruise ships brought more than 10,000 tourists to Japanese shores (JNTO 2008b: 45). From 2003 to 2008, the number of cruise ships calling into Japanese ports increased by about 100 to almost 600 annually. In particular, Hiroshima (from 18 ships in 2003 to 45 in 2008), ports in Kyûshû and Okinawa, Kobe (from 74 to 97) and Yokohama (from 91 to 120) have seen large increases, the last of these at the cost of Tokyo (JPM 2009). In Hiroshima a citizen group constituted in 2002 by residents and companies in the harbour area supplies information services to visiting cruise ships in cooperation with the prefectural harbour administration, thus adding a personal touch to the cruise experience.

Information and Images: The Role of Guidebooks and Internet Sites

The 'Visit Japan' campaign certainly had one very visible effect: an increase in foreign-language information on Japan on the internet. The campaign consisted of promotion abroad and of policies implemented inside the country by regional blocks, where each government ministry is represented through a regional bureau, and by prefectures and municipalities. Each received their share of funds from the campaign, and many of these were spent on providing information material in the form of homepages and pamphlets.

JNTO itself maintains a homepage in several languages and it is also possible to access the local sites maintained by the respective regional offices of JNTO around the world. For example, JNTO North America offers a special site for American customers, where the content is grouped under four themes – Heritage, Indulgence, Adventure and Modern Art – on which reports from individual travellers add a personal note. The UK site promotes 'Cool Japan: Fusion with Tradition'. The German and French sites are similar in content, but themes are grouped slightly differently. All sites feature not only traditional culture, but also modern art, and the popular sub-cultures of *animé* and *manga*. They also provide information on outdoor sports.

Although the information available on the internet plays an important role in preparing trips, the influence of guidebooks on the choice of destination and accommodation by individual travellers is still strong. For visitors from America and Europe, the Lonely Planet and Rough Guides and their translated versions are the most common choice. If an accommodation facility is included in these books, a sudden increase of foreign guests can be observed. Some countries have their own established guidebooks. When Michelin published its first Japan guide in 2007 (Brabis et al. 2007), French tourists flocked to the destinations ranked with three stars. French interest in Japan was further induced by Michelin's famous restaurant evaluation in the same year, which accredited Tokyo's restaurants with the most stars of any city worldwide (Michelin 2008).

While the JNTO sites certainly put the emphasis on traditional Japan, they also prominently feature modern aspects like shopping, theme parks, *animé*, *manga* and modern architecture. In contrast, the list of twenty-one 'highlights' of Japan in the 2007 edition of the Lonely Planet guide to Japan (Lonely Planet 2007) consisted of sixteen traditional locations and experiences, four nature destinations and outdoor activities, and only one representing modern Japan. As was mentioned in Chapter 4, outdoor sports have decreased in popularity in Japan. However, indoor and outdoor golf and skiing facilities were developed abundantly during the 1980s and 1990s and now attract tourists from Korea, Taiwan, Hong Kong and China, where either the climatic conditions or the facilities are not available. Some locations in Hokkaidô have also successfully attracted skiers from Australia and New Zealand. 'Outdoor' therefore has become a new international keyword for Japan, promoted by skiing brochures from JNTO and foreigners offering their experience and information as a business, such as the internet site Outdoor Japan.

From Foreigners for Foreigners? The Role of Expatriate Residents

When Prime Minister Koizumi was looking for new ideas for the 'Visit Japan' campaign in 2006, he recruited a group of foreigners resident in Japan active in the tourism business. One of them was an American who offers accommodation in *machiya*, traditional Kyoto housing, combined with Japanese cultural experiences like lessons in Noh theatre and calligraphy. Another American married into a Japanese family now runs a traditional *ryokan*. An Australian provides kayaking, climbing and other outdoor experiences in Hokkaidô with his adventure company. A Korean runs a travel agency. A group of Americans runs the site Outdoor Japan on the internet. These committee members form just the visible tip of a – still rather small – iceberg. They do not exclusively cater for foreign tourists; in fact, some of these businesses have proved to be more popular with Japanese domestic tourists. However, they do play an important role in establishing certain locations on the international tourist map of Japan and making their names known.

A case in point is the small island of Shiraishi, located on the Seto Inland Sea in Okayama Prefecture. The prefecture, in cooperation with local government, established the International Villa Group in 1988 as a non-profit organization to provide international guests with a place to stay in rural Japan. Prices were subsidized to below actual cost. The villas are simple but architecturally attractive houses where guests share the facilities with other visitors and can prepare their own meals. Among the five villas scattered around the prefecture, the one located on Shiraishi became the most popular as a summer escape for expatriates living in the Kansai area. An American writer living on the island has contributed regular columns about life there to one of Japan's biggest English-language newspapers and recently started to offer sailing cruises. Local residents have adjusted to the situation and receive foreign guests in their *minshuku* even when they arrive without reservations, and the international villa is fully booked. They adjust meals accordingly and provide kayak and surfboard rental. In 2009, Okayama Prefecture decided to abandon the programme for financial reasons; however, the villa in Shiraishi had become sufficiently important for Kasaoka City to take over its management. The combination of regional or local administration providing facilities, foreigners spreading information and local residents seeing a new business chance has thus created a small-scale international island resort on the Seto Inland Sea that is now even featured in the Lonely Planet guide (Lonely Planet 2007: 446).

A Case Study in Public–Private Cooperation in Inbound Tourism: Hida Takayama

Like Shiraishi Island, most of the famous inbound locations mentioned above have been successful due to a combination of policies by local or regional administrations and private tourism businesses. One destination that has witnessed a more than fourfold increase in foreign visitors since the mid 1990s is Hida Takayama, a town tucked away in the mountains of Gifu Prefecture (Funck 2012a).

Hida Takayama is located in the central region of Japan at the foot of the Japanese Alps. To cite the Lonely Planet guide, 'Takayama is a rarity: a twenty-first century city that's also retained its traditional charm' (Lonely Planet 2007: 255). The number of foreign visitors to Takayama City increased from 23,766 in 1993 to at least 111,400 in 2007 (the latter number only includes overnight visitors). Overall visitor numbers grew from 2,080,000 in 1993 to 2,817,000 in 2004. Unfortunately for statistical purposes, the city merged with surrounding municipalities in 2005, so the number of 3,067,000 visitors in 2007 is not comparable to earlier ones. While international tourists therefore only account for a few per cent of all visitors, they are highly visible and are provided with public infrastructure like multilingual signs and private services like accommodation and restaurants. The multilingual homepage supported by the Takayama Tourism Association advertises the city in eleven languages as a place with the atmosphere of a castle town, of an ancient city (Takayamashi 2010). In a monitored tour by twelve foreign residents in Japan organized by the city in 2006, five participants praised the friendliness towards foreign visitors, four called it real, authentic Japan, and the remaining three also made positive remarks about the historic townscape (HTTJ 2006). Hida Takayama can thus be classified as a 'traditional' destination, with the additional attraction of easy access to the Japanese Alps (Figure 7.6).

The same traditional atmosphere attracted Japanese tourists in the 1970s, when historic townscapes were rediscovered in an age of rapid urban development.

Figure 7.6: Hida Takayama offers 'something interesting' for international visitors.

Takayama first attracted national attention in a magazine article about 'the town behind the mountains' in 1963. The National Railway's 'Discover Japan' campaign brought one million visitors in 1971, and the establishment of an outdoor folk museum with a spectacular array of old houses gathered from around the region, and the designation of preservation districts for groups of historic buildings in the city centre laid the groundwork for a sustainable management of historic resources. Organized tourism management based on cooperation between the public and the private sectors was established in 1982 with the foundation of the Takayama Tourism Association. The 1990s saw the development of new sightseeing facilities in the suburbs by the private sector. At this time too hotels began to replace traditional *ryokan* and *minshuku*, although the numbers of older style accommodation establishments is still high for a city of this size, as almost half of all visitors stay overnight.

Using this background of development as a domestic tourist destination based on its well-preserved townscape, the city started early on to promote international tourism. Takayama City allocated a substantial budget to tourism promotion; English-language pamphlets and maps, as well as a manual in five languages for tourist facilities on how to receive foreign tourists, were produced in the 1980s. In 1986, the city was designated an International Tourism Model District. In the 1990s, promotion aimed at Asian markets started with multilingual pamphlets, regular promotion visits to Taiwan's annual international tourism fair from 1997, and later also to South Korean and Chinese fairs. As a result, numbers of tourists from Asia, especially Taiwan, increased rapidly from 1999 onwards (Tsuchida and Hanyu 2006). The World Expo 2005 in nearby Nagoya further attracted international tourists to the central area of Japan. From 1996, the city combined welfare planning with tourism, as it started to promote an inclusive town that would eliminate barriers to physical movement under the slogan of 'a town comfortable to live in is a town comfortable to travel in'. Regular monitoring tours were conducted to ensure that services and facilities met the needs of users.

These policies have been supported by the private sector. Some accommodation facilities started to accept foreigners about twenty years ago. *Minshuku* are popular among foreigners, as they offer a Japanese atmosphere at a reasonable price. According to the president of the *minshuku* association, about ten out of twenty-seven registered *minshuku* in Takayama accept foreigners, but only three or four actively recruit international tourists. Nowadays, facilities popular among foreign visitors cover the whole range: classical *ryokan*, traditional *minshuku*, an Asian-style budget inn, resort hotels popular with Taiwanese tour groups, and new business hotels conveniently located in front of the station. Especially in smaller facilities, international tourists often account for more than half of all nights spent, as they make early reservations and stay for several nights. A similar pattern can be observed with restaurants, where a few places are almost exclusively frequented by foreigners. However, some facilities stumble across the inbound sector by chance: one restaurant owner recounted that she started to receive foreign guests when she added an outside terrace to her place; only after that did she prepare an English menu.

Public–private cooperation, concentration on promotion in certain markets, gathering and sharing information on these markets, and a coherent strategy connecting efforts abroad and at the destination are some of the elements listed by JNTO (2006: 12) as common features of destinations successful in the inbound market. Takayama has so far implemented many of these elements. It is now an international tourist destination where tour groups from Taiwan and other Asian countries share the historic townscape with individual travellers from Europe and America. The fact that foreign – especially Western – tourists are highly visible in the streets of Takayama further adds to the attraction of the city for domestic tourists.

Issues of Reception

Takayama City was one of the first local administrations to develop an inclusive concept of a barrier-free town that addressed the problems of physical and language barriers together. This was an important step towards the integration of tourism with the more vernacular daily life of the city, and it marked an improvement in the reception of all types of visitors. Issues of reception are wide ranging, from visa restrictions through language services to adjustments to special needs at tourist facilities. Visa problems have been explained in detail at the beginning of this chapter, but the adjustment of services in accommodation and other facilities depends largely on the initiative of owners and staff. However, as one of the central agencies involved in the 'Visit Japan' campaign, JNTO offered information on each country of origin, both on its homepage and in a handbook on how to attract foreign tourists (JNTO 2006), ranging from data on the number of holidays to detailed advice on the type of meals appreciated. Language services, on the other hand, have been initiated by the public sector at the national, regional and local level and form an important part of the management of inbound tourism. Private companies providing public services like transportation also play an important role in making the country 'travelable' for foreign visitors.

The first obstacle for foreigners entering the country is certainly language, as Japanese has a unique writing system. Since it developed from Chinese characters, it is often assumed that visitors from China, Taiwan and Hong Kong can understand the content of written Japanese. However, the meanings of words have shifted and changes have been made to the written form of the characters in all of these countries, so that this form of comprehension has its limits. Efforts to make the linguistic landscape of Japan comprehensible to foreigners have evolved in several steps. During the Meiji period, transcription using the Roman alphabet (*romaji*) and translation into English became common.

After 1945, four phases in the development of language services and management of the linguistic landscape can be distinguished. In a first phase, concerted efforts had to be made for the Occupation forces, so English was the dominant language promoted. The Tokyo Olympics of 1964 and the World Expo 1970 in Osaka started the second phase, in which the use of place names in Roman script and English signs in railway and subway stations spread throughout the country. This was especially so for the *shinkansen* trains and stations, inaugurated in 1964, which offered English signage and announcements as standard from the beginning. National road signs also offer transcriptions of place names.

The third phase, starting in the 1980s with the promotion of internationalization and the designation of International Tourism Model Districts in 1986, is distinguished by the expansion from English to other languages. It could be termed the four-language phase, with signs in English, Chinese, Taiwanese and Korean mushrooming in tourist destinations. This phase also saw the emergence of voluntary action in language services. Resident foreigners have taken the initiative to create books about regional cities like Kanazawa (Stevens 1979) and Matsuyama (Vergin 1985), often in cooperation with local volunteer groups. These groups have increasingly diversified into the provision of volunteer guides for foreign tourists, monthly magazines for foreign residents, and Japanese language teaching. As was explained at the beginning of this chapter, this period is characterized by an official emphasis on outbound tourism and, at the same time, changes in immigration legislation that allow for the restricted entry of foreign workers in the form of trainees, entertainers and *nikkeijin*. While the public sector provides multilingual signs and establishes international centres at the regional and local levels, citizen groups are filling these centres with activities and taking over advisory and educational services. Thus, citizens are taking the lead in creating a multicultural society, receiving tourists as well as foreign residents (Tsuji 2007).

The fourth phase coincided with the beginning of the twenty-first century. In inbound tourism, the 'Visit Japan' campaign takes a more thorough approach to language services. For foreign residents, local and regional administrations are taking a more active role in providing services connected to daily life, especially municipalities with high concentrations of foreigners. In the context of the 'Visit Japan' campaign, the regional offices of the MLIT conducted checks on airports and stations around the country to assess their usability by foreign tourists. Foreign residents with sufficient Japanese language skills to communicate their opinions to the administration and companies in charge of facilities tested items like visibility and information content, but also the possibility of barrier-free movement. Positive results were achieved for airports and regional train stations, but connecting services like local buses remained almost inaccessible without

Japanese language skills. Even in train stations and airports, different phases of 'internationalization' and different authorities in charge have led to a variety of sign types, incoherent translation and different languages being used. This pattern can also be observed in destinations. Currently, efforts are being promoted to replace text with international symbols to simplify the information available. Although translations, types of signs and languages are often incoherent, sometimes unclear and almost non-existent on local transport like ferries and buses, foreign visitors nowadays can use transportation hubs more easily than in the past.

As a general trend through all of these phases, emphasis has been put on making the written landscape comprehensible rather than providing information in spoken form in foreign languages. Attractions too rely on pamphlets and rarely offer guided tours. However, a qualification for tour guides in foreign languages has existed since 1949, and in theory guides should possess this qualification when guiding foreign tourists. Japanese travel agencies use these qualified guides for foreign tour groups because a lack of comprehension can create trouble when foreign visitors enter everyday life in Japan and discover tourist attractions that are not meant to attract large numbers of people. A case in point is the auction at Tsukiji, Japan's largest fish market in Tokyo. Auctions had to be closed to visitors in 2008, as increasing numbers of foreign visitors flashed their cameras and tried to touch the fish. Restricted areas, and signs and pamphlets explaining correct behaviour were introduced and the auctions were reopened a few months later. Foreigners trying to take pictures of Kyoto's famous *geisha* and *maiko* and thus bothering them on their way to work are another example of inappropriate behaviour that makes it into newspaper headlines and proves the need for tourism management beyond signs. Finally, it should be mentioned that one issue that creates problems for inbound tourists in many countries is of little significance to the ordinary foreign visitor in Japan: crime levels, although perceived as rising by the Japanese, are still low, and in tourist destinations there is little fear of theft, cheating or other security threats.

Are They Satisfied?

We now turn to the important questions of how foreign tourists perceive Japan, what motivates them to visit, and whether they are satisfied with their visit. Since foreign visitors still form a minority at most destinations and arrive from a variety of language backgrounds, few surveys have been conducted at the local level. Results from the annual survey on departing tourists conducted by JNTO give some interesting hints, although it is questionable whether tourists will be able to recall their image of Japan prior to their visit, a question asked in the questionnaire.

Table 7.1: Motives of overseas visitors for visiting Japan by country of origin, 2007.

Motivation (per cent)	Country of Origin						
	Korea	Taiwan	China	Hong Kong	USA	Britain	France
Historical Architecture	15.9	26.9	25.3	21.1	56.2	63.2	56.2
Experience traditional culture	12.7	9.6	13.6	5.4	29.0	35.1	34.3
Hot springs	42.6	38.1	40.8	34.6	10.2	7.5	6.1
Scenic natural landscapes	17.3	33.2	24.5	25.7	16.0	10.3	13.2
Japanese food	36.4	34.9	23.9	50.3	35.4	42.5	34.2
Communicating with Japanese	9.0	4.9	4.0	2.4	14.3	13.7	14.0
Streetwalking through entertainment districts	23.1	11.4	12.1	9.4	12.0	9.6	23.7
Urban landscapes	17.4	14.0	21.8	8.8	6.2	10.3	13.2
Shopping	36.8	42.0	50.2	61.0	22.9	19.9	27.2
Theme Parks	14.8	15.1	21.7	18.1	3.1	0.7	0.0

Note: The question about motivation is only asked of visitors who give 'leisure' as the purpose of their visit.

Source: JNTO (2009).

A short look at motivations for visits to Japan soon shows a clear difference between tourists from different areas. As can be seen in Table 7.1, relaxation and hot springs as well as shopping and Japanese food rank highly among Asian visitors. For the Chinese and Taiwanese, nature is also an attraction, whereas Koreans are interested in streetwalking through entertainment districts. On the other hand, visitors from the USA and the UK put their emphasis on culture and history as well as people and their lifestyle. Unlike Asian visitors, they show no interest in theme parks. For all groups, modern Japanese culture like *manga* and *animé* is becoming more popular, even though the percentage of those interested is still low.

Motivations for visiting Japan clearly connect to ideas and images held about the country. In 2006, 87.9 per cent of respondents had a positive image of Japan, while 94.2 per cent were satisfied with their trip. The top five items listed as positive images prior to a visit include Japanese people, listed by 28.9 per cent of respondents, the city landscapes (25.6 per cent), culture and history (18 per cent), food (15.6 per cent) and services (13.2 per cent). On the other hand, negative images were held on prices (15 per cent), language (3.0 percent) and food (1.6 percent). Needless to say, these perceptions vary widely according to country or

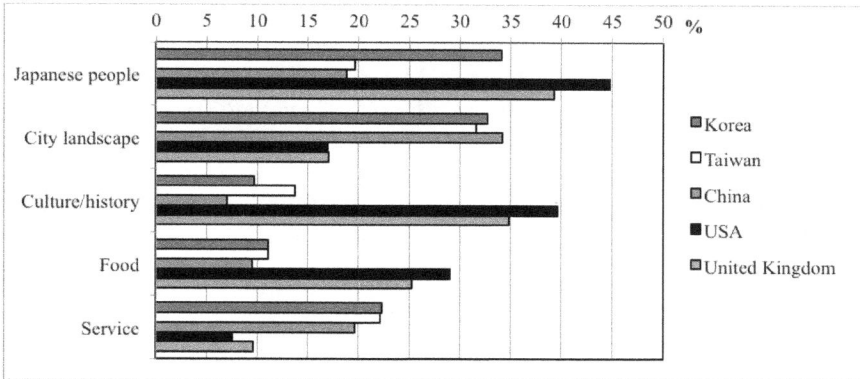

Figure 7.7: Overseas visitors' positive perceptions of Japan by country of origin.
Source: JNTO (2005).

region of origin, as can be seen in Figure 7.7. A clear separation between Asian and other visitors is visible: Asian visitors hold city landscapes and services in high esteem, whereas tourists from Western countries have a positive image of Japanese people and food as well as culture and history. Koreans form an exception as they have a more favourable perception of Japanese people than other Asian tourists.

Among the top ten positive items, four – namely city landscapes, culture and history, living standards, and industry and products – are less positively perceived after a visit. The decline concerning culture and history is especially strong among tourists from Europe and America. While the overall decrease in these categories is only a few percent, Japanese people are seen in a 9 per cent more favourable light at the end of a trip to Japan. Food, services, transportation, safety, nature and shopping also increase by from 1 to 5 per cent each. As for negative images, prices are seen as more realistic and less expensive after a visit, whereas the language barrier is perceived as being more of a problem than before. Generally, visitors hold a rather favourable image of Japan that improves further after their visit. However, as city landscapes for Asian tourists and culture and history for Western tourists are important motives for making a visit to Japan, an unfavourable impression in these areas will have a negative impact on future visitors or visits, and therefore needs to be addressed by the relevant sectors of the tourism industry.

A New Sector of Inbound Tourism: Foreign Capital

The deregulation of capital markets since the late 1980s finally bore fruit in the tourism sector in the early years of the twenty-first century, when international investment funds turned their attention to the ailing remnants of the bubble economy. As mentioned in Chapter 4, in 2001 Ripplewood Holdings took over the Phoenix Group's Seagaia resort in Miyazaki Prefecture. Next in line was Goldman Sachs in 2002, then followed by Lone Star in 2003, both buying up golf courses from two Japanese companies. With more than 100 golf courses each under their belts, these two corporations for a while were the numbers one and two in the Japanese golf market (Anon. 2008a: 119). Both created subsidiaries that have since been listed on the stock market, and they hoped to turn business around through economies of scale and the introduction of a more casual American style of golf. South Korean investors followed their lead, making use of a strong won and a keen interest in golf among Koreans, and in 2012 they owned forty-nine courses in Japan (Anon 2012: 47). Ski resorts also saw their share of foreign investment, although on a much smaller scale than golf courses. However, Goldman Sachs and Lone Star both sold their subsidiaries to Japanese investors in 2011 and thus retired from the Japanese golf market after less than ten years.

The second focus of foreign investment was established domestic hotel brands like Prince Hotels (acquired by Citigroup in 2006) and ANA Hotels (acquired by Morgan Stanley in 2007), but also destination flagships like the Kobe Oriental Hotel and individual hotels across the country, either in famous resort locations like Hokkaidô and Okinawa or in metropolitan centres. Between 2003 and 2006 alone, 42 hotels were acquired by five investment groups, seventeen by Ishin Hotels Group, ten by Lone Star, eight by Morgan Stanley, six by Goldman Sachs and one by Colony Capital (Kitamura and Okamura 2007: 2). The hotel market has also been influenced by franchises and investments by international hotel chains. The luxury part of the market has been restructured by international hotel brands rushing into Tokyo, with Hilton (2003), Conrad (2005), Mandarin Oriental (2006), Ritz Carlton (2007) and Peninsula (2007) opening in connection with large urban development projects. The business hotel sector, on the other hand, saw the start of a franchise system by Solare Hotels and Resorts (Anon. 2008a).

Like the foreign tourists themselves, some of these investments are concentrated in certain regions or locations. The influx of Australian skiers to Niseko in Hokkaidô has already been mentioned; they were followed by investment companies developing resort apartments and by travel agencies. Another example is the concentration of Korean projects in Kyûshû, which is conveniently located close to South Korea and where a mild climate allows for year-round golf. Foreign investment in the Japanese tourist industry thus has expanded from pure investment purposes to active involvement in the industry by a variety of companies. They bring their networks, their experience in branding, financing and management and international visitors to Japan; on the other hand, neglect of local conditions like landscape regulations and the local workforce can cause problems (Kitamura and Okamura 2007: 7). While mainly visible in certain sectors like golf courses and hotels, and in limited locations, foreign capital has started to transform the sheltered Japanese domestic tourism market at the same time as foreign tourists bring new images, demand and needs.

Summary and Conclusions

Inbound tourism was promoted at various points during the late nineteenth and twentieth centuries, mainly to improve the image of Japan abroad and to attract foreign currency into the country. However, due to its distance from the major tourist generating countries, high price levels and diplomatic and economic disputes between Japan and her neighbouring countries, travel to Japan, apart from business trips, remained a pastime for wealthy travellers from Western countries. Inbound tourism entered a new phase in the twenty-first century, when the Japanese government started to actively encourage foreign tourists to visit. Attempts to increase the number of visitors and address the imbalance between inbound and outbound tourism are nevertheless hampered by strict immigration policies. It remains to be seen how long the distinction between the 'good' tourist and the 'bad' migrant can be uphold.

One of the aims of the new concentration on inbound tourism promotion policies is the revitalization of regional economies. However, caution is advised in accepting the idea that the concept of a 'tourism nation' promoted in the Tourism Nation Promotion Basic Law of 2007 will easily come to pass. As revealed by a survey conducted in 2007 of 1,015 local government authorities and 4,808 accommodation facilities, 37.8 per cent of facilities had no foreign guests at all, and of these 72.3 per cent didn't expect to do so in the future. Furthermore, only 28.8 per cent of local public authorities were involved in policies to adjust destinations to the needs of international tourists (Anon. 2008b: 31–32). These data suggest that there may be difficulties in reconciling the interests of local communities and the tourist industry to the needs of foreign tourists.

On the other hand, some communities and entrepreneurs are actively engaged in the promising field of inbound tourism in a way that can make up for some of the shortcomings of the domestic market – especially the high concentration on public holidays and short trips. Many destinations have grappled with policies that might pull them out of the cycle of decline of mass-tourism resorts, while others have seen new possibilities through local or even foreign investment. Inbound tourism certainly has reached a critical mass for it to work as a trigger in the life cycle of tourist destinations, pushing them to the next stage of development. However, due to the uneven distribution of tourists on the one hand and very few active entrepreneurs, developers and administrators on the other, for the time being this will be a localized effect that appears in many different guises throughout the country.

The effects of inbound tourism on regional economies in Japan have become even more difficult to calculate since the number of visitors started to fluctuate in late 2008. A steep decline in 2009, a recovery starting in 2010 and then a sharp dip in numbers after the 11 March 2011 disaster prove that inbound tourism is not a stable growth sector at present. Even though the 2011 earthquake, tsunami and nuclear accident at Fukushima occurred in a region that is only rarely visited by foreign tourists, fear of the spread of radiation was unpredictably widespread and its effects are still far from clear. JNTO data from September 2011 show that tourist numbers dropped by 50.3 per cent in March and 62.5 per cent in April. In August, they were still 31.9 per cent below the level of the previous year. Within this general trend, some Asian markets like Malaysia, Thailand and Taiwan recovered much faster, and by March 2012 inbound tourism to Japan had bounced back to 96 per cent of March 2010 levels. Lagging behind were tourist numbers from South Korea and Europe; that is, countries suffering from poor exchange rates against the yen. In the long run, it will therefore be difficult to distinguish between effects of the disaster and of the high value of the yen.

8

MULTIPLE FUTURES FOR JAPAN'S TOURISM

In Japan and elsewhere, several new forms of tourism have emerged in the twenty-first century. Some of these, like green (rural) tourism, adventure tourism, and *manga* and *animé* tourism figure prominently in advertisements, media and policies but in reality form a rather small market segment. Others have yet to be officially adopted in Japanese, but can be clearly distinguished as phenomena; for example, the emergence of local volunteer guides or visits to sites of destruction connected to war and environmental hazards. Finally, World Heritage Site designation has developed into a powerful tool in a market highly sensitive to cultural markers and offers interesting insights into changing concepts of heritage. This chapter examines new forms of tourism that contain opportunities for Japanese communities and policy makers to solve some of the difficulties we have outlined in this book and take tourism in Japan to even greater heights.

Green Tourism

The antecedents of rural tourism were introduced to Japan during the nineteenth century, when Europeans working in diplomatic, scientific, technical, trade-related or missionary fields discovered mountain villages as a place to escape from the hot, humid summers along the coast. However, although this kind of holiday had previously become established among all social classes in Europe, it remained a pastime only for wealthy citizens in Japan. On the other hand, picking fruit directly on the farm became a cheap and easy way to spend leisure time outdoors during the period of rapid economic growth and urbanization in the 1960s. Trips to rural areas for hiking, skiing or swimming became popular among urbanites, made possible through the development of cheap accommodation in *minshuku*. Since many inhabitants of the metropolitan areas were first generation urban dwellers, a number still had a home and parents somewhere in the countryside that could be visited during holidays.

This connection loosened over the years so that in the 1980s the rural areas were sufficiently distant in reality and memory to be reinterpreted as the 'real Japan', where community ties would be strong and a simple lifestyle could be enjoyed. At the same time, rural areas suffered from the double impact of ageing communities as a result of decades of depopulation and the global liberalization of trade in agricultural products. Although rice, the symbol of Japanese agriculture, is still exempted from free trade, the system of guaranteed prices has been abolished so that farmers face difficulties running their businesses. In this situation, the urban and political attitude on rural areas has shifted from one on agricultural products to a perception of the whole village and rural setting as the product (Arahi 2008: 10).

The expression *gurîn tsûrizumu* (green tourism) served as a keyword to summarize this new interest in rural spaces and experiences in the 1990s. Whereas in Europe, green tourism was just one among many antecedents of sustainable tourism and thus has almost disappeared as a term, in Japanese it has taken on meanings of rural tourism, *furusato*, and agri-tourism, culminating in the twenty-first century in the *satoyama* and *satoumi* movements. During this process, emphasis has shifted from an environmentally friendly type of tourism towards activities where tourists can enjoy nature, culture and interaction in a rural, green environment (Yokoyama 1998: 87; Nakamura 2010).

The term *gurîn tsûrizumu* was officially introduced in 1992, when the Ministry of Agriculture, Forestry and Fisheries (MAFF) established a research committee on green tourism. This committee came to the conclusion that rural space is not only a space for production and daily life for rural inhabitants; at the same time it answers the needs of citizens for a relaxed life rich in humanity, and that therefore it should be considered as a common good. Green tourism, to the committee, served as a bridge to connect the rural need for development and the urban need for leisure space (Arahi 2008: 16). With this purpose in mind, between 1993 and 1997, MAFF designated 203 sites as model districts for rural vacations. This was followed up with a law to promote holidays in villages in 1998. On the basis of this law, a system for the registration of *minshuku* that offer hands-on rural experiences was established.

By the end of the 1990s, green tourism had become an integrated part of agricultural and regional policies, mentioned in the National Development Plan of 1998 as well as in the Basic Law on Food, Agriculture and Villages in 1999 as an important tool for diversifying regional development and for exchange between urban and rural areas. Several organizations were established to promote the idea, like the Organization for Urban–Rural Interchange Revitalization in 2000. From the national level, policies spread to prefectures and municipalities. A central pillar of the systematic promotion of green tourism has been the education of leaders and supporters. Programmes include courses for farm-inn operators, the direct sale of agricultural products, and the training of local instructors so that they can give the tourist better rural experiences in general.

The establishment of the idea of green tourism was helped by the necessity for new economic activities in rural areas and a reversal of the rural population outflow, a renewed interest in rural areas among urban people, and an uninterrupted series of favourable policies from the government over the course of more than a decade. An increasing concern for food safety and quality among consumers strengthened the desire to buy and consume at the source of production. However, perhaps the most important factor was the active involvement of stakeholders in rural areas. In Japan's agricultural structure, small holdings dominate. Due to the absence of large-scale agricultural owners, groups of farmers, agricultural cooperatives and neighbourhood organizations have taken the initiative in developing activities and facilities. Starting from the direct sale of products and fruit picking on farms, activities expanded to food processing, the development of special products and the operation of restaurants, rental farm plots (where urban citizens can rent a piece of land and try their hand at farming supported by the local farmers), rural experience events and *minshuku*. In 2002, 26,972 facilities and activities of this type were counted nationwide (Eguchi 2005: 129).

Although these projects were often initiated by existing local organizations, the founding of enterprises with investment by farmers and the integration of new-comers and non-farming inhabitants into rural areas have led to new organizational forms and social structures there. Heavy involvement of female farmers and women's associations and groups is another feature of green tourism activities. The number of businesses started by women in rural areas has increased from 1,255 in 1994 to 9,050 in 2006 (Miyaki 2008: 103). Even though food processing and sales, including in restaurants, are the most common types of business, *minshuku* and other forms of urban–rural contact also feature prominently. Many older rural properties are suitable for conversion into *minshuku*. If empty properties in rural Japan can be rehabilitated rather than abandoned, they could form the basis of a flourishing rural tourism, with tourists coming to see the rehabilitated landscapes and their biodiversity. Most of these green tourism businesses are small-scale, operated by groups, and are not incorporated. Generally, though, green tourism has contributed to positive changes in the traditional village and household structures. Figures 8.1 and 8.2 give two examples from the town of Uchiko in Ehime Prefecture.

At Karari, the farmer's market (Figure 8.1), individual farmers sell their products directly to the public, setting the price for each product and checking by fax and mobile phone if their products have sold out. Detailed information on the production process, like the amount and type of pesticides used, is contained on the labels of each product and can be checked on a computer screen. Karari's

Figure 8.1: Direct sale of agricultural products at Karari in Uchiko (photo courtesy of Carolin Funck).

environmentally friendly architecture, bakery and restaurant, and its pleasant setting next to a river, are designed to make the place an attractive day-trip destination for citizens from nearby Matsuyama City. Figure 8.2 shows a meal at a *minshuku* run by a village community: local farm women take turns in preparing the meals for guests, using local ingredients and recipes.

In contrast to these endogenous developments in green tourism, larger companies have also profited from budgets for the promotion of green tourism provided by MAFF. One company called Farm Group has specialized in agricultural theme-park projects and has completed fifteen such parks nationwide since 1986, many of them as joint ventures with municipalities. These parks include food-processing facilities, making such things as sausages, cheese, jam and soba noodles. Visitors can watch the process, participate in production and consume the results in restaurants on the spot or take them away as souvenirs. These initiatives and others like the 'One Village, One Product' initiative pioneered in Ôita Prefecture (Kyûshû) have led to efforts to use green tourism for the revitalization of Japan's rural areas being closely watched in South Korea and other East and South-east Asian countries with similar agricultural sectors, such as a dominance of small-scale holdings and a strong tradition of communal management (Hong et al. 2003).

Figure 8.2: A meal prepared by local farm women for guests of Ikadaya public lodge in Uchiko (photo courtesy of Carolin Funck).

Satoyama and *Satoumi*

Many industrial societies face similar problems of maintaining their rural environments, but the case of Japan is particularly acute because Japanese society is ageing faster than almost any other in the world (Chapter 4). If it is possible to maintain the rural landscape and its biodiversity in Japan despite this, the country may hold lessons for societies elsewhere in the region. The fact that the International Partnership for the *Satoyama* Initiative, initiated by the Ministry of the Environment of Japan and the United Nations University Institute of Advanced Studies, was launched at the Tenth Meeting of the Conference of the Parties to the Convention on Biological Diversity in October 2010 in Nagoya, shows that *satoyama* is increasingly attracting international interest as a model to conserve biodiversity in human-influenced natural environments. Tourism can assist in this as has been pointed out many times in the literature (Funck 1999a). In this section we describe a Japanese version of rural or green tourism using the areas of managed rural land between the mountains with their forests and the villages, known as *satoyama*, and the areas along the coast also exploited by local villagers known as *satoumi*.

Rural households in Japan before the Second World War were generally poor, and therefore gained great skill over time in exploiting the environmental resources around them. The most diverse and productive areas in the landscape were not untouched forests, mountains and rivers but the managed woodlands on the periphery of the villages, the watercourses and irrigation channels which fed the paddy fields, the paddy fields themselves, and the pastures on the banks of rivers. It should be noted that in 1994, only 18 per cent of Japanese land area was covered with natural forests, compared to 25 per cent planted forest and 24.1 per cent secondary forests, showing strong human influence even in forest areas (MoE 2013). These elements of humanly managed nature, in various combinations, made up the *satoyama* landscape, a mosaic of land-use types, each of them productive in different ways (Nakamura 2010). Between them, they produced many of the resources on which rural families depended for survival: fuel wood, mulberry trees for silk production, fruit, mountain vegetables and mushrooms, fish and frogs from the water courses and the paddy fields, and reeds from the river banks with a variety of uses, from fishing rods to window screens. Among these elements, forests, pasture and river banks were mainly managed by the local community as common land (*iriaichi*), while the sea in front of coastal villages was also seen as a common resource.

However, legislation after the Meiji Restoration and again after the Second World War changed the status of common resources. While most forest and grassland came under national, prefectural or municipal ownership, it is estimated that about two million hectares are still managed by locally based organizations. Some of these made huge profits from urban development on former common land, whereas others promoted the development of golf courses and ski slopes (Ike 2006). However, as the rural population went into decline during the period of rapid urbanization after 1945, many of the rice fields, water courses, pastures and woodlands ceased to be properly managed, leading to a loss of biodiversity and productivity, and a less attractive rural landscape, the management of which is an increasing problem as time goes by.

Satoyama can refer to the whole traditional rural Japanese landscape, but mostly denotes the secondary grasslands and woodlands adjacent to rural settlements (McDonald et al. 2009). *Satoumi* is its coastal counterpart, involving both land and coastal marine environments and activities. The regeneration cycle of *satoyama* forest land in particular used to provide a variety of additional resources to farmers, including fuel wood, charcoal and fertilizer in the form of litter and leaves from the forest floor. However, now that woodlands are not managed as part of the agricultural cycle due to rural depopulation and ageing, other species such as deer, the native bear and wild boar have spread into them. Woodlands have become crowded and the forest-floor biomass has become depleted. As a result soil erosion has become more common during the rainy season.

These changes affect the benefits that the *satoyama* ecosystem traditionally provided (Nakamura 2010). These include support of the nutrient cycle or soil formation as well as provisioning services in the form of food such as mountain vegetables, fresh water, wood and fuel. *Satoyama* also supported the regulation of the local climate, flood and disease, as well as water purification. Cultural services included aesthetic, spiritual, educational and recreational services for the human communities involved. All of these are threatened as the traditional *satoyama* system collapses. To be effective and sustainable in environmental terms it has to be kept in good condition, through continuous agriculture, forestry and conservation activities.

There are three biodiversity crises happening in Japan at the moment: the destruction of the landscape due to urban-based human activities; the under-management of rural land due to the ageing population and loss of manpower; and the intrusion of alien species and chemical pollution. A fourth crisis, triggered by global warming, may be just over the horizon, involving sea-level rises in the sea around Japan. But the most important is Japan's own 'inconvenient truth', the ageing population (Nakamura 2010: 31). The percentage of commercial farmers above the age of 65 was 60.3 per cent in 2012 nationwide, but as high as 72.3 per cent in the Chûgoku area in the Western part of Honshu (MAFF 2012). The average age is expected to rise to 77 by 2018. It is also expected that 70 per cent of farmers will leave agriculture within the next ten years because of retirement or death (Nakamura 2010: 31). As a result, paddies and other fields are being abandoned and bamboo and weeds are spreading into forest areas. If trees, especially the Japanese cedar (*sugi*) and cypress (*hinoki*) planted for timber production, are not tended properly they grow too dense. As a consequence, wild animals are increasingly coming into contact with humans, as bears, boars and other dangerous large animals invade previously humanly managed space.

The problem, therefore, is how can *satoyama* and *satoumi* biodiversity be conserved and the community revitalized in the face of present social and economic conditions. In order to create a win-win situation both for the environment and local residents, the question is how to create business opportunities through conservation of the environment and rural culture. Two possibilities can be mentioned here. The first is the stimulation of green tourism as explained above; the second could be ecotourism through the conservation of key local species. Changes in the environment have led to the endangering or the extinction of well-known local species such as the Japanese crested ibis, which is now extinct in certain areas, and the Oriental white stork. The reintroduction and conservation of these species is generating widespread interest among ornithologists as well as the general public, and the result could be an influx of tourists wanting to observe them. The ibis is now used as the symbol of environmentally friendly agriculture, forestry and fisheries projects involving the conservation and regeneration of *satoyama* and *satoumi* landscapes in the Noto Peninsula in Ishikawa Prefecture, but breeding attempts are concentrated on Sato Island in Niigata Prefecture. Meanwhile, the storks that were once common around Japan survived longest in the Tajima area of Hyôgo Prefecture, but even there became extinct in 1971. Efforts to bread and release storks in combination with measures to create a stork-friendly environment with many biotopes have since been successful in this area, and the birds now attract more than 400,000 tourists a year (Asano et al. 2009). They became especially popular after the younger brother of the crown prince and his wife visited the area in 2005 to take part in the release of the first storks from the breeding centre into the wild. Soon afterwards the couple produced a son and potential heir to the throne, confirming the popular belief that storks carry babies and therefore their protection will not only support the environment, but also the Japanese population.

How far these activities are economically sustainable depends on the successful organization and marketing of tourist attractions by the tourist industry, but a successful tourism industry will in turn ensure the income and population to sustain the environment as well. It should be noted that in the context of abandoned rural landscapes, the distinction between green tourism and ecotourism, as described below, becomes blurred. So-called ecotourism activities in Japan nowadays often focus on the *satoyama* environment, as very few areas in Japan have truly unmanaged natural environments available for tourism development otherwise.

Ecotourism

With a few minor earlier exceptions, ecotourism made its appearance in Japan in the late 1990s. Unlike green tourism, which uses the almost ubiquitous rural landscape strongly influenced by human activities as its main resource, ecotourism in its original interpretation relied on natural surroundings with few traces of human activity. In a highly developed country like Japan, locations with a high potential for ecotourism are therefore scattered around the peripheries: on the islands of Ogasawara or Okinawa, in Hokkaidô and other remote parts of the country. Another difference from green tourism lies in its structure of development, as ecotourism is often initiated by local communities, scientists, environmental protection groups and urban inhabitants relocating to areas of outstanding natural quality and beauty for a better lifestyle.

One of the first organizations active in ecotourism was the Ogasawara Whale Watching Association. Founded in 1989, it introduced regulations for correct whale watching tours as early as 1994, when an increase in tour operators put increasing strain on whales and their habitats (Nakai 2002). Nationwide, the Japan Ecotourism Society was founded in 1998. Its definition of ecotourism emphasizes a balance between three elements: preservation of regional nature, history and culture; the promotion of tourism; and regional revitalization (JES 2010). Local and regional initiatives and travel agents are dominant among its members, which include few environmental organizations. Therefore, emphasis is more on tourism than on the preservation of natural resources in the Japanese version of ecotourism.

In a densely inhabited country like Japan, all types of nature preservation play an important role as ecotourism resources. National parks have been in existence since 1939. However, since designation of these was originally based on aspects of visual landscape rather than ecological components, many designated locations have developed into mass-tourism destinations. Since Japan signed the World Heritage Convention in 1992, natural world heritage registration has become the most important branding exercise for ecotourism. Yakushima Island in Kagoshima Prefecture and the Shirakami Mountains in the north of Honshû were registered in 1993 together with two cultural sites. The Shiretoko Peninsula in Hokkaidô joined them in 2005. It is not a exaggeration to say that since then Yakushima has developed into Japan's most famous ecotourism location.

The landscape of Japan also features abundant flora and fauna, with many indigenous species. However, with the exception of whales, few of its animals attract the general tourist. In the absence of iconic animals (although, with the reversion of parts of the country to wilderness as the rural population declines, the native bear and wild boar are becoming more prominent), it is mainly trees that have attracted the ecotourist gaze. Yakushima, for example, features a rich and distinct flora, from subtropical elements along the coastline to alpine areas around its 2000 metre high mountain range, which receives up to 10 metres of rain per year. Nevertheless, it is the singular cedar trees said to be several thousand years old that attract the bulk of tourists (Figure 8.3). The strenuous ten-hour walk to *jômon sugi*, a cedar said to date back to the *jômon* period, has become a kind of pilgrimage, undertaken by more than 92,000 persons in 2008 (YWHCC 2009).

Yakushima's forests have been logged for their precious cedar wood for centuries. By the end of the nineteenth century, when feudal domains were dissolved, the forests were transferred almost completely to the state. Although large parts of Yakushima were designated early as a national park (1964), wilderness area (1975) and biosphere reserve (1981), logging continued until the early 1980s. At the same time, tourism development started in the 1970s, when two areas of forest were equipped with access roads, parking, hiking trails and signs explaining the nature of Yakushima. Visitor arrivals on the island grew from 46,000 in 1969 to 122,149 in 1988, and 406,387 in 2007. It is estimated that about 58 per cent of these are tourists and 100,000 persons visit the two forest parks each year (Makita 2008). Arrivals are restricted by the availability of transport to the island, which has expanded from ferries to include high-speed boats and planes. About 140 predominantly small-scale accommodation facilities and a few resort

Figure 8.3: Cedar trees on Yakushima Island: *Kinensugi* (photo courtesy of Carolin Funck).

hotels cater for tourists. In addition, the island's nature attracts not only tourists but also new inhabitants. The number of residents has stabilized since 1993, a rare phenomenon among remote Japanese islands which tend to lose inhabitants constantly. Immigrants from urban areas make a living as eco-tour guides or operators of accommodation and restaurants; but some of them simply come to retire. Before World Heritage registration, local residents occasionally worked as mountain guides as a supplementary job. Nowadays, about 180 guides are said to be active on the island, and about 80 per cent of them migrated from other parts of the country, making Yakushima the leading ecotourism area of Japan (Yakushimachô 2008).

A number of national, prefectural and local organizations are involved in protecting or promoting Yakushima Island, supplemented by a variety of individual stakeholders, mainly eco-tour guides and operators of tourist facilities. To promote the shift from forestry to tourism and environmental conservation, Kagoshima Prefecture developed an environmental and cultural plan for Yakushima in 1992. Based on this, the Yakushima Environmental and Cultural Village Foundation opened a visitor centre to inform tourists about the nature of the island and a training centre to promote educational programmes for visitors and locals. In 2004, the island was chosen as a model district for the promotion of ecotourism, a project of the Ministry of the Environment. Following the introduction of the Law on the Promotion of Ecotourism in 2008, Yakushima is now designated as an Ecotourism Promotion District. The Ecotourism Promotion Council founded within this project consists of representatives of local, regional and national administration connected to tourism and environmental issues, as well as local organizations like the chamber of commerce, the tourism association, and fishing, agricultural and forest cooperatives. Guides were involved in a subcommittee that addressed problems created through the increase in eco-tour operators, and they designed a guide registration system. Registered guides have to have insurance, training in first aid and nature protection law, two years residence in Yakushima and two years of guiding experience. They also have to make available information on the content of their tours and fees and agree to the common rules for Yakushima tour guides set by the council. The system started operation in 2006; as of 2008, 120 guides were registered. However, their number decreased to 86 when registration had to be renewed in 2009, as most guides saw little merit in going through the accreditation process when it is possible to operate without it (Kanetaka and Funck 2012).

The Yakushima Tourism Association also maintains a list of guides, but sets no requirements except membership fees for the association. Other agencies involved in Yakushima's ecotourism are the national park office and the forest agency. Eco-tour guides form the most visible and distinctive part of the island's tourism industry. The first guide group, the Yakushima Guide Association, was founded in 1989; in 1993, the Yakushima Nature Activity Centre (YNAC) separated from this group. These two groups consist almost completely of new residents with some kind of training in ecology or long experience with outdoor sports, so they offer a wide range of tours including diving, kayaking, canoeing, hiking and mountain biking. Together with a few similar guide groups, these organizations also guide tour groups for travel agents. On the other hand, a large number of individual guides often work as specialists on one activity but combine guide work with other jobs. It is thus clear that the need for and desirability of tour guide registration and qualification differs between locals and newcomers, and between specialists and semi-professionals looking for an easy way to supplement their living; therefore, the introduction of a more thorough, comprehensive and exclusive qualification system has not yet been possible (Kanetaka and Funck 2012).

Yakushima Island faces a series of threats as an ecotourism location. In the absence of land-use planning regulations for most parts of the non-forested rural areas, immigrants and accommodation operators in search of natural environments have scattered the landscape with new buildings, and transport relies almost exclusively on rental cars. High visitor concentration around the longer public holidays in May and August creates congestion on the mountain roads accessing forest parks and at the entrances to hiking trails. During peak times, the most popular trail to *jômon sugi* is hiked by up to a thousand people a day, whose deposits in the toilets along the trail have to be carried out by park rangers. On the other hand, eco-tour guides in search of new attractions for their customers increasingly enter areas so far untouched by tourism. Apart from humans, the number of deer has also increased, taking their toll on forest vegetation. The establishment of counting devices at mountain trails in 1999 and restrictions on access by private cars to the forest parks since 2008 are just the first steps in the process of managing ecotourism on the island. Policies are caught in the dilemma between attempts to control access to the most popular trails and diversify attractions on the one hand, and fears that diversification will have negative impacts over a wider area.

Guides and Interpretation in Tourism

Yakushima is a rare case in Japan, in so far as guiding has developed into an important sector of the local tourism industry there. Otherwise, guides are generally provided by travel agencies who recruit their own, mostly part-time staff and rely on freelance qualified interpreter-guides for foreign customers. Attractions rarely offer guided tours themselves as part of their total visitor experience, and as a result, since vernacular heritage sites like townscapes and rural landscapes have joined the ranks of tourist attractions, volunteer guide organizations have sprung up around the country. The number of such organizations doubled from 600 to 1,200 between 2001 and 2007. More than half of them started their activities encouraged by municipalities, as towns and villages seeking designation as preservation districts for groups of historic buildings frequently offer courses on local history and initiate guide groups (Kato et al. 2003) The history of towns that once flourished as ports, mines, pilgrimage towns or production centres for goods

Figure 8.4: A volunteer guide explains the history of Mitarai (Kure City, Hiroshima Prefecture), a sleepy island settlement that once flourished as a port town and entertainment district (photo courtesy of Carolin Funck).

no longer used is not easily comprehended by visitors. Guides can paint a more vivid picture of a rich past, embellished with stories garnered from local memory (Figure 8.4).

Travel agencies were quick to pick up the new view of local history and use volunteer guide services. This is one of the reasons why guide groups have started to charge fees, mostly small amounts for transport expenses and office costs. However, as many guides are retired senior citizen or housewives, they have a stronger interest in meeting tourists and explaining their local area than in earning money. Only in famous destinations like the old routes of Kumano and the Iwami silver mine, both registered as World Heritage sites, are higher fees charged. At Iwami, Ôta City has run guide classes since 2005. By 2008 there were about fifty guides acting as interpreters of the past, explaining the rich and vivid history of the small mountain town where more than ten thousand people used to work in the mines. The number of tours per year increased to more than 700 in 2006.

A common feature of guide groups is their traditional view of history. Stories and legends about famous people abound, rather than accounts which touch on ordinary life in the past. Guides often carry plates showing the names of historic persons or explaining historical terminology, sometimes carefully illustrated with hand-drawn pictures. Legends become history and recent historical knowledge is not touched upon, or is even unknown. While many senior visitors, who constitute the main target group for these destinations, can connect easily to these accounts because of their educational background, younger visitors have difficulties in following the explanations and quickly lose interest. To be attractive to a wider audience, for example foreign visitors, changes in content and presentation are an urgent task for these guide groups. However, the fact that they are mostly volunteers means that the time they can invest in rectifying the situation is limited.

In some areas, professionals in the form of Non Profit Organizations (NPOs) have taken on the task of interpreting local identities and histories. The possibility of registering NPOs as legal entities was established in Japan only in 1998. While most work in the welfare and education sector, some now coordinate tours and promote local initiatives. On Shodoshima Island (Kagawa Prefecture) in the Seto Inland Sea, the NPO Dream Island was established in 2006 with a staff of three. They offer to make arrangements and organize guides for tours in small groups of up to six people, providing such groups with a 'safe, enjoyable, relaxed and carefree' experience of what they call the 'slow world Setouchi', Setouchi being another expression for Seto Inland Sea, and of an 'island culture that developed in coexistence with nature' (Dream Island, personal communication). Their half-day tours include elements like visits to traditional soy sauce producers and noodle makers, terraced rice fields and an outdoor *kabuki* stage, hiking along a pilgrimage route, and even kayaking (Figure 8.5).

Thus, whereas official tourist associations have to promote all the members of their association equally, NPOs work as coordinators for local producers and guides and can choose experiences and enterprises freely to create high quality tours with a special character. As a result of these developments, the interpretation of local heritage and local identities is occurring in increasingly varied forms,

Figure 8.5: Hands-on experience of local products: noodle making in Shodoshima, part of a tour arranged by Dream Island (photo courtesy of Carolin Funck).

from volunteer guides to NPOs to professional tour guides, offering the tourist a wide choice in experiences. However, in the absence of visible third-party quality control there is little comparative information available to guide this choice in practice.

World Heritage Sites

As mentioned above, the professionalization of tour guides has occurred mainly at World Heritage sites like Yakushima and the Iwami silver mine – proof of the power of the World Heritage Site label as a brand name and an initiator of tourism development in the Japanese market. Japan joined the World Heritage Convention in 1992; by 2012 it had registered sixteen sites, four natural and twelve cultural. However, recent registrations have experienced difficulties, as sites were criticized for insufficient management or did not receive a positive

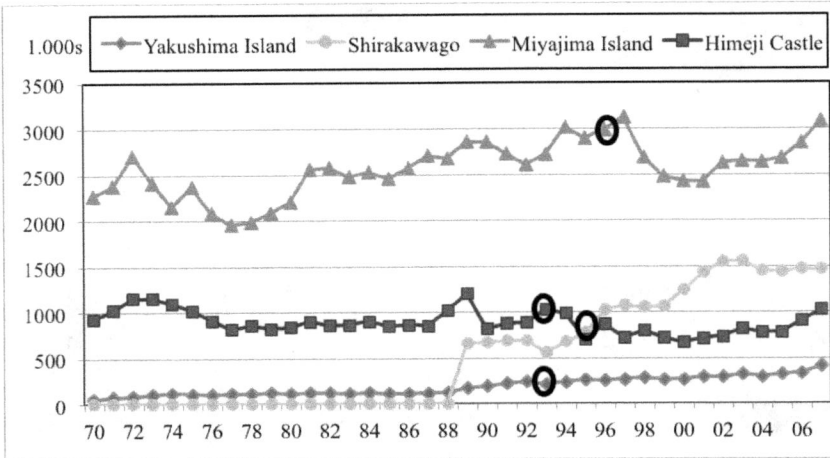

Figure 8.6: Visitor numbers for selected World Heritage sites: Yakushima, Miyajima Island, Himeji Castle and Shirakawago.

Note: the circles in the graph show the year of World Heritage Site registration.

Source: NKK (yearly a); Yakushimachô (n.y.); Hyôgoken (yearly).

recommendation from the International Council on Monuments and Sites (ICOMOS). When the Iwami mine and its cultural landscape was proposed as a World Heritage Site in 2007, Japan managed to overcome the fact that ICOMOS had not given a positive judgement of the universal value of the site and received a positive vote. However, the following year the registration of Hiraizumi, a religious heritage site, had to be postponed for the same reason, dealing a blow to the other sites on Japan's tentative list.

Japan's registered World Heritage sites fall into two categories. 'High' value sites include mainly castles, temples and shrines, and were initially selected by the Agency for Cultural Affairs and the Agency (now Ministry) for the Environment. The second category consists of sites that have been proposed by local movements or governments aiming to protect their heritage or stimulate regional development. Naturally, registration has a much stronger impact on the second category of sites, which so far have seen little or no tourism development. To illustrate this, Figure 8.6 shows changes in visitor numbers to four destinations registered in the mid 1990s: Itsukushima shrine on Miyajima Island (Hiroshima Prefecture); Himeji Castle (Hyôgo Prefecture), which had been an established tourist destination for centuries; Yakushima, which was a secret destination for nature lovers before registration; and the historic village of Shirakawago (Gifu Prefecture), hardly known at all before it was registered in 1995. Clearly, registration has a stronger direct impact on unknown destinations. In the case of Miyajima, registration coincided with the broadcast of a historical drama on national television that was set partly on the island. This had a stronger effect than registration itself.

In tourism that is heavily influenced by cultural markers for must-visit destinations, World Heritage Site designation adds a further, highly recognizable level of branding in addition to the national categories of protected sites, such as national parks, preservation districts for groups of historic buildings or important cultural properties in the domestic Japanese market. Television programmes, books, travel journals and travel agents have therefore promoted these sites as destinations that will not disappoint visitors. Regional and local agencies quickly recognized the potential for tourism promotion. Prefectures and cities set up divisions for World Heritage Site registration; citizen groups fighting destruction of natural or historic environments looked for World Heritage Site status. In 2006, only three cultural sites were left on the tentative list. The national government decided to open up the list to proposals by local government to increase the number and to respond to the increased interest in World Heritage Site registration as a tool for regional development. Thirty-seven locations were proposed, including cultural landscapes, local cultural sites, archaeological remains and industrial heritage sites, and nine of these were chosen for the tentative list. The variety of proposals mirrors the tendency of World Heritage Site registration to include vernacular heritage and complex sites with networks of items spread over a wider area. The nine chosen sites represent archaeological, religious and industrial heritage. Discussion is also underway on the introduction of a national heritage designation, to satisfy regional and local interests and address the regional imbalance of registered sites across the country.

Case Study: Hiroshima and Dark Tourism

The A-bomb Dome in Hiroshima City is a good example of World Heritage Site registration promoted by local movements. At the same time, it connects the two categories of world heritage and dark tourism (Cooper 2007). With one million inhabitants, Hiroshima faces the usual problems of regional metropolitan centres, like inadequate infrastructure, loss of central functions to larger centres like Osaka and Tokyo, and suburbanization and financial problems, and can therefore be seen as just an ordinary city in Japan (Funck et al. 2005). On the other hand, the dropping of an atomic bomb on the city on 6 August 1945 made it the second most famous Japanese city after Tokyo, visited by about eleven million people in 2007, of which 312,000 were foreigners. The A-bomb Dome (which marks the impact point of the explosion), registered as a World Heritage Site in 1996, the Peace Memorial Museum (opened in 1955) and the Peace Memorial Park, designed by the famous architect Tange Kenzo, form the centre pieces of Hiroshima's 'dark tourism'. They are one of the earliest examples of a memorial for victims of mass violence constructed as a reminder for future generations (Schäfer and Funck 2012).

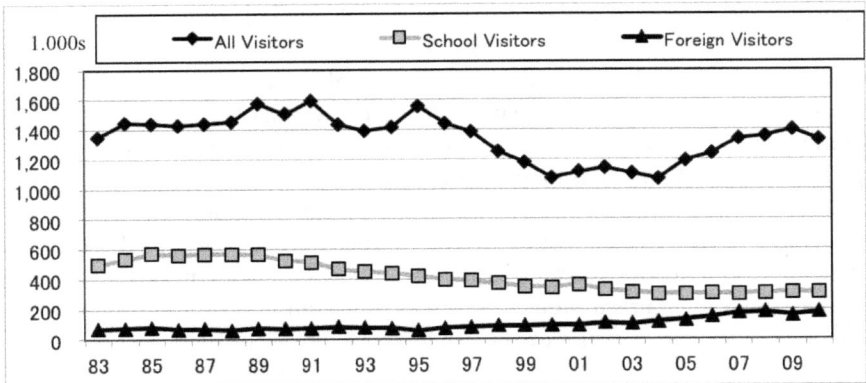

Figure 8.7: Visitor numbers for Hiroshima Peace Memorial Museum.

Source: Hiroshimashi (2009).

Since the dome and park are open access, only visitor data for the museum offer a glimpse of changes in Hiroshima's tourism. From its foundation until 2004, fifty-two million visitors had entered the museum. However, numbers peaked in 1991 with 1.59 million visitors, declined to just about 1 million in 2004 and since then have picked up again to an average of around 1.4 million annually. The number of foreigners has risen from 47,043 in 1970, when data for foreign visitors were collected for the first time, to a maximum of 181,727 in 2008. On the other hand, school excursions, which accounted for about one third of all visitors at peak times, have declined from 570,000 students in 1985 to 308,550 in 2010 (Figure 8.7). Among them, the number of elementary students has remained constant, whereas numbers of senior-high-school students have declined by one third. Overall, educational tourism and foreign visitors, especially tourists from Europe, North America, Australia and New Zealand, are characteristic of Hiroshima. Together with nearby Miyajima Island, the city has developed as the major international tourist attraction in this part of Honshû.

The building now known as the A-bomb Dome, located at ground zero in the centre of Hiroshima City, received its name in 1950 from its dome-shaped roof. Discussion about the ruins continued until the 1960s between peace activists requesting its protection as a memorial, and parts of the administration and citizen groups who hoped to free the city of its terrible memories by tearing down the structure. Finally, in 1966 the city decided to preserve the ruins. When the Japanese government drew up its first list of sites for world heritage registration in 1992, Itsukushima shrine on Miyajima Island in Hiroshima Prefecture, famous for the shrine's red buildings built upon the sea bed, was included, but the A-bomb Dome was not. In 1993, the mayor of Hiroshima City suggested that the A-bomb Dome should be put on the list. However, this proposal was declined by the

Figure 8.8: Apartment buildings looking down on the A-bomb Dome, Hiroshima. These became a target of critics in 2006 and induced discussion about buffer zones in the urban context (photo courtesy of Carolin Funck).

Agency for Cultural Affairs on account of the lack of rules for preserving the building. Up to this point, no modern building had been registered as a cultural property in Japan, so a discussion began about changes in the system of heritage protection. At the same time, public pressure increased when 1.5 million people across the country signed a petition for the inclusion of the A-bomb Dome on the proposed list, and a resolution was passed by both houses of Parliament in 1994 (Chûgoku Shinbunsha 1997). In 1995, the A-bomb Dome was the first modern building to become protected as a national cultural property in Japan and was proposed to the UNESCO World Heritage Site committee together with Itsukushima shrine in 1996. Both sites were approved; however, China and the USA expressed concerns about the registration of war heritage sites in general, and possible distortions of history in relation to Japan's wartime activities in particular.

Although the building itself was sufficiently protected by national law, regula-tions for the buffer zone proved to be rather loose. Hiroshima City created an ordinance concerning types of buildings and design, but no height regulations. As the A-bomb Dome is situated in the central business district of the city, office and apartment buildings soon started to encroach (Figure 8.8). The relocation of the nearby baseball stadium in 2009 set off discussions on the further use of the area adjacent to the Peace Park and the integration of Hiroshima's dark past with its modern city centre. Originally, about 150 other buildings had survived the bombing. However, many of them have since been demolished or are in a state of decay. On the other hand, A-bomb survivor organizations have tried to keep history alive by visiting schools and passing on their personal experience as a *kataribe*, which can be literally translated as storyteller. Archives of letters, diaries and tapes from *kataribes* have been established in a fight with time, as the last survivors reach a critical age. Naturally, the personal side of memory has emphasized the role of victims, as did the exhibitions at the Peace Memorial Museum until the 1990s. In 1991 for the first time, the mayor of Hiroshima apologized for Japan's war responsibilities at the annual memorial ceremony. The present exhibition at the museum also clearly points out Hiroshima's past as a military city and Japan's wartime activities, thus setting the A-bomb properly in the context of the city's history. So, nearly seventy years after the bomb, Hiroshima is facing the shift from direct to indirect memory, the acceptance of historical responsibility and the integration of dark tourism into the concept of a modern city. Seen critically, an increasing emphasis on the bright side of peace – as represented in the colourful parades of the annual flower festival – might turn the city into 'an icon of harmlessness and the well-being of postwar Japan' rather than the site of a terrible tragedy (Yoneyama 1999: 65).

Dark Tourism: Learning from Disaster

Wartime Events

As the example of Hiroshima shows, sites connected to the Second World War constitute an important part of dark tourism and peace education in Japan. In addition to Nagasaki, the second city to be hit by an atomic bomb in 1945, Okinawa is another important destination in this regard. Since school trips by plane became permitted, sites of the only ground battles fought on Japanese soil have been the target of educational tours from the rest of the country. In the case of Okinawa, however, the interpretation of this history is far more complex as it includes not only the Second World War but also the earlier absorption of the kingdom of the Ryukyus into Japan, and the subsequent and continuing occupation of Okinawa's territory after the war by the US military. So, while the hotly debated role of the Japanese Army in forcing Okinawa's civilian population to fight or even to commit suicide in 1945 is part of dark tourism to the Islands, it is just one part of Okinawa's version of history that is seeking exposure in the twenty-first century.

Environmental Disasters

Another theme for tourism based on the dark side of the past lies in environmental pollution. Locations range from where the internationally famous Minamata disease occurred (Ariake Sea, Kyûshû) to islands that suffered from large-scale illegal toxic waste disposal. Their life span as tourist destinations varies, though, according to the scale of pollution and the length of public memory. Here too, *kataribe* narrating the results of pollution and their fight against it play an important role in the tourist's experience. Minamata disease, one of Japan's four major pollution scandals, has regressed from public memory into history since a cleanup at the site occurred and has now become part of the school curriculum for the majority of Japanese. However, since the company that caused the mercury pollution employed many citizens from the city, which was also home to the fishing families along the coast who suffered most from it, Minamata illustrates the complex social background of pollution scandals.

Where victims and offenders share the same living environment, presenting local history to a general public that includes tourists is a difficult task. Some support groups for Minamata disease patients, consisting mainly of newcomers to the area, take a more radical stance, and court cases concerning responsibility for the pollution and recognition of the victims continue to the present. It took until the 1990s for the approach of the area's local government to change from silence to a more active confrontation with the past. In 1993, a municipal museum for Minamata disease was established, visited by thirty to fifty thousand persons a year. The next year, the city invited victims to register as *kataribe*. In 1994 for the first time, the city's mayor apologized for the government's insufficient response to pollution and called on all citizens to rebuild community relations so that the city could go forward. This call also reflects the fact that even now, fifty years after Minamata disease was officially recognised as being caused by mercury included in the discharge waters of the Chiso factory, interpretation and therefore reconciliation is still contested.

Natural Disasters

The third category of dark tourism includes sites of natural disasters, unfortunately a common phenomenon in Japan. While fast and effective reconstruction rarely leaves traces of the majority of typhoons, earthquakes and volcanic eruptions, efforts have been made by local and regional administrations to preserve memories of the Great Hanshin Awaji (Kobe) Earthquake of 1995. The earthquake museum on Awaji Island took on the difficult task of preserving the geological fault which had shifted. The Disaster Reduction Museum in Kobe City recreates the experience through three-dimensional theatre and movies and detailed documentation of records, pictures and things affected by the earthquake. NPOs and neighbourhood associations guide school trips through the affected, now mostly rebuilt, areas, telling local histories of mutual aid and reconstruction efforts (Funck 2012b).

As interpretation of nature and local history has become a major part of the diversifying tourist experience, the focus of dark tourism too has expanded from visits to sites of tragic war events to include more complex topics like environmental pollution and natural hazards. From a one-sided emphasis on victims' sufferings, interest has shifted to citizens' involvement in environmental movements and efforts to create a better living environment. However, with the attention of the general public and the media shifting fast, only a few famous locations will be able to establish sustainable tourism development based on a dark past.

Connecting Real and Virtual Worlds: Manga, Animé and Video-game Tourism

Japanese *manga* and *animé* art forms have gained a worldwide reputation in recent years. The Mecca of the international crowds arriving in Tokyo to visit the *manga* and *animé* kingdom is the district of Akihabara, but in the domestic market, *manga*, *animé* and even video games have created new tourism destinations all around the country. The popularity of Yakushima, Japan's most famous ecotourism site, has increased enormously through its connection with the *animé* character Princess Mononoke. This internationally famous film, created in 1997 by Miyazaki Hayao and Studio Ghibli, is mainly set in a forest landscape inspired by the forests of the island. The small port town of Tomonoura in Hiroshima Prefecture recently experienced a similar rush in visitors when it became the scene for another Ghibli *animé*, *Ponyo on a Cliff* (2008).

As for manga, *GeGeGe no Kitaro*, first published in 1959, has had a huge spin-off in follow-ups, *animé* and video games based on its rich supply of spirit-monsters called *yokai*. Sakaiminato in Tottori Prefecture, the place of birth of its creator Mizuki Shigeru, has adorned its main street with one hundred bronze statues of *yokai*. In the Mizuki Shigeru Museum, visitors can feel the existence of *yokai* through models, sound and lighting effects. A yearly competition for the best *yokai* performance or costume attracts participants from around the country. Even video games have pulled their users out of the virtual into the real world. *Sengoku Basara*, known internationally as *Devil Kings*, is a video game featuring dashing samurai warriors. The Japanese version of the game has close connections to historical persons and sparked a surge of interest in regional feudal history. In consequence, some localities enjoyed a sharp rise in tourism from young fans, many of them women, since the company who produced the game estimates that about 40 per cent of the players are female (*Asahi Shimbun* 25/26 July 2009: 22).

This increase in *manga, animé* and video-based tourism has strong connections with the structural changes in the internet world. Video-sharing sites have made access to *animé* omnipresent: online game groups, blogs and social networking sites help to spread information among fans. Many destinations have been taken by surprise when visiting fans arrive on a 'pilgrimage to sacred places' of their favourite oeuvre (Yamamura 2009: 34), but have succeeded in connecting their new popularity to successful tourism development by involving fans in the production of goods and events. Yamamura (2009) sees this new type of tourism as a form of emotional networking created by sub-cultures making full use of individual information technologies, in contrast to mass tourism based on the commodification of destinations. Media-content tourism has thus shifted from TV series that were watched by almost the entire nation to multiple contents taken up by different sub-groups in society. Since backpacker tourism never played a decisive role in the discovery of Japanese tourist destinations, *manga, animé* and video-game tourism is for the first time bringing young domestic tourists to the forefront of tourism development, where they can play a role as producers of place (Kelly 2004: 7).

Summary and Conclusions

Changes in Japanese society, as well as new trends in international tourism experienced by outbound Japanese tourists, have resulted in new forms of tourism that have not previously been seen in the domestic market, or at least not clearly identified. As the domestic tourism industry adapts, new forms of tourism such as ecotourism, green tourism, marine tourism and youth tourism will continue to develop their own distinctive patterns, often strongly linked with particular destinations. Our analysis of these at the local level has shed further light on the localization of global trends and processes within Japanese tourism.

9

CONCLUSIONS
RETROSPECT, CHALLENGES AND THE FUTURE

The Development of Japanese Tourism

Our analysis of tourism in Japan has shown that it has a long and varied history, with several lines of continuity that define its nature even today. For example, the fundamental contours of present-day domestic tourism are found in the earlier patterns of religious pilgrimage and *onsen* visits during the Edo period, even though the duration of the latter has been significantly shortened due to changes in the world of paid work, and the former has metamorphosed into local festivals (*matsuri*) and away from religion. The bulk of visitor flows in Japan, however, remain clearly directed towards the former religious, cultural, economic, political and transport centres (and their *onsen* resources). In that sense, domestic tourism development in Japan represents not a movement away from the known to discovery of the 'other' but serves instead to affirm the existing order. Historically speaking, Japanese domestic tourism has thus always demonstrated a strong centralist tendency, unlike the European emphasis on the periphery.

As elsewhere, historical developments created the conditions under which several different types of tourist destinations developed that are still the nuclei of the most important tourist regions today. Cultural and religious tourism created *monzen machi*, the towns around temples and shrines, where the visitor's needs for board and lodging, entertainment and souvenirs were satisfied. The *onsen* resorts with their hot springs evolved into the bathing culture of today. Here a range of accommodation establishments were formed to cater to different social classes of users, creating contrasts which are still reflected today in the standards of the various types, ranging from *ryokan* to hotels. The resorts with the greatest number of overnight stays almost all look back on a long tradition as spas. On the other hand, the former post stations along the old overland roads (such as the Tôkaidô) have lost their original function since the building of railways and modern roads along other routes, although some have regained importance as places with historically valuable architecture and today draw visitors by virtue of their historical image. Finally, the mountain tourism that began during the early decades of the twentieth century brought the idea of 'summer holidays' to Japan. In this period, outdoor sport also began to play a growing role in recreation in the mountains and at the seaside. In principle these types and their derivatives form – individually or in combination – the foundations of most existing tourist regions in Japan.

Two periods thus shaped the development of present tourism spaces, visitor flows and travel cultures in Japan. While religious travel and *onsen* visits date back many centuries, it was the political system of the Edo period from 1600 to the mid 1800s that gave birth to a system of roads, post stations, shipping routes, guide maps, souvenirs, luggage services and other travel institutions that shaped domestic tourism once the country entered the Meiji Restoration period. When the country opened up to international influences in the Meiji period, new forms of transport, accommodation and recreation were adapted to the needs of foreign and domestic tourists. To gain international recognition as well as foreign currency, government and industries have actively promoted inbound and outbound tourism since then, even if the emphases have changed over time, as we have shown.

Tourism Today

In order to understand these processes we outlined the role of the state in the development and promotion of tourism in Japan and then examined the actual patterns of domestic, inbound and outbound tourism that have occurred since the Meiji Restoration (Chapters 3 to 7). To do this we began with a close look at how tourism policy has developed since the beginning of the Meiji era, and outlined the principal methods used in tourism promotion, development and control. The most recent Tourism Nation Promotion Basic Plan (2007) proposes a much more balanced promotion of tourism than that which occurred after the Second World War, one that will more fully integrate inbound tourism with domestic and outbound tourism, and with the rest of the economy. In summary, as a result of the economic and social upheavals of the past twenty years, tourism has become much more important to policy makers at national, regional and local levels.

Even so, there are particular interconnections, constraints and trends that have influenced the patterns of Japanese tourism as we see them today. In our discussion we identified population distribution and structure as one factor shaping tourism in Japan, as the continuing concentration of population in the capital metropolitan area and along the Pacific axis contrasts with a declining and ageing population in other parts of the country, especially in rural areas and former industrial cities. In combination with the restricted time budgets that still face most Japanese tourists, this unbalanced distribution makes tourism destinations dependent on fast – and cheap – access from the major cities. In particular, the failure to guarantee employees the legal right to take holidays of more than two consecutive days has created a very unbalanced domestic market relying on short trips, weekends and the pattern of national holidays.

A recent shift in societal relationships from an emphasis on organizations like companies and schools as the main locus for leisure activities to family members and friends has also forced mass-tourism destinations to rejuvenate their facilities and services. There are now fewer groups and more free independent travellers (FITs) in the domestic market, and in connection with the extension of high-speed transport networks this tendency has opened the market to new destinations. Finally, the cultural re-evaluation of things Japanese, supported by efforts to reinvent a common Japanese heritage and by the growing number of foreign tourists, has affected the appearance of destinations and facilities. So although the basic problems of unbalanced population distribution and a restricted time budget for domestic travel have not changed, a stronger emphasis on personal social ties, 'traditional' culture and individual forms of recreation in recent years have offered development opportunities to particular destinations while reducing that of others.

The Economics of Tourism

One of the main objectives of this book was to document the role of tourism in Japanese local, regional and national economic development. The discussion shows that the economic and social impacts from major tourism developments are virtually always assumed to be positive, and that government at all levels will do almost anything to ensure that development proposals are approved even if the likely returns on investment are less than clear. In the recent past this type of outcome has been framed and achieved through direct investment by national government institutions in support of the private sphere, a process which also often requires local community land-use regulations to be suspended. For example, by using the financial resources established under such programmes as the Resort Law of 1987, developers were able to obtain land cheaply, and local and prefectural governments were able to issue bonds to finance tourism infrastructure without much reference to the wishes of their constituents or to the likely longevity of the investment. Unfortunately, when tourism-based major development projects fail, which they often do due to unpredictable market changes and the difficult structure of a domestic tourism market which relies almost completely on short trips, it is usually local communities that are left with unfinished projects and debts.

Our analysis also showed that the relationship between tourism investment and economic development policies and management practices in Japan is actually no different from that involving any other industry able to influence the state's policy-making process. In this respect major tourism facility development has been the most recent beneficiary of the *dokken kokka*, the Japanese 'construction state' ideology. In this system decisions on many major tourism projects are made centrally by the state to the benefit of political and business interests that operate at that level. It remains to be seen whether recent changes in local government structures through large-scale community mergers, new legal systems to allow for stronger and more individual land and building regulations by municipalities, and the so-called regionalization of responsibilities will offer better chances for sustainable tourism development at the local level for the benefit of the country as a whole.

Recent Tourism Patterns

We have outlined how Japanese domestic and outbound travel rapidly developed in the decades following 1964 when travel was finally liberalized after the Second World War and Occupation. By the 1980s the Japanese overseas traveller had become one of the major source markets for international tourism, and this remains true today for many countries. Nevertheless, the nature of Japanese outbound tourism has changed over the years, with an expansion and then contraction in the 'office lady' singles group, the rise of the 'silver market', and the even sharper rise in the FIT group. The latter has taken over from the group tour as the main way of travelling (couples and individuals travelling with their own agenda), although travel agencies and the airline and accommodation sectors continue to provide services on a group basis to many individuals. This change is more related to the financial and operational requirements of service providers though, not the desire of the Japanese traveller to travel in a close-knit group to an overseas destination.

We also identified the fact that a major factor in the growth of outbound tourism was the willingness of the Japanese government to encourage it in an effort to contribute to international society and to improve the quality of people's lives, including the promotion of internationalization at home, and to announce to the rest of the world that Japan was once more an advanced industrialized country. Encouraging Japanese overseas travel in the early days was also helped by a strong yen during much of this period, and the fact that overseas travel was seen as politically preferable to the opening up of Japan's domestic markets, widely seen as closed by outsiders, to foreign competition.

Inbound tourism was of course promoted sporadically during the late nineteenth and twentieth centuries, mainly to improve the image of Japan abroad and to bring foreign currency into the country (Chapters 5 and 7). However, due to its distance from the major tourist generating countries, high price levels and diplomatic and economic disputes with her neighbours, travel to Japan, apart from business trips, long remained a pastime for wealthy travellers from Europe and America. Inbound tourism has definitely entered a new phase in the twenty-first century though, as the Japanese government began to actively encourage foreign tourists to visit from 2003. Attempts to increase the number of visitors and address the imbalance between inbound and outbound tourism are nevertheless hampered by strict immigration policies trying to uphold the distinction between the 'good' tourist and the 'bad' migrant.

Some communities and entrepreneurs are now actively engaged in inbound tourism in a way that can make up for some of the shortcomings of the domestic market. Many destinations have followed policies that might pull them out of the domestic cycle of decline, while others have received a new stimulus through local or even foreign investment. However, the standstill in inbound tourism after the triple disaster of March 2011 also drives home the point that it is not advisable for destinations and facilities to rely on international tourists alone, but rather keep a balance between domestic and foreign visitors.

Multiple Futures for Japan's Tourism

In the twenty-first century, changes in Japanese society, as well as new international tourism trends experienced by outbound Japanese tourists, have resulted in new forms of tourism that have not previously been seen in the domestic market, or at least have not been clearly identified. As the domestic tourism industry adapts, new forms of tourism – such as ecotourism, green tourism, marine tourism and youth tourism – will continue to develop their own distinctive patterns, often strongly linked with particular destinations. Our analysis of these at the local level has shed further light on the localization of global trends and processes within Japanese tourism.

As has become clear during the process of writing this book, tourism in, to and from Japan has developed over the centuries into a highly diversified phenomenon, with overlapping and sometimes contrasting interpretations of space and place. The beginning of the twenty-first century has seen the growing influence of inbound tourism and affiliated investment on the one hand and attempts at a comprehensive tourism policy on the national level on the other. As spaces formerly used for agricultural and industrial production open up for tourism due to depopulation and deindustrialization, regions and municipalities will increasingly compete to attract tourists from inside and outside the country. Since the domestic market is limited by population trends, economic conditions and tight time budgets, tourism will turn international. In a country where foreigners make up less than two per cent of the population, these trends might have important cultural and social implications.

The beginning of the twenty-first century has also brought some turmoil to Japan's national politics. Since 2006, prime ministers have changed annually, and the natural and nuclear disaster of March 2011 has left the country with many pressing issues to solve. Given this political situation, tourism will most certainly remain on the sidelines of the national agenda for the foreseeable future, although Japan's Tourism Agency, established in 2008, has created many waves in tourism policy and administration. However, as the rise in numbers of education courses, conferences, publications and organizations shows, and as recent changes to the Immigration Act indicate, tourism is now well established as a topic worthy of serious attention, which was not the case twenty years ago. And as some established destinations disappear due to lack of appeal, others will be shared by mass tourism and new forms of special-interest tourism, and new ones will be added constantly to the changing map of Japanese tourism.

Glossary

Daimyô	feudal lord
Furusato	home town
Gurîn tsûrizumu	green tourism
Han	feudal domain
Hoteru	Western-style hotel
Kaisuiyoku	sea bathing
Kataribe	a person telling her/his story
Kô	mutual cooperative organization associated to a shrine or temple
-ken	prefecture
-mairi	pilgrimage
-machi, -chô	town
Machizukuri	literally 'making a town' – neighbourhood and citizens' activities to improve the local environment
Matsuri	festival
Minshuku	Japanese-style pension
Monomi yusan	sightseeing
Monzen machi	towns formed around shrines and temples mainly catering to visitors
-mura	village
Onsen	hot spring, spa
Ryokan	Japanese-style hotel
-shi	city
Satoyama	literally 'home mountains' – wooded areas close to villages, often managed as commons
Satoumi	literally 'home sea', coined after *satoyama*
Shinkansen	high-speed bullet train
Yamabushi	mountain priest

REFERENCES

ABTR. 1990. *Japanese Tourism in Australia: Marketing Segmentation*. Canberra: Bureau of Tourism Research.

Aburakawa, H., et al. 2009. *Atarashii shiten no kankô senryaku* [Tourism strategies from a new aspect]. Tokyo: Gakubunsha.

ACA. 2009. 'Administration of Cultural Affairs in Japan, Fiscal 2009', Agency for Cultural Affairs. Retrieved 4 March 2010 from: http://www.bunka.go.jp/english/index.html.

———. 2010. 'Our Treasure: Cultural Landscapes for Future Generations', Agency for Cultural Affairs. Retrieved 4 March 2010 from: http://www.bunka.go.jp/bunkazai/pamphlet/pamphlet_en.html.

Agrusa, J., et al. 2005. 'Japanese Runners in the Honolulu Marathon and their Economic Benefits to Hawaii', *Tourism Review International* 9(3): 261–70.

Ahmad, S. 2004. 'Japanese Invaders in the East Coast', *New Straits Times*, 23 April.

An, J. 2012. 'A Comparative Study of Views on Overseas Travel between Japanese and Korean University Students', *Tourism Studies* 24(1): 69–79.

Anon. 2008a. 'Nihon no rejâ sangyô 40 nen' [Forty years of leisure industry in Japan], *Rejâ Sangyô Shiryô* 500: 35–122.

———. 2008b. 'Chakuchigata kankô ni yoru bijinesu moderu no kôchiku ga jiritsu shita kankôchi o tsukuru' [Business models based on destination type tourism will create independent tourist destinations], *Rejâ Sangyô Shiryô* 506: 30–33.

———. 2012. 'Kigyô grûpu betsu gorufujô shoyû ranking' [Golf course ownership ranking by enterprise group]. *Gorufu manejimento* 354: 46–49.

Aoki, E. 1973. 'Kankô kaihatsu to kôtsû' [Tourism development and transport], *Chiri* 18(3): 57–63.

Aoki, E., and J. Yamamura. 1976. 'Nihon ni okeru kankô chirigaku kenkyû no keifu' [A genealogy of tourism geography research in Japan], *Human Geography* 28: 57–80.

Arahi, Y. 2008. 'The Development of Green Tourism Study in Japan', *Annual Bulletin of Rural Studies* 43: 7–42.

Arayama, M. 1995. 'Authenticity of Cultures and the Establishment of National Parks: Geographical Problematics of Tourism', *Geographical Review of Japan* 68A(12): 792–810.

———. 1998. 'Shizen no fûkeichi e no manazashi' [The gaze on natural landscapes], in M. Arayama and N. Ôshiro (eds), *Kûkan kara basho e* [From space to place]. Tokyo: Kokon Shôin, pp. 128–41.

Asahi Shinbunsha (ed.). 1987. *Shûkan Asahi Hyakka. Nihon no rekishi. Tabi: shinkô kara monomi yusan e* [Weekly Asahi Encyclopedia. Japanese history. Travel: from religious activity to sightseeing]. Tokyo: Asahi Shinbunsha.

Asaka, Y., and J. Yamamura (eds). 1974. *Kankôchirigaku* [Tourism geography]. Tokyo: Daimeidô.

Asamizu, M. 1998. 'Kankyô, senjumin, kokusaika: 1990 nendai ôsutoraria ni okeru kankô seisaku' [Environment, indigenous people and globalization: Australia's tourism policy in the 1990s], *Ôsutoraria Kenkyû Kiyô* 24: 227–38.

———. 2005. *World Travel and Japanese Tourists*. Tokyo: Gakubunsha.

———. 2007. 'Tourism Trends in Japan', in M. Asamizu (ed.), *Human Mobility in Asia Pacific*. Tokyo: Sakuta, pp. 100–35.

Asano, T., et al. 2009. 'Reintroduction Project of the Oriental White Stork and Tourism: A Survey of Visitors' Attitudes', *Studies in Environmental Science* (Bulletin of the Graduate School of Integrated Arts and Sciences, Hiroshima University, II) 4: 35–50.

Ashiba, Y. 1994. *Shin kankôgaku gairon* [A new outline of tourism studies]. Kyoto: Mineruva Shobô.

Befu, H. 2000. 'Globalization as Human Dispersal: From the Perspective of Japan', in J. Eades et al. (eds), *Globalization and Social Change in Contemporary Japan*. Melbourne: Trans-Pacific Press.

Bestor, T.C. 2004. *Tsukiji: The Fish Market at the Center of the World*. Berkeley: University of California Press.

Biao, Y. 2005. 'Historical Memory in Australia and Japan', in S. Alomes (ed.), *Islands in the Stream: Australia and Japan Face Globalisation*. Hawthorn: Maribyrnong Press, pp. 115–24.

Bird, I.L. 1888. *Unbeaten Tracks in Japan*. London: John Murray.

Bisignani, G. 2005. 'We Remain a Strange but Wonderful Industry', unpublished speech delivered at the Foreign Correspondent's Club of Japan, Tokyo, 12 April 2005. Retrieved 7 December 2005 from: http://www.iata.org/pressroom/speeches/2005-04-12-01.htm.

Blacker, C. 1986. *The Catalpa Bow: A Study of Shamanistic Practices in Japan*. London: Allen and Unwin.

Blanke, J.W., and I. Mia. 2007. 'Global Competitiveness Report 2007'. Retrieved 12 March 2010 from: http://www.weforum.org.gcr28.09.2007.

Bolkus, N. 1991. 'Answer Given by the Minister Representing the Minister for Immigration, Local Government and Ethnic Affairs to a Question Regarding the Holiday Worker Program: 18 Feb 1991', in *Parliamentary Debates (Hansard) Senate*, Parl. 36, Sess.1, Per. 3: 688.

Bornoff, N. 1991. *Pink Samurai: Love, Marriage and Sex in Contemporary Japan*. New York: Pocket Books.

Brabis, D., et al. 2007. *Guide Michelin Voyager Pratique: Japon*. Paris: Michelin.

Brannen, M.Y. 1992. 'Bwana Mickey: Constructing Cultural Consumption at Tokyo Disneyland', in J. Tobin (ed.), *Remade in Japan*. New Haven: Yale University Press.

Brown, P.C. 2009. 'Unification, Consolidation and Tokugawa Rule', in W.M. Tsutsui (ed.), *A Companion to Japanese History*. Chichester: Wiley-Blackwell, pp. 69–85.

Brumann, C., and R. Cox. 2010. *Making Japanese Heritage*. London: Routledge.

Buckley, R.C. 2004. *Environmental Impacts of Ecotourism*. Wallingford: CAB International.

Buhrs, T. 2000. 'The Environment and the Role of the State in New Zealand', in P. Ali Memon and H. Perkins (eds), *Environmental Planning and Management in New Zealand*. Palmerston North: Dunmore Press, pp. 27–35.

Buruma, I. 1994. *The Wages of Guilt: Memories of War in Germany and Japan*. New York: Farrar, Straus and Giroux.

Butler, R.W., and B. Mao. 1996. 'Conceptual and Theoretical Implications of Tourism between Partitioned States', *Asia Pacific Journal of Tourism Research* 1(1): 25–34.

Callies, D.L. 1994. 'Land Use Planning and Control in Japan', in P. Shapira et al. (eds), *Planning for Cities and Regions in Japan*. Liverpool: Liverpool University Press, pp. 59–69.

Carle, R. 2003. 'The Development and Social Impact of Heritage Tourism in Ogimachi', *Ritsumeikan Journal of Asia Pacific Studies* 12: 31–60.

Carlile, L.E. 1996. 'Economic Development and the Evolution of Japanese Overseas Tourism, 1964–1994', *Tourism Recreation Research* 21(1): 11–18.

Cha, S., et al. 1995. 'Travel Motivations of Japanese Overseas Travelers: A Factor-cluster Segmentation Approach', *Journal of Travel Research* 34(1): 33–39.

Chon, K.S., et al. 2000. *Japanese Tourists: Socio-economic, Marketing and Psychological Analysis.* New York: Haworth Press.

Chûgoku Shinbunsha (ed.). 1997. *Yunesuko sekai isan genbaku dômu* [UNESCO World Heritage A-bomb Dome]. Hiroshima: Chûgoku Shinbunsha.

Clammer, J. 1997. *Contemporary Urban Japan: A Sociology of Consumption.* Oxford: Blackwell.

———. 2000. 'Management of the Emotions in Contemporary Japan', in J. Eades et al. (eds), *Globalization and Social Change in Contemporary Japanese Society.* Melbourne: Trans-Pacific Press.

Cooper, M. 2000. 'Destination Vietnam', in C.M. Hall and S. Page (eds), *Tourism in South East Asia: Issues and Cases.* Oxford: Butterworth-Heinemann, pp. 167–77.

———. 2005. 'Japanese Outbound Tourism and the SARS Epidemic of 2003', in B. Prideaux and E. Laws (eds), *Tourism Crises: Management Responses and Theoretical Insight.* New York: Haworth Hospitality Press, pp. 117–32.

———. 2006. 'The Pacific War Battlefields: Tourist Attractions or War Memorials?' *International Journal of Tourism Research* 8(3): 213–22.

Cooper, M., and J.S. Eades. 2007. 'Landscape as Theme Park: Demographic Change, Tourism, Urbanization and the Fate of Communities in Twenty-first Century Japan', *Tourism Research International* 11(1): 9–18.

———. 2009. 'Migrating Capitals: Diverging Images of Tradition and Modernity in Japanese Urban Tourism', in B. Ritchie and R. Maitland (eds), *National Capital Tourism.* New York: CABI, pp. 50–61.

Cooper, M., and P. Erfurt. 2007. 'Tsunamis, Earthquakes, Volcanism and Other Problems: Disasters, Responses and Japanese Tourism', in E. Laws et al. (eds), *Crisis Management and Tourism.* Wallingford: CABI, pp. 234–51.

Cooper, M., and P. Erfurt-Cooper. 2009. 'Beppu Reconstruction: A Domestic Hot Spring Destination in Search of a Twenty-first Century Global Role', *Geographical Sciences* 64(3): 127–39.

Cooper, M., and M. Flehr. 2006. 'Government Intervention in Tourism Development: The Case of Japan and South Australia', *Current Issues in Tourism* 9(1): 69–85.

Cooper, M., and K. Vafadari. 2008. 'Non-institutionalized Working Tourists in Japan: The Case of Iranians in Tokyo as a Social Phenomenon of the Early 1990s', *International Journal of Tourism and Travel* 1: 7–12.

Cooper, M., et al. 2007. 'The Politics of Exclusion? Japanese Cultural Reactions and the Government's Desire to Double Inbound Tourism', in P. Burns and M. Novelli (eds), *Tourism and Politics: Global Frameworks and Local Realities.* London: Elsevier, pp. 71–82.

———. 2008. 'Heritage Tourism in Japan: A Synthesis and Comment', in B. Prideaux et al. (eds), *Culture and Heritage Tourism in the Asia Pacific.* London: Routledge, pp. 107–17.

Coulmas, F., et al. (eds). 2008. *The Demographic Challenge: A Handbook about Japan.* Leiden: Brill.

D'Amore, L. 1989. 'Tourism: The World's Peace Industry', *Annals of Tourism Research* 27: 35–40.

Douglas, N., et al. (eds). 2001. *Special-interest Tourism: Context and Cases.* Milton, Qld: Wiley Australia.

Douglass, M. 2000. 'The Singularities of International Migration of Women to Japan: Past, Present and Future', in M. Douglass and G. Roberts (eds), *Japan and Global Migration.* London: Routledge, pp. 91–119.

Douglass, M., and G. Roberts. 2000. 'Japan in a Global Age of Migration', in M. Douglass and G. Roberts (eds), *Japan and Global Migration*. London: Routledge, pp. 3–37.

Dower, J. 1979. *Empire and Aftermath*. Cambridge, MA: Harvard East Asian Monographs.

Dredge, D. 2001. 'Local Government Tourism Planning and Policy-making in New South Wales: Institutional Development and Historical Legacies', *Current Issues in Tourism* 4(2–4): 355–80.

Eades, J.S. 2007. 'Sex Tourism and the Internet: Information, Amplification, and Moral Panics', in W. Pease, M. Rowe and M. Cooper (eds), *Information and Communication Technologies in Support of the Tourism Industry*. Hershey: Idea Group, pp. 260–85.

Eades, J.S., and S. Yamashita. 2003. *Globalization and Culture in Southeast Asia*. Oxford: Berghahn.

Eades, J.S., et al. (eds). 2000. *Globalization and Social Change in Contemporary Japan*. Melbourne: Trans-Pacific Press.

Eguchi, N. 2005. *Sôgôteki genshô toshite no kankô* [Tourism as an integrated phenomenon]. Kyoto: Shôyô Shôbo.

Erfurt-Cooper, P., and M. Cooper. 2009. *Health and Wellness Spa Tourism*. London: Channel View Press.

Euromonitor. 2005. 'Travel and Tourism in Japan – Executive Summary: Growing Business over the Internet'. Retrieved 7 December 2005 from: http://www.euromonitor.com/Travel_and_Tourism_in_Japan#toc.

Faier, L. 2009. *Intimate Encounters: Filipina Women and the Remaking of Rural Japan*. Berkeley: University of California Press.

Faulkner, W. 2001. 'Towards a Framework for Tourism Disaster Management', *Tourism Management* 22: 135–47.

Fawcett, C. 1995. 'Nationalism and Postwar Japanese Archeology', in P.L. Kohl and C. Fawcett (eds), *Nationalism, Politics and the Practice of Archeology*. Cambridge: Cambridge University Press, pp. 232–48.

———. 1996. 'Archaeology and Japanese Identity', in D. Denoon et al. (eds), *Multicultural Japan*. Cambridge: Cambridge University Press, pp. 60–77.

Fichtner, U., and R. Michna. 1987. *Freizeitparks*. Freiburg: Selbstverlag des Verfassers.

Figal, G. 2012. *Beachheads: War, Peace, and Tourism in Postwar Okinawa*. Lanham, MD: Rowman and Littlefield.

Formanek, S. 1998. 'Pilgrimage in the Edo Period', in S. Linhart and S. Frühstück (eds), *The Culture of Japan as Seen through Its Leisure*. New York: State University of New York Press, pp. 165–93.

Fujii, S., et al. 2007. 'Inner-city Redevelopment in Tokyo', in A. Sorensen and C. Funck (eds), *Living Cities in Japan*. London: Routledge, pp. 247–66.

Fukuda, J. 2008. 'Naganoken Hakubamura: gaishi mane to inbaundo kyaku de sukîjô saisei ha naru ka?' [Nagano Prefecture Hakuba village: will foreign capital and inbound tourists contribute to ski resort reconstruction?], *Rejâ Sangyô Shiryô* 4(7): 156–61.

Funabiki, T. 1992. 'From Rice to Money: The Communal and the Social in Japan with Reference to a Village, Kurokawa', *Proceedings of the Department of Humanities, College of Arts and Sciences, University of Tokyo* 96(6): 47–66.

Funck, C. 1994. 'The Use of Tourism Statistics for Comparative Studies in Japan', *Kôbe Gakuin Daigaku Keizaigaku Ronshû* 25(3/4): 93–114.

———. 1999a. *Tourismus und Peripherie in Japan: Über das Potential Touristischer Entwicklung zum Ausgleich regionaler Disparitäten*. Bonn: Verlag Dieter Born.

———. 1999b. 'When the Bubble Burst: Planning and Reality in Japan's Resort Industry', *Current Issues in Tourism* 2(4): 333–53.

———. 2002. 'Tourismus an der japanischen Inlandsee', *Geographische Rundschau* 54(6): 44–49.

———. 2004. 'Diversifizierung im innerjapanischen Tourismus', *Petermanns Geographische Mitteilungen* 2004(5): 36–43.

———. 2006. 'Conflicts over Space for Marine Leisure: A Case Study of Recreational Boating in Japan', *Current Issues in Tourism* 9(4/5): 459–80.

———. 2007. 'Machizukuri, Civil Society, and the Transformation of Japanese City Planning', in A. Sorensen and C. Funck (eds), *Living Cities in Japan*. London: Routledge, pp. 137–56.

———. 2008. 'Ageing Tourists, Ageing Destinations: Tourism and Demographic Change in Japan', in F. Coulmas et al. (eds), *The Demographic Challenge: A Handbook about Japan*. Leiden: Brill, pp. 579–98.

———. 2012a. 'The Innovative Potential of Inbound Tourism in Japan for Destination Development – A Case Study of Hida Takayama', *Contemporary Japan* 24(2): 121–47.

———. 2012b. 'Erinnerungsstätten des Großen Hanshin-Awaji Erdbebens 1995', in H.-D. Quark and A. Steinecke (eds), *Dark Tourism*. Paderborn: Paderborn Selbstverlag des Faches Geographie Universität Paderborn, pp. 309–20.

Funck, C., et al. 2005. 'Hiroshima 60 Jahre danach: eine ganz normale Großstadt?' *Geographische Rundschau* 57(7/8): 56–64.

Garcia Dizon, J. 2006. 'Revisiting the ODA Phenomenon: What's Next for Filipino Migrant Workers to Japan?' *Ritsumeikan Journal of Asia Pacific Studies* 20: 69–84.

Garreau, J. 1991. *Edge City: Life on the New Frontier*. New York: Doubleday.

Gilman, T. 2001. *No Miracles Here: Fighting Urban Decline in Japan and the United States*. New York: State University of New York Press.

Glosserman, B. 2004. 'Fog of Politics Obscures War', *Japan Times*, 27 January, p. 19.

Graburn N. 1983. *To Pray, Pay and Play: The Cultural Structure of Japanese Domestic Tourism*. Aix en Provence: Centre des Hautes Études Touristiques.

———. 1995. 'The Past in the Present in Japan: Nostalgia and Neo-traditionalism in Contemporary Japanese Tourism', in R. Butler and D. Pearce (eds), *Change in Tourism: People, Places, Processes*. London: Routledge, pp. 47–70.

Guichard-Anguis, S. 2002. 'From Curing and Playing to Leisure: Two Japanese Hot Springs: Arima and Kinosaki Onsen', in J. Hendry and M. Raveri (eds), *Japan at Play*. London: Routledge, pp. 245–58.

———. 2009. 'Japanese Inns (*ryokan*) as Producers of Japanese Identity', in S. Guichard-Anguis and O. Moon (eds), *Japanese Tourism and Travel Culture*. London: Routledge, pp. 76–101.

Guichard-Anguis, S., and O. Moon (eds). 2009. *Japanese Tourism and Travel Culture*. London: Routledge.

Hall, C.M. 1997. *Tourism in the Pacific Rim*. Melbourne: Longman Australia.

———. 2000. *Tourism Planning: Policies, Processes and Relationships*. Harlow: Prentice Hall.

———. 2003. 'Spa and Health Tourism', in S. Hudson (ed.), *Sport and Adventure Tourism*. New York: Haworth Hospitality Press, pp. 273–92.

Hamada, T. 1999. 'Kinsei no kaiun to kôkai' [Maritime traffic and navigation in modern times], in Y. Shirahata (ed.), *Setonaikai no bunka to kankyô*. Kôbe: Kôbe Shuppan Sentâ, pp. 61–83.

Havens, T.R. 1994. *Architects of Affluence*. Cambridge, MA: Harvard University Press.

Hebbert, M. 1994. 'Sen-biki amidst Desakota: Urban Sprawl and Urban Planning in Japan', in P. Shapira et al. (eds), *Planning for Cities and Regions in Japan*. Liverpool: Liverpool University Press, pp. 70–92.

Hendry, J. 2009. 'Fantasy Travel in Time and Space: A New Japanese Phenomenon?' in S. Guichard-Anguis and O. Moon (eds), *Japanese Tourism and Travel Culture*. London: Routledge, pp. 129–44.

Hendry, J., and M. Raveri (eds). 2002. *Japan at Play*. London: Routledge.

Hiroshimashi. 2009. 'Heiwa kinen shiryôkan no nyûkanshato no gaikyô ni tsuite' [About the general situation of visitors to the Peace Memorial Museum]. Retrieved 31 March 2010 from: http://www.city.hiroshima.lg.jp/www/contents/0000000000000/1146017987771/index.html.

Hisada, M. 1992. *Firipina wo Aishita Otokotachi* [The men who loved Filipinas]. Tokyo: Bunshun Bunko.

Hohn, U. 2000. *Stadtplanung in Japan: Geschichte-Recht-Praxis-Theorie.* Dortmund: Dortmunder Vertrieb für Bau- und Planungsliteratur.

Hong, S., et al. 2003. 'Implications of Potential Green Tourism Development', *Annals of Tourism Research* 30(2): 323–41.

Horie, T. 2006. *Kankô to Kankô sangyô no genjô (Kaichôban)* [The situation of tourism and the tourism industry]. Tokyo: Bunka Shôbô Hakubunsha,

HTTJ. 2006. 'Hida Takayama zainichi gaikokujin monitâ ryokô jisshi hôkokusho' [Report on the monitor tour in Hida Takayama by foreign residents of Japan]. Takayama: Hida Takayamashi Tôkyô Jimushô.

Hyôgoken. Yearly. 'Hyôgoken kankô dôtai chôsa hôkokusho' [Hyôgo prefecture report on the survey on tourist dynamics]. Kôbe: Hyôgoken.

Ike, S. 2006. *Sonraku kyoyû kûkan no kankôteki riyô* [Touristic uses of common spaces in rural communities]. Tokyo: Kazama Shobô.

Imai S., et al. 2004. *Kankô gairon* [An outline of tourism]. Tôkyô: JHRS.

IPSS. 2006. 'Population Projections for Japan: 2006–2055', National Institute of Population and Social Security Research. Retrieved 4 February 2013 from: http://www.ipss.go.jp/site-ad/index_english/population-e.html.

Ishii, H. 1980. 'The Formation of Minshuku Regions in Japan', *Tsukuba Studies in Human Geography* 4: 115–50.

———. 1982. 'Distribution of Major Recreational Areas in Japan', *Frankfurter Wirtschafts und Sozialgeographische Schriften* 41: 187–201.

Ishii, H., and S. Shirasaka. 1988. 'Recent Studies on Recreational Geography in Japan', *Geographical Review* (Series B) 6(1): 141–49.

Ishimori, S. 1989. 'Popularization and Commercialization of Tourism in Early Modern Japan', *Senri Ethnological Studies* 29: 179–94.

Iverson, T.J. 1997. 'Japanese Visitors to Guam: Lessons from Experience', *Journal of Travel and Tourism Marketing* 6(1): 41–54.

Iwabana, M. 1987. 'Sangaku shinkô no tabi [Travel in mountain religions]', in Asahi Shinbunsha (ed.), *Shûkan Asahi Hyakka. Nihon no rekishi. Tabi: shinkô kara monomi yusan e* [Weekly Asahi Encyclopedia. Japanese history. Travel: from religious activity to sightseeing]. Tokyo: Asahi Shinbunsha, pp. 268–75.

Iwashita, C. 2003. 'Media Construction of Britain as a Destination for Japanese Tourists: Social Constructionism and Tourism', *Tourism and Hospitality Research* 4(4): 331–40.

JATA. 2008. 'Jûyô ryokô gyôsha no ryokô toriatsukai jôkyô sokuhô' [Report about the handling of trips by leading travel agencies], Japan Association of Travel Agents. Retrieved 15 June 2009 from: http://www.jata-net.or.jp/tokei/001/1_1904_2003.htm.

JCO. 2005. 'Report on the Aging Society 2005', Japan Cabinet Office. Retrieved 19 March 2006 from: http://www8.cao.go.jp/kourei/english/annualreport/2005/05wp-e.html.

———. 2007. *Population Projections for Japan, Courses and Strategies for the Japanese Economy.* Tokyo: Japan Cabinet Office.

Jeffreys, E. 2004. *China, Sex and Prostitution.* London: Routledge.

JES. 2010. 'Ekotsûrizumu ni tsuite' [About ecotourism], Japan Ecotourism Society. Retrieved 31 March 2010 from: http://www.ecotourism.gr.jp/what/.

JNTO. 2005a. *Hônichi gaikokujin ryokôsha manzokudo chôsa hôkokusho* [Report on the satisfaction of foreign visitors to Japan]. Tokyo: International Tourism Center of Japan.

———. 2005b. *Sekai to nihon no kokusai kankô kôryû no dôkô* [Tendencies of international tourism worldwide and in Japan]. Tokyo: International Tourism Center of Japan.

———. 2006. *Hônichi ryokô yûchi handobukku* [Handbook for attracting foreign trips to Japan]. Tokyo: International Tourism Center of Japan.

———. 2008a. *Statistics on Tourism for Japan*. Tokyo: International Tourism Centre of Japan.

———. 2008b. *Kokusai kankô hakusho* [White Paper on international tourism]. Tokyo: International Tourism Center of Japan.

———. 2009. *Destination Survey of Overseas Visitors to Japan 2007/2008*. Tokyo: International Tourism Center of Japan.

———. 2013. '2012 nen 12 gatsu suikeichi' [Estimated figures, December 2012]. Retrieved 8 February 2013 from: http://www.jnto.go.jp/jpn/news/data_info_listing/index.html.

———. yearly a. 'Visitor Arrivals and Japanese Overseas Travellers'. Retrieved 31 March 2010 from: http://www.jnto.go.jp.

———. yearly b. 'Destination Survey of Overseas Visitors to Japan'. Tokyo: International Tourism Center of Japan.

Johnson, L. 1989. 'Have Yen, Will Travel: Japanese Youth on Working Holidays in Australia', *Bulletin*, 7 November, pp. 104–6.

JPCSED. 2007. *White Paper of Leisure 2007*. Tokyo: Japan Productivity Centre for Socio-economic Development.

JPM. 2009. 'Japanese Port Manual'. Retrieved 13 March 2010 from: http://www.japantravelinfo.com/ongoing/ports/.

JTA. 2013. 'The Tourism Nation Promotion Basic Plan'. Japan Tourism Agency, Retrieved 4 April 2013 from: http://www.mlit.go.jp/kankocho/en/kankorikkoku/kihonkeikaku.html.

JTB. 2000. 'Hanemûn dôkô chôsa 2000 haru' [Survey on trends in honeymoons, spring 2000], Japan Travel Bureau. Retrieved 31 March 2010 from: http://www.jtb.co.jp/koho/00/news09.html.

———. 2001. *JTB Report: All about Japanese Overseas Travelers*. Tokyo: Japan Travel Bureau.

———. 2003. *JTB Report 2003: All about Japanese Overseas Travellers*. Tokyo: Japan Travel Bureau.

JTBB. 1986. *Overview of Japanese Overseas Travel*. Tokyo: Japan Travel Blue Book.

Kaempfer, E. 1964[1777]. 'Geschichte und Beschreibung von Japan, Originalausgabe Lemgo 1777-1779', *Quellen und Forschungen zur Geschichte der Geographie und des Reisens*, 2. Stuttgart: Brockhaus.

Kanda, K. 2001. 'The Development Process of Nanki-Shirahama Spa Resort and Images of Other Places: A Consideration of the Production of Tourism Space in the Modern Period', *Human Geography* 53(5): 24–45.

Kanetaka, F., and C. Funck. 2012. 'The Development of the Tourism Industry in Yakushima and its Spatial Characteristics', *Studies in Environmental Science* (Bulletin of the Graduate School of Integrated Arts and Sciences, Hiroshima University, II) 6: 65–82.

Kanzaki, N. 1991. *Monomi yusan to nihonjin* [Sightseeing and the Japanese]. Tokyo: Kodansha Gendai Shinsho.

Kato, M., et al. 2003. 'A Study on the Actual Condition and Trend of the Activities and Organization of Voluntary Tour Guides by Local Residents', *Japanese Institute of Landscape Architecture* 66(5): 799–802.

Kelly, W.W. 1992. 'Finding a Place in Metropolitan Japan', in A. Gordon (ed.), *Postwar Japan as History*. Berkeley: University of California Press, pp. 189–238.

———. (ed.). 2004. *Fanning the Flames: Fans and Consumer Culture in Contemporary Japan*. Albany: State University of New York Press.

Kerr, A. 2001. *Dogs and Demons: Tales from the Dark Side of Japan*. New York: Hill and Wang.

Kibata, Y. 2005. 'Unfinished Decolonisation and Conflicts over Historical Memory', in S. Alomes (ed.), *Islands in the Stream: Australia and Japan Face Globalisation*. Hawthorn: Maribyrnong Press, pp. 103–14.

Kim, D.-Y., et al. 2005. 'Modeling Tourism Advertising Effectiveness', *Journal of Travel Research* 44(1): 42–49.

Kitamura, M., and A. Okamura. 2007. 'Gaishi ni yoru kankô fudôsan tôshi no kakudai to sore o katsuyô shita kankôchi shinkô' [The expanding foreign investment in tourism property and its application for regional development), *NRI Public Management Review* 43: 1–7.

KKS (ed.). 2007. *Airport Handbook*. Tokyo: Gekkan Dôyûsha, Kansai Kûkô Chôsakai.

Klamann, E. 1990. 'Can Mouse Ears Fit Steel Hats?' *Japan Economic Journal*, 28 April.

Klemers, D. 2011. 'Technologietransfer oder Import von Arbeitskräften? Politische und wirtschaftliche Dimensionen des Trainings und Praktikums für Ausländer in Japan 1982 bis 2010', in D. Chiavacci and I. Wieczorek (eds), *Japan 2011*. Berlin: Vereinigung für sozialwissenschaftliche Japanforschung e.V., pp. 147–85.

Knight, J. 1993. 'Rural Kokusaika? Foreign Motifs and Village Revival in Japan', *Japan Forum* 5(2): 203–16.

———. 1994. 'Town Making in Rural Japan: An Example from Wakayama', *Journal of Rural Studies* 10(3): 249–61.

———. 1998. 'Selling Mother's Love: Mail Order Village Food in Japan', *Journal of Material Culture* 3(2): 153–73.

———. 2003a. 'Repopulating the Village?', in J.W. Traphagen and J. Knight (eds), *Demographic Change in Japan's Aging Society*. Albany, NY: State University of New York Press, pp. 107–24.

———. 2003b. *Waiting for Wolves in Japan: An Anthropological Study of People–Wildlife Relations*. Oxford: Oxford University Press.

Knight, J., and J.W. Traphagen. 2003. 'The Study of the Family in Japan: Integrating Anthropological and Demographic Approaches', in J.W. Traphagen and J. Knight (eds), *Demographic Change in Japan's Aging Society*. Albany, NY: State University of New York Press, pp. 3–23.

Kobayashi, A., and T. Aikô. 2008. *Riyôsha no kôdô to taiken* [Visitor use and experience]. Tokyo: Kokon Shôin.

Kobayashi, H. 2003. 'Trends and Potential of the Japanese Outbound Travel Market', unpublished paper given at the Japan Association of Travel Agents World Tourism Congress, 2–3 October, Yokohama.

Kodama, K., and T. Toyoda (eds). 1970. *Kôtsûshi* [History of traffic]. Tokyo: Yamakawa Shuppansha.

Kômoto, K. 2004. 'Kintsû no shôsan: Kurabu tsûrizumu baikyaku to iu kake ni deta nambâ tsû kigyô no korekara', *Travel Journal* 41(19): 10–14.

Kono, M. 2008. *Consumption and Travel Trends for Japanese Youth in Their Twenties*, Parts 1 (April), 2 (May), 3 (June). Tokyo: JTM.

Kotler, P., and D. Gertner. 2004. 'Country as Brand, Product and Beyond: A Place Marketing and Brand Management Perspective', in N. Morgan et al. (eds), *Destination Branding: Creating the Unique Destination Proposition*. Oxford: Elsevier Butterworth-Heinemann.

Kremers, D. 2011. 'Technologietransfer oder Import von Arbeitskräften? Politische und wirtschaftliche Dimensionen des Trainings und Praktikums für Ausländer in Japan 1982 bis 2010', in D. Chiavacci and I. Wieczorek (eds), *Japan 2011. Politik, Wirtschaft und Gesellschaft*. Berlin: Vereinigung für sozialwissenschaftliche Japanforschung, pp. 147–85.

Kureha, M. 1995. *Wintersportgebiete in Japan und Österreich*. Innsbruck: Selbstverlag des Instituts für Geographie der Universität Innsbruck.

———. 2002. 'Regional Characteristics of Ski Population in Japan', *Tsukuba Studies in Human Geography* 26: 103–23.

———. 2009. 'Sukîjô no ritchi to sono hensen' [Location of ski slopes and their transition], in K. Kanda (ed.), *Rejâ no kûkan* [Spaces for leisure]. Kyoto: Nakanishiya Shuppan, pp. 38–47.

Le, A.T., and M. Cooper. 2009. 'Vietnam's Image as a Tourism Destination in Japan: An Analysis of Japanese Travel Guidebooks and Brochures, and Attribute Importance-Performance', *Ritsumeikan Journal of Asia Pacific Studies* 25: 37–54.

Leheny, D. 2003. *The Rules of Play: National Identity and the Shaping of Japanese Leisure.* Ithaca, NY: Cornell University Press.

Lennon, J., and M. Foley. 2000. *Dark Tourism: The Attraction of Death and Disaster.* London: Continuum.

Leupp, G. 1995. *Male Colors: The Construction of Homosexuality in Tokugawa Japan.* Berkeley: University of California Press.

Lie, J. 2000. 'The Discourse of Japaneseness', in M. Douglass and G. Roberts (eds), *Japan and Global Migration.* London: Routledge, pp. 70–90.

Linhart, S., and S. Frühstück. 1998. *The Culture of Japan as Seen through Its Leisure.* New York: State University of New York Press.

Liu-Farrer, G. 2009. 'Educationally Channeled International Labor Mobility: Contemporary Student Migration from China to Japan', *International Migration Review* 43(1): 178–204.

Lonely Planet. 2007. *Japan.* London: Lonely Planet Publications.

Lund, J.W. 2002. *Balneological Use of Geothermal Waters.* Oregon: Geo-Heat Center.

MAFF. 2012. 'Heisei 24 nendô nôgyô kôzô hendô chôsa kekka no gaiyô', Ministry of Agriculture, Forestry and Fisheries. Retrieved 9 February 2011 from: http://www.maff.go.jp/j/tokei/kouhyou/noukou/pdf/nougyou_kouzou_12.pdf.

McCormack, G. 1996. *The Emptiness of Japanese Affluence.* New York: Sphere.

McDonald, A., et al. 2009. 'Harvest Time in Satoyama', *OurWorld 2.0*, United Nations University. Retrieved 13 January 2009 from: http://ourworld.unu.edu/en/harvest-time-in-satoyama/.

McQueen, I. 1986. *Japan: A Travel Survival Kit.* South Yarra: Lonely Planet Publications.

Mak, J. 2004. *Tourism and the Economy: Understanding the Economics of Tourism.* Honolulu: University of Hawaii Press.

Mak, J., and K. White. 1992. 'Comparative Tourism Development in Asia and the Pacific', *Journal of Travel Research* 31: 14–23.

Mak, J., et al. 2004. 'Impact of Population Aging on Japanese International Travel to 2025', East–West Center Working Papers, Economic Series, No. 73. Honolulu: East-West Center.

———. 2005. 'Impact of Population Aging on Japanese International Travel', *Journal of Travel Research* 44: 151–62.

Makita, K. 2008. 'Kauntâ ni yoru riyôsha no haaku' [Catching users through counters], in A. Kobayashi and T. Aikô (eds), *Riyôsha no kôdô to taiken* [Visitor use and experience]. Tokyo: Kokon Shoin, pp. 59–71.

Maksay, A. 2007. 'Japanese Working Holiday Makers in Australia: Subculture and Resistance', *Tourism Review International* 11(1): 33–44.

Manzenreiter, W. 1995. *Leisure in Contemporary Japan.* Vienna: Universität Wien.

———. 2000. *Die soziale Konstruktion des japanischen Alpinismus.* Vienna: Universität Wien.

March, R. 2000. 'The Japanese Travel Life Cycle', in K.S. Chon et al. (eds), *Japanese Tourists: Socio-economic, Marketing and Psychological Analysis.* New York: Haworth Hospitality Press, pp. 185–200.

Martinez, D.L. 2004. *Identity and Ritual in a Japanese Diving Village: The Making and Becoming of Person and Place.* Honolulu: University of Hawai'i Press.

Mason, P., and S. Leberman. 2000. 'Local Planning for Recreation and Tourism: A Case Study of Mountain Biking from New Zealand's Manawatu Region', *Journal of Sustainable Tourism* 8(2): 97–115.

MHLW. 2006. 'White Paper on the Labour Economy 2005', Ministry of Health, Labour and Welfare. Retrieved 19 July 2006 from: http://www.mhlw.go.jp/wp/hakusyo/index.html.

———. yearly a. 'Shuro jôken sôgô chôsa kekka' [Results of the comprehensive survey of labour conditions], Ministry of Health, Labour and Welfare. Retrieved 4 February 2013 from: http://www.mhlw.go.jp/toukei/itiran/.

———. yearly b. 'Vital Statistics', Ministry of Health, Labour and Welfare. Retrieved 5 May 2009 from: http://www.mhlw.go.jp/english/database/db-hw/vs01.html.

———. yearly c. 'Report on Public Health Administration and Services', Ministry of Health, Labour and Welfare. Retrieved 5 May 2009 from: http://www.mhlw.go.jp/english/database/db-hw/vs01.html.

MIAC. 1996. *1996 Survey on Time Use and Leisure Activities*. Tokyo: Ministry of Internal Affairs and Communication Statistics Bureau.

———. 2000. '2000 Population Census of Japan 2006', Ministry of Internal Affairs and Communication Statistics Bureau. Retrieved 5 February 2013 from: http://www.stat.go.jp/english/data/kokusei/index.htm.

———. 2001. '2001 Survey on Time Use and Leisure Activities', Ministry of Internal Affairs and Communication Statistics Bureau. Retrieved 25 May 2006 from: http://www.stat.go.jp/english/data/shakai/2001/kodo/zenkoku/travel.htm.

———. 2005. '2005 Population Census of Japan', Ministry of Internal Affairs and Communication Statistics Bureau. Retrieved 5 February 2013 from: http://www.stat.go.jp/english/data/kokusei/index.htm.

———. 2006a. '2006 Survey on Time Use and Leisure Activities', Ministry of Internal Affairs and Communication Statistics Bureau. Retrieved 25 February 2009 from: http://www.stat.go.jp/english/data/shakai/2006/h18kekka.htm.

———. 2006b. 'Establishment and Enterprise Census of Japan 2006', Ministry of Internal Affairs and Communication Statistics Bureau. Retrieved 31 March 2010 from: http://www.stat.go.jp/data/jigyou/2006/index.htm.

———. n.y. 'Historical Statistics of Japan, Ch. 12 Transportation', Ministry of Internal Affairs and Communication Statistics Bureau. Retrieved 5 February 2013 from: http://www.stat.go.jp/english/data/chouki/12.htm.

Michelin. 2008. *Michelin Guide Tokyo: Restaurants & Hotels*. Tokyo: Michelin.

Milne, S., et al. 2002. 'New Zealand Residents and Japanese Tourists: Can the Internet Improve Relationships and Linkages?' in P. Morris (ed.), *Dynamics of Japanese Tourism in New Zealand*. Wellington: Asian Studies Institute, pp. 83–92.

Mimura, T. 2008. 'Japan's Travel Industry towards Productivity Improvement', monthly JTM report, August. Retrieved 9 December 2009 from: http://www.tourism.jp/english/report/2008/08/112088-2e.php.

MITI. 1974. *Leisure Development Industrial Office Policy Recommendations*. Tokyo: Ministry of International Trade and Industry.

Miyaki, M. 2008. 'Rural Women Who Carry Out Green Tourism', *Annual Bulletin of Rural Studies* 43: 96–126.

MLIT. 1987. *Annual Report of Transport Economy 1987*. Tokyo: Transport Policy Bureau, Ministry of Land, Infrastructure and Transport.

———. 1991. *Annual Report of Transport Economy 1991*. Tokyo: Transport Policy Bureau, Ministry of Land, Infrastructure and Transport.

———. 1994. *Annual Report of Transport Economy 1994*. Tokyo: Transport Policy Bureau, Ministry of Land, Infrastructure and Transport.

————. 1998. 'The Fifth Comprehensive National Development Plan: Grand Design for the Twenty-first Century', Ministry of Land, Infrastructure and Transport. Retrieved 19 July 2009 from: http://www.mlit.go.jp/kokudokeikaku/zs5-e/part1chap1.html.

————. 2002a. *White Paper on Tourism*. Tokyo: Ministry of Land, Infrastructure and Transport.

————. 2002b. *The Inbound Tourism Initiative of Japan*. Tokyo: Ministry of Land, Infrastructure and Transport.

————. 2004. *Gaikokijin kankôkyaku ni kakawaru tôkei jôhô no arikata ni kansuru kenkyû* [Research on the concept of statistic information on foreign tourists]. Tokyo: Policy Research Institute, Ministry of Land, Infrastructure and Transport.

————. 2006. *White Paper on Tourism*. Tokyo: Ministry of Land, Infrastructure and Transport.

————. 2007. *White Paper on Tourism*. Tokyo: Ministry of Land, Infrastructure and Transport.

————. 2008a. 'Overnight Trip Statistics Survey 2007', Ministry of Land, Infrastructure and Transport. Retrieved 6 December 2009 from: http://www.mlit.go.jp/kankocho/siryou/toukei/shukuhakutoukei.html.

————. 2008b. *White Paper on Tourism*. Tokyo: Ministry of Land, Infrastructure, Transport and Tourism.

————. 2009a. 'Japan Tourism Policy', Ministry of Land, Infrastructure, Transport and Tourism. Retrieved 20 January 2009 from: http://www.mlit.go.jp/sogoseisaku/kanko/english/overview.html.

————. 2009b. *White Paper on Tourism*. Tokyo: Ministry of Land, Infrastructure, Transport and Tourism.

————. 2010. 'Keikanryoku sanpô' [Three laws on landscape and greenery], Ministry of Land, Infrastructure, Transport and Tourism. Retrieved 4 March 2010 from: http://www.mlit.go.jp/crd/townscape/keikan/index.htm.

————. 2012. 'Tôkei jôhô' [Statistics information], Ministry of Land, Infrastructure, Transport and Tourism. Retrieved 1 March 2012 from: http://www.mlit.go.jp/kankocho/siryou/toukei/index.html.

MoE. 2013. 'State of Japan's Environment at a Glance: Natural Vegetation', Ministry of the Environment. Retrieved 8 February 2013 from: http://www.env.go.jp/en/nature/npr/forest/vege.html.

Moeran, B. 1997. *Folk Art Potters of Japan*. London: Curzon.

MoJ. 2006. 'Kongo no gaikokujin no ukeire ni kansuru kihonteki na kangaekata' [Basic stance on the admittance of foreigners in the future], Ministry of Justice. Retrieved 19 February 2006 from: http://www.moj.go.jp/NYUKAN/nyukan51-3.pdf.

————. 2008. '2008 Immigration Control Report', Ministry of Justice Immigration Bureau. Retrieved 19 February 2009 from: http://www.moj.go.jp/NYUKAN/nyukan80.html.

————. 2009. 'Permission for Permanent Residence', Ministry of Justice Immigration Bureau. Retrieved 3 February 2009 from http://www.immi-moj.go.jp/english/tetuduki/index.html.

————. 2010. *2010 Immigration Control Report*. Retrieved 26 May 2012, from: http://www.moj.go.jp/nyuukokukanri/kouhou/nyuukokukanri01_00015.html.

Moon, O. 1989. *From Paddy Field to Ski Slope: The Revitalization of Tradition in Japanese Village Life*. Manchester: Manchester University Press.

————. 1997. 'Tourism and Cultural Development: Japanese and Korean Contexts', in S. Yamashita et al. (eds), *Tourism and Cultural Development in Asia and Oceania*. Bangi, Malaysia: Penerbit UKM, pp. 178–94.

————. 2002. 'The Countryside Reinvented for Urban Tourists: Rural Transformation in the Japanese Muraokoshi Movement', in J. Hendry and M. Raveri (eds), *Japan at Play*. London: Routledge, pp. 228–44.

Mouer, R., and Y. Sugimoto. 1995. 'Nihonjinron at the End of the Twentieth Century: A Multicultural Perspective', in J.P. Arnason and Y. Sugimoto (eds), *Japanese Encounters with Postmodernity*. London: Kegan Paul International, pp. 237–69.

Muraoka, M. 1981. *Nihon no hoteru shoshi* [A short history of Japan's hotels]. Tokyo: Chûkôshinsho.

Nakai, T. 2002. 'Ecotourism on the Local Level: Attempts and Problems on the Ogasawara Islands', *Geographical Sciences* 57(3): 187–93.

Nakamura, K. 2010. 'The Satoyama and Satoumi Initiatives for the Conservation of Biodiversity and the Reactivation of Rural Areas in Japan: The Case of the Noto Peninsula', *Asia Pacific World* 1(1): 29–36.

NCS. 2008. *Naraken kankôkyaku dôtai chôsa hôkokusho Heisei 19 nen* [Nara Prefecture report on the survey on tourist dynamics in 2007]. Nara: Naraken Chiiki Shinkôbu.

NDKSK. 2003. 'Jiyûjikan to kankô ni kansuru seron chôsa' [Survey on free time and tourism], Naikakufu Daijin Kanbô Seifu Kôkokushitsu. Retrieved 20 February 2010 from: http://www8.cao.go.jp/survey/h15/h15-jiyujikan/index.html.

Nihon Kôtsû Kôsha. 2006. *Ryokôsha dôkô 2006* [Travellers trends 2006]. Tokyo: Nihon Kôtsû Kôsha.

———. 2007. *Ryokôsha dôkô 2007* [Travellers trends 2007]. Tokyo: Nihon Kôtsû Kôsha.

NIPSS . 2002. *Population Projections for Japan: 2001–2100*. Tokyo: National Institute of Population and Social Security.

Nishigaki, H. 1987. 'Isemairi' [Pilgrimage to Ise], in Asahi Shinbunsha (ed.), *Shûkan Asahi Hyakka. Nihon no rekishi. Tabi: shinkô kara monomi yusan e* [Weekly Asahi Encyclopedia. Japanese history. Travel: from religious activity to sightseeing]. Tokyo: Asahi Shinbunsha, pp. 260–65.

NKK. 1995. *Kankô jiten* [Tourism dictionary]. Tokyo: Nihon Kankô Kyôkai.

———. 2004. *Kankô no jittai to shikô* [Situation and tendency of tourism]. Tokyo: Nihon Kankô Kyôkai.

———. 2005. *Kankô no jittai to shikô* [Situation and tendency of tourism]. Tokyo: Nihon Kankô Kyôkai.

———. 2009. *Kankô no jittai to shikô* [Situation and tendency of tourism]. Tokyo: Nihon Kankô Kyôkai.

———. yearly a. *Zenkoku kankô dôkô* [National tourism trends]. Tokyo: Nihon Kankô Kyôkai.

———. yearly b. *Kankô no jittai to shikô* [Situation and tendency of tourism]. Tokyo: Nihon Kankô Kyôkai.

NKSKK. 2003. 'Certificated Ships and Inspection Records', Nihon Kogata Senpaku Kensa Kikô (Japan Craft Inspection Organization). Retrieved 12 April 2004 from: http://www.jci.go.jp/index.htm.

NSRK. 2005. 'Shûgaku ryokô no subete 2005' [All about school trips 2005]. Tokyo: Nihon Shûgaku Ryokô Kyôkai.

———. 2007. 'Kyôiku ryokô hakusho 2007' [White book on school trips 2007]. Tokyo: Nihon Shûgaku Ryokô Kyôkai.

Oedewald, M. 2009. 'Meanings of Tradition in Contemporary Japanese Domestic Tourism', in S. Guichard-Anguis and O. Moon (eds), *Japanese Tourism and Travel Culture*. London: Routledge, pp. 105–28.

Oguchi, C. 1985. 'Sea Bathing and the Process of its Acceptance in the Late Nineteenth Century in Japan', *Human Geography* 37(3): 23–37.

Okamoto, N. 2001. *Kankôgaku nyûmon* [Introduction to tourism]. Tokyo: Arma.

Okata, J. 1999. 'Land Use Control Type Machizukuri Ordinances', in S. Kobayashi (ed.), *Local Community Building Ordinances in the Era of Local Rights*. Kyoto: Gakugei Shuppansha, pp. 111–49.

Onodera, J. 1987. 'Tabi no moderu rûto' [Model routes for travel], in Asahi Shinbunsha (ed.), *Shûkan Asahi Hyakka. Nihon no rekishi. Tabi: shinkô kara monomi yusan e* [Weekly Asahi Encyclopedia. Japanese History. Travel: from religious activity to sightseeing]. Tokyo: Asahi Shinbunsha, pp. 274–80.

Ponting, H.G. 1910. *In Lotus Land Japan*. London: Macmillan.

PSR. 2008. 'Phoenix Seagaia Resort'. Retrieved 6 June 2009 from: http://www.seagaia.co.jp/english/guidance/news/20070807.html.

Raz, A.E. 2002. 'Japan at Play in TDL', in J. Hendry and M. Raveri (eds), *Japan at Play*. London: Routledge, pp. 285–99.

Reisinger, Y., and L.W. Turner. 2003. *Cross-cultural Behaviour in Tourism: Concepts and Analysis*. Oxford: Butterworth Heinemann.

Richardson, B. 1994. 'Crisis Management and Management Strategy: Time to "Loop the Loop"?' *Disaster Prevention and Management* 3(3): 59–80.

Rimmer, P.J. 1992. 'Japan's "Resort Archipelago": Creating Regions of Fun, Pleasure, Relaxation, and Recreation', *Environment and Planning A* 24: 1599–625.

Roberts, G.S. 2008. 'Immigration Policy: Framework and Challenges', in F. Coulmas et al. (eds), *The Demographic Challenge: A Handbook about Japan*. Leiden: Brill, pp. 765–80.

Robertson, J. 1995. 'Hegemonic Nostalgia, Tourism and Nation-making in Japan', *Senri Ethnological Studies* 38: 89–103.

Ryan, C. 2007. *Battlefield Tourism: History, Place and Interpretation*. Amsterdam: Elsevier.

Ryang, S., and J. Lie. 2009. *Diaspora without Homeland: Being Korean in Japan*. Berkeley: University of California Press.

Sakai, M., et al. 2000. 'Population Aging and Japanese International Travel in the Twenty-first Century', *Journal of Travel Research* 38(3): 212–20.

Sakakibara, F. 2003. 'The Trend of Middle and Elderly Market in Japan', unpublished paper given at the Japan Association of Travel Agents' World Tourism Congress, 2–3 October, Yokohama.

Satô, D. 2003. 'Diffusion of Yachts and Change of Their Acceptance in Modern Japan', *Geographical Review of Japan* 76(8): 599–615.

Satô, D., and I. Saitô. 2004. 'Formation Process of Hill Stations and Changes of Landowners in Modern Karuizawa', *Rekishichirigaku* 46(3): 1–19.

Satô, M. 1990. *Rizôto rettô* [Resort archipelago]. Tokyo: Iwanami Shinsho.

Schäfer, S., and C. Funck. 2012. 'Der Atombombentourismus und der "Hiroshima Friedensgedächtnispark"', in H.D. Quark and A. Steinecke (eds), *Dark Tourism*. Paderborn: Selbstverlag des Faches Geographie Universität Paderborn, pp. 291–308.

Schöller, P. 1980. 'Tradition und Moderne im innerjapanischen Tourismus', *Erdkunde* 34(2): 134–50.

Schumann, F. 2006. 'Changing Trends in Japanese Overseas Travel: Implications for Guam as a Resort Destination', *Ritsumeikan Journal of Asia Pacific Studies* 21: 125–49.

Seaton, A.V., and M.M. Bennett. 1996. *The Marketing of Tourism Products: Concepts, Issues and Cases*. London: International Thompson Business Press.

Seigle, C.S. 1993. *Yoshiwara: The Glittering World of the Japanese Courtesan*. Honolulu: University of Hawaii Press.

Shapira, P. 1994. 'Industrial Restructuring and Economic Development Strategies in a Japanese Steel Town: The Case of Kitakyushu', in P. Shapira et al. (eds), *Planning for Cities and Regions in Japan*. Liverpool: Liverpool University Press, pp. 155–83.

Shimoura, S., et al. 2006. 'A Case Study of the Influence of Rural Tourism on Farm Village Endogenous Development', *Shoku to Midori no Kagaku* 60: 67–73.

Shinjô, T. 1971. *Shomin to tabi no rekishi* [History of common people and travel]. Tokyo: Nihon Hôsô Shuppan Kyôkai.

Shirahata, Y. 1996. *Ryokô no susume* [Travel suggestions]. Tokyo: Chûô Kôronsha.

Shiratsuka, S. 2003. 'Asset Price Bubble in Japan in the 1980s: Lessons for Financial and Macroeconomic Stability', IMES Discussion Paper No.2003-E-15. Tokyo: IMES.

Shono, S., et al. 2005. 'The Changing Gaze of Japanese Tourists', *Tourism Review International* 9(3): 237–46.

Siddle, R., and B. Hook (eds). 2003. *Japan and Okinawa: Structure and Subjectivity*. New York: Routledge.

Siebold, P.F. von. 1897. *Nippon: Archiv zur Beschreibung von Japan*. Würzburg/Leipzig: Leo Woerl.

SJS. 2002. *Statistical Data of Leisure and Resort 2002*. Tokyo: Seikatsu Jôhô Sentâ.

———. yearly. *Zenkoku kankôchi kankôkyaku dêtabukku* [Databook of tourists and tourist resorts in Japan]. Tokyo: Seikatsu Jôhô Sentâ.

SKSH. 2008. *Rejâ hakushô* [White book on leisure]. Tokyo: Shakai Keizai Seisansei Honbu.

———. yearly. *Rejâ hakushô* [White book on leisure]. Tokyo: Shakai Keizai Seisansei Honbu.

Slattery, L. 'Man Over Board: What an Australian Surfing Odyssey Means to Japanese Dreamers', *Weekend Australian* (Review Section), 8–9 January, pp. 5–7.

Sorensen, A. 2002. *The Making of Urban Japan*. London: Routledge.

Sorensen, A., and C. Funck (eds). 2007. *Living Cities in Japan*. London: Routledge.

Soshiroda, A. 2005. 'Inbound Tourism Policies in Japan from 1859 to 2003', *Annals of Tourism Research* 32(4): 1100–20.

SRI [Sanro Research Institute]. 1999. 'Shain ryokô no jittai 1999' [The situation of company trips 1999], *Kigyô Fukushi* 503: 5–36.

———. 2004. 'Shain ryokô no jittai ni kansuru chôsa 2004' [Survey of the situation of company trips 2004], *Ryômu Jijô* 1055: 4–21.

Stevens, R.P. 1979. *Kanazawa: The Other Side of Japan*. Kanazawa: Society to Introduce Kanazawa to the World.

Sudô, H. 2009. 'Nihonjin no hawai imêji to kankô patân no henyô' [Changes of the Japanese image of Hawaii and travel patterns], in K. Kanda (ed.), *Rejâ no kûkan* [Spaces for leisure]. Kyoto: Nakanishiya Shuppan, pp. 221–33.

Sunamoto, F. 2009. 'Kokusai rizôto no seibi to kokusai kankô rûto no keisei' [The construction of international resorts and the development of international tourism routes], in K. Kanda (ed.), *Rejâ no kûkan* [Spaces for leisure]. Kyoto: Nakanishiya Shuppan, pp. 202–10.

Sutherland, M., and D. Britton. 1980. *National Parks of Japan*. Tokyo: Kodansha.

Suzuki, S., and M. Kobuchi. 1991. *Rizôto no sôgôteki kenkyû* [Comprehensive research on resorts]. Kyoto: Shôyô Shobô.

Suzuki, Y. 1967. 'Tourism in Japan', in J. Beckel and H. Lecjleitner (eds), *Festschrift Leopold Scheidl zum 60*. Vienna: Geburtstag II. Teil, pp. 204–15.

Takada, M. 1995. 'The City and Its Model: A Civilization's Mechanism for Self-expression as the Object of Tourism', *Senri Ethnological Studies* 38: 105–24.

Takahashi, Y. 2004. 'Kinsei no onsen shiryô ni miru sôron' [Conflicts that can be detected in documents about early modern hot springs], *Tôhoku Bunka Kenkyûshitsu Kiyô* 46: 15–50.

Takai-Tokunaga, N. 2007. 'The Dialectics of Japanese Overseas Tourists: Transformation in Holiday Making', *Tourism Review International* 11(1): 67–83.

Takano, Y. 1994. 'Rizôtohô daiichigo shitei miyazakiken shîgaia' [Miyazaki Prefecture Seagaia: first designated under the Resort Law], *Sangyô Ritchi* 33(1): 46–55.

Takayamashi. 2010. 'Takayamashi kankô jôhô' [Tourist information on Takayama City]. Retrieved 31 March 2010 from: http://www.hida.jp/.

Takeuchi, K. 1984. 'Some Remarks on the Geography of Tourism in Japan', *Geo Journal* 9(1): 85–90.

Talmadge, E. 2004. 'Echoes of War Haunt Iwojima', *Japan Times*, 18 March, p. 3.

Tanaka, T. 1987. 'Saikoku junrei to saikoku henro' [Pilgrims and pilgrimage to the western temples), in Asahi Shinbunsha (ed.), *Shûkan Asahi Hyakka. Nihon no rekishi. Tabi: shinkô kara monomi yusan e* [Weekly Asahi Encyclopedia. Japanese history. Travel: from religious activity to sightseeing]. Tokyo: Asahi Shinbunsha, pp. 276–78.

Tanno, A. 1998. *Kankô chiiki no keisei to gendaiteki kadai* [The development of tourist regions and their current problems]. Tokyo: Kokon Shôin.

———. 2004. *Urban Tourism*. Tokyo: Kokon Shôin.

Tanno, A., and T. Tanaka. 1993. *Tabi no echûdo* [Studies on travel]. Kyoto: Shôwadô.

Thompson, C.S. 2003. 'Depopulation in Rural Japan: "Population Politics" in Towa-cho', in J.W. Traphagen and J. Knight (eds), *Demographic Change in Japan's Aging Society*. Albany, NY: State University of New York Press, pp. 89–106.

———. 2008. 'Population Decline, Municipal Amalgamation and the Politics of Folk Performance Preservation in Northeast Japan', in F. Coulmas et al. (eds), *The Demographic Challenge: A Handbook about Japan*. Leiden: Brill, pp. 361–86.

Tokuhisa, T. 1980. 'Tourism within, from and to Japan', *International Social Science Journal* 32(1): 125–50.

Tosun, C., and D.J. Timothy. 2003. 'Arguments for Community Participation in the Tourism Development Process', *Journal of Tourism Studies* 14(2): 2–15.

Traphagen, J.W. 1998. 'Emic Weeds or Etic Wild Flowers? Structuring "The Environment" in a Japanese Town', in K. Aoyagi et al. (eds), *Towards Sustainable Cities*. Leiden: University of Leiden Development Studies, pp. 37–52.

———. 2000. *Taming Oblivion: Aging Bodies and the Fear of Senility in Japan*. Albany, NY: State University of New York Press.

———. 2003. 'Demographic Change in Japan's Aging Society', in J.W. Traphagen and J. Knight (eds), *Demographic Change in Japan's Aging Society*. Albany, NY: State University of New York Press, pp. 89–106.

Treuren, G., and D. Lane. 2003. 'The Tourism Planning Process in the Context of Organized Interests, Industry Structure, State Capacity, Accumulation and Sustainability', *Current Issues in Tourism* 6(1): 1–22.

Tsuchida, Y., and F. Hanyu. 2006. 'The Transition of Residents' Opinions about Tourism-based Community Development in Articles on Local Newspaper Takayama Shimin Jiho', *Journal of the City Planning Institute of Japan* 41(3): 439–44.

Tsuji, K. 2007. 'Kanazawa no kokusai kôryû no rekishi to genjô' [History and present situation of international exchange in Kanazawa], in T. Kawahara and H. Noyama (eds), *Gaikokujin jûmin he no gengô sâbisu* [Language services for foreign residents]. Tokyo: Akashi Shoten, pp. 122–45.

Tsuruta, E. 1994. 'Current Trends in Japanese Tourism Geography and the Post Resort-Boom Era', *Human Geography* 46(1): 66–84.

Turner, L., and J. Ash. 1975. *The Golden Hordes: International Tourism and the Pleasure Periphery*. London: Constable.

UNWTO. 2009. *World Tourism Barometer 2009*. Madrid: UNWTO.

Urry, J. 1990. *The Tourist Gaze*. London: Sage.

Uyama, M., and T. Urade. 2002. 'Effects and Problems of Green Tourism in Asuka Village', *Memoirs of the Faculty of Agriculture of Kinki University* 35: 31–41.

Vafadari, K., and M.J. Cooper. 2007. 'Japan–Iran Tourism Relations: Opportunities and Limitations in Promoting Iran's Cultural and Heritage Tourism in the Japanese Market', *Ritsumeikan Journal of Asia Pacific Studies* 23: 75–88.

Vaporis, C. 1995. 'The Early Modern Origins of Japanese Tourism', *Senri Ethnological Studies* 38: 25–39.

Vergin, R. 1985. *The Land of Iyo*. Matsuyama: Aoba Tosho.

Wakuda, Y. 1981. *Nihon no Shitetsu* [Japan's private railways]. Tokyo: Iwanami Shinsho.

Weaver, D., and L. Lawton. 2002. *Tourism Management*. Milton Keynes: Wiley.

Witherick, M., and M. Carr. 1993. *The Changing Face of Japan: A Geographical Perspective*. Sevenoaks: Hodder and Stoughton.

Witt, S.F., and L. Moutinho. 1995. *Tourism Marketing and Management Handbook*. London: Prentice Hall.

Wolferen, K. von. 1989. *The Enigma of Japanese Power: People and Politics in a Stateless Nation*. London: Macmillan.

Wood, C. 2005. *The Bubble Economy: Japan's Extraordinary Speculative Boom of the 1980s and the Dramatic Bust of the 1990s*. New York: Solstice Publishing.

Yakushimachô. 2008. *Gyôsei shisatsu shiryô* [Material for administrative visits]. Yakushima: Yakushimachô.

———. n.y. *Yakushima nendô betsu irikomi kyakusû* [Visitor numbers to Yakushima]. Yakushima: Yakushimachô.

Yamamoto, D., and A.W. Gill. 1999. 'Emerging Trends in Japanese Package Tourism', *Journal of Travel Research* 38(2): 134–52.

Yamamoto, E. 2004. 'Nihon kinsei onsenshi kenkyû no genjô to kadai: kankô to chiiki no shiten kara' [Problems and situation of research on Japanese onsen history in early modern times: from the viewpoint of tourism and regions], *Minshûshi Kenkyû* 67: 23–28.

Yamamura, J. 1982. 'The Course of Development of Tourism and Recreation in Japan', *Frankfurter Wirtschafts- und Sozialgeographische Schriften* 41: 175–86.

———. 1990. *Kankô chiiki ron* [Theory of tourism areas]. Tôkyô: Kokon Shôin.

———. 1995. *Shin kankô chirigaku* [New tourism geography]. Tôkyô: Kokon Shôin.

———. 1998 *Nihon no onsenchi* [Japan's spas]. Tôkyô: Nihon Onsen Kyôkai.

Yamamura, T. 2009. 'Kankô jôhô kakumei to bunka sôshutsugata kankô no kanôsei: anime seichi junrei ni miru jisedai tsûrizumu no hôga' [The revolution of tourism information and possibilities of creative cultural tourism], *Chiikikaihatsu* 533: 32–36.

Yamashita, S. 2003. *Bali and Beyond: Explorations in the Anthropology of Tourism*, trans. J.S. Eades. Oxford: Berghahn.

Yamori, K. 1987. 'Nichijô kara no dassô' [Escaping daily life], in Asahi Shinbunsha (ed.), *Shûkan Asahi Hyakka. Nihon no rekishi. Tabi: shinkô kara monomi yusan e* [Weekly Asahi Encyclopedia. Japanese history. Travel: from religious activity to sightseeing]. Tokyo: Asahi Shinbunsha, pp. 266–73.

Yanagida, K. (ed.). 1957. *Japanese Manners and Customs in the Meiji Era*, trans. C.S. Terry. Tokyo: Ôbunsha.

Yanagita, K. 2008[1910]. *The Legends of Tono*, trans. R.A. Morse. Lanham, MD: Lexington Books.

Yasumura, K. 2001. *Kankô: shinjidai wo tsukuru shakai genshô* [Tourism: a social phenomena creating a new age]. Tokyo: Gakubunsha.

YKS. 1994. *Rejâ hakushô* [White book on leisure]. Tokyo: Yoka Kaihatsu Sentâ.

———. yearly. *Rejâ hakushô* [White book on leisure]. Tokyo: Yoka Kaihatsu Sentâ.

Yokoyama, H. 1998. 'Waga kuni ni okeru gurîn tsûrizumu no tenkai to sono kadai: yôroppa to no hikaku kentô' [The development of green tourism in our country and its problems: a comparison with Europe], *Kyûshû Sangyô Daigaku Sankei Ronshû* 39(1): 81–97.

Yoneyama, L. 1999. *Hiroshima Traces: Time, Space, and the Dialectics of Memory*. Berkeley: University of California Press.

Yoo, J., and D. Sohn. 2003. 'The Structure and Meanings of Intercultural Interactions of International Tourists', *Journal of Travel and Tourism Marketing* 14(1): 1054–8408.

You, X., and J. Leary. 2000. 'Age and Cohort Effects: An Examination of Older Japanese Travelers', *Journal of Travel and Tourism Marketing* 9(1): 21–24.

Yu, H., and K. Shimoyama. 2010. 'A Study of the Trend of Chinese Tourists Visiting Japan', *Bulletin of Beppu University Junior College* 29: 89–99.

YWHCC. 2009. 'Tozan ni tsuite' [About mountaineering], Yakushima World Heritage Conservation Centre. Retrieved 25 May 2009 from: http://www.env.go.jp/park/kirishima/ywhcc/.

ZNKK. 1997. *Nôka no yoka/ryokô hakusho* [White book on leisure and travel by farmers]. Tokyo: Zenkoku Nôkyô Kankô Kyôkai.

ZSRK. 2010. 'Heisei 22nendô zenkoku kôshiritsu kôtô gakkô no kaigai shûgaku ryokô jisshi jôkyô' [The situation of school trips to foreign countries at public and private senior high schools nationwide], Zenkoku Shûgaku Ryokô Kyôkai. Retrieved 20 February 2012 from: http://shu gakuryoko.com/chosa/kaigai/index.html.

INDEX

www.ingramcontent.com/pod-product-compliance
Lightning Source LLC
Chambersburg PA
CBHW060033030426
42334CB00019B/2306